SOUS VIDE MASTERY

300 Recipes for the Best in Modern, Low Temperature Cooking

By
Renee Dufour

Legal Disclaimer
The information contained in this book is the opinion of the author and is based on the author's personal experience and observations. The author does not assume liability whatsoever for the use of or inability to use any or all information contained in this book, and accepts no responsibility for any loss or damages of any kind that may be incurred by the reader as a result of actions arising from the use of information in this book. Use this information at your own risk. The author reserves the right to make any changes he or she deems necessary to future versions of the publication to ensure its accuracy.

TABLE OF CONTENTS

INTRODUCTION

By definition, the term "sous vide" means "under vacuum" in French. This refers to the vacuum sealed bags that many French chefs used when they would cook food using the sous vide method. Modern day sous vide cooking has come to mean food that is cooked at a precise and constant temperature in a water bath. The invention of the Immersion Circulator has made cooking using the sous vide method not only attainable for the home chef, but almost fool-proof.

If you have bought this book I assume you have basic knowledge of the sous vide process. You will need an immersion circulator, a Cambro container or other suitable pot filled with water, bags for your food and some time. Because of the low temperature that is called for in most recipes, the process of cooking sous vide can take longer than traditional methods. But this process ensures that your food will be cooked evenly and turn out tender and juicy every time.

This book has 300 recipes, so you will find that there is quite the variety. Everything from basic chicken breasts and corn on the cob to much more complex and extravagant meals, such as osso bucco or quail with pancetta, lemon and thyme. I hope that as your comfort level with sous vide grows, so will your excitement to try some of these more elaborate dishes.

Just a word about the cooking times of the recipes. Because of the nature of sous vide using lower temperatures to cook, food will rarely become over done. With many recipes, it is really up to the chef to determine how rare or well done they like their food. With meat in particular, once it has reached the temperature that will kill the food's bacteria, thus making it safe to eat, the meat goes through slow subtle changes over a long period of time. These changes determine the overall texture and moisture content of the food, which really become personal preference. In some recipes, I have listed a wide cooking time range. For these, a good rule of thumb to cook the food somewhere between the minimum and maximum time listed. Anywhere in between will be up to you as the chef to determine your personal taste.

As you make your way through this book, I hope you will find many recipes that suit your taste and your desire to create delicious food using the sous vide method. Happy cooking!

1

BREAKFAST DISHES

Easy Eggs Benedict

Preparation Time: 10 mins
Cooking Time: 1 hour
Cooking Temperature: 147°F
Servings: 2

Ingredients:

4 large eggs, room temperature

4 slices of precooked Canadian bacon

4 toasted English muffins, cut into halves

pinch of paprika

2 sprigs parsley, for garnish (optional)

Hollandaise Sauce:

4 large egg yolks

2 teaspoons lemon juice

4 teaspoons water

2 sticks unsalted butter, melted

champagne vinegar, to taste

salt, to taste

Directions:

1. Attach the sous vide immersion circulator to a Cambro container or pot with water using an adjustable clamp and preheat the water bath to 147°F.

2. Gently drop the eggs into the water bath and set the time to 1 hour.

3. Prepare the Hollandaise sauce while the eggs are cooking. Prepare a double-boiler setup by placing a mixing bowl on a pot with boiling

water. Combine the egg yolks, lemon juice, and water in the mixing bowl and whisk constantly until thick and well combined. Remove the bowl from the pot, and gradually add in the melted butter and vinegar while whisking constantly until the ingredients are well incorporated. Season with salt and whisk until thick and smooth. Cover and set aside.

4. Prepare an ice bath and set aside. Reheat the bacon and muffins in an oven, cover and set aside.

5. When the eggs are ready, briefly immerse in the ice bath to stop further cooking and gently remove the eggshells. Set aside.

6. Place the bottom halves of the muffin on a serving plate, add 2 slices of bacon and top with the eggs. Drizzle with Hollandaise sauce, sprinkle with paprika and garnish with parsley before serving.

PERFECT SOFT-BOILED EGGS

Preparation Time: 10 mins
Cooking Time: 1½ to 2 hrs
Cooking Temperature: 145°F
Servings: 2

INGREDIENTS:

4 large eggs

salt, to taste

DIRECTIONS:

1. Attach the sous vide immersion circulator to a Cambro container or pot with water using an adjustable clamp and preheat the water to 145°F.

2. Gently drop the eggs into the water bath and set the time to 110 mins for soft-boiled eggs with slightly runny yolks and 155 mins for soft-boiled eggs with slightly firm yolks.

3. When the eggs are ready, immerse them in an ice bath or rinse with cool running water to stop further cooking. Gently crack the eggs or use an eggshell cutter to remove the shells.

4. Transfer into individual egg cups, season with salt, and serve warm.

HAM AND QUAIL EGG BREAKFAST SANDWICH

Preparation Time: 10 mins
Cooking Time: 45 mins
Cooking Temperature: 140°F
Servings: 4

INGREDIENTS:

8 quail eggs

one loaf of baguette, sliced into 8 portions (diagonal cuts or bias-cuts)

4 slices of smoked ham, cut into strips

ripe red tomatoes, sliced into rounds

cheddar cheese, sliced

DIRECTIONS:

1. Attach the sous vide immersion circulator to a Cambro container or pot with water using an adjustable clamp and preheat the water to 140°F. Carefully immerse the eggs in the water bath and set the cooking time to 30 minutes. Remove the eggs from the water bath and immerse in an ice bath for about 3 minutes to stop further cooking. Transfer to a plate and set aside.

2. While cooking the eggs, fry the ham in a non-stick skillet for about 3 to 4 minutes or until golden brown. Repeat on other side. Transfer to a serving plate and set aside. Reheat the baguette slices in separate batches in the same pan until crisp and lightly golden. Remove from heat and set aside.

3. Add a slice of cheese, a layer of ham, and tomatoes on four slices of baguette and place two eggs on top. Cover with the remaining bread and secure the sandwich by inserting a toothpick in the center. Serve immediately.

VEGETABLE FRITTATA CUPS

Preparation Time: 35 mins
Cooking Time: 1 hour
Cooking Temperature: 176°F
Servings: 4

INGREDIENTS:

1 tablespoon extra-virgin olive oil

1 medium onion, chopped

kosher salt

4 cloves garlic, minced

1 small rutabaga, peeled and diced

2 medium carrots, peeled and diced

1 medium parsnip, peeled and diced

1 cup butternut squash, peeled and diced

6 ounces oyster mushrooms, trimmed and roughly chopped

¼ cup fresh parsley leaves, minced

pinch red pepper flakes

5 large eggs

¼ cup whole milk

DIRECTIONS:

1. Attach the sous vide immersion circulator to a Cambro container or pot with water using an adjustable clamp and preheat the water to 176°F. Prepare four canning or mason jars and brush the inner part with oil or cooking spray.

2. Add the oil to a large skillet over medium-high heat. Add the onion, sprinkle with salt, and cook until the onion is soft and translucent, stirring regularly. Add the garlic and cook for an additional 30 seconds, or until lightly brown and fragrant.

3. Add the remaining vegetables except mushrooms, season with salt, and cook for about 10 minutes or until the vegetables are soft and tender. Add the mushrooms, cook for another 3 to 5 minutes and stir in the parsley and red pepper flakes. Remove from heat and let cool completely.

4. While cooling the vegetables, mix the milk and eggs in a large bowl and whisk until well combined.

5. Divide the cooled vegetables into four equal portions and transfer into the prepared jars. Pour the egg mixture into the jars to cover the vegetables fully and cover with lids.

6. Immerse the jars into the water bath and set the cooking time for 1 hour. Remove the jars from the water bath, transfer onto a wire cooling rack and let cool completely.

7. Carefully open the lids, let rest for 5 minutes and transfer to a plate before serving.

BASIC STEEL CUT OATS

Preparation Time: 5 mins
Cooking Time: 8 hours
Cooking Temperature: 155°F
Servings: 4

INGREDIENTS:

3 cups of water

1 cup of steel cut oats, rolled oats, or oat groats

¼ teaspoon salt

DIRECTIONS:

1. Attach the sous vide immersion circulator to a Cambro container or pot with water using an adjustable clamp and preheat the water to 155°F.

2. Combine all ingredients in a cooking pouch, remove any excess air and seal the bag. Immerse bag into the water bath and set the cooking time to 8 hours. Remove from the water bath and let rest for about 5 minutes before opening.

3. Divide the oats into four equal portions and transfer into separate serving bowls. Top with desired ingredients and serve warm.

BACON AND GRUYERE EGG CUPS

Preparation Time: 5 mins
Cooking Time: 1½ hours
Cooking Temperature: 172°F
Servings: 4 to 6

INGREDIENTS:

6 eggs

¼ cup milk or cream

2 to 3 strips of bacon, halved and cooked

¼ cup Gruyere cheese

¼ cup Monterey jack cheese

DIRECTIONS:

1. Attach the sous vide immersion circulator to a Cambro container or pot with water using an adjustable clamp and preheat the water to 172°F. Lightly brush 4 or 6 small canning/mason jars with oil or cooking spray and set aside.

2. Add the milk and eggs to a mixing bowl and whisk until well combined.

3. Place one slice of bacon on the bottom of each jar and top with Gruyere cheese. Pour in egg mixture and add a layer of Monterey jack cheese. Cover with lid or seal the jars, immerse the jars into the water bath, and set the cooking time to 1½ hours.

4. Remove the jars from the water bath and let rest for about 5 minutes before opening. Carefully transfer onto a serving platter and serve warm.

CHEDDAR BACON EGG BITES

Preparation Time: 10 mins
Cooking Time: 1 hour
Cooking Temperature: 167°F
Servings: 2

INGREDIENTS:

For the Egg Bites:

4 eggs

4 tablespoons cottage cheese

1/4 cup Monterey Jack cheese, shredded

1/4 cup Gruyère cheese, shredded

For serving:

4 pieces crispy thin bacon, precooked

1/4 cup Gruyère cheese, shredded, for broiling

DIRECTIONS:

1. Attach the sous vide immersion circulator to a Cambro container or pot with water using an adjustable clamp and preheat the water to 167°F. Lightly grease four mason or canning jars with oil or cooking spray and set aside.

2. Place all egg bite ingredients in a blender and pulse until smooth and well combined.

3. Break one slice of bacon and place it on the bottom of each greased jar. Fill jars with egg mixture and cover with lids. Immerse in the water bath and set the cooking time to 1 hour.

4. Remove the jars from the water bath and let rest for 5 minutes before serving. Transfer onto a serving platter and serve immediately.

Jalapeno Egg Cups

Preparation Time: 5 mins
Cooking Time: 1½ hours
Cooking Temperature: 172°F
Servings: 4

INGREDIENTS:

6 large eggs

¼ cup milk or cream

4 strips precooked pancetta bacon

1 jalapeño, seeded and sliced

¼ cup Cheddar cheese

DIRECTIONS:

1. Attach the sous vide immersion circulator to a Cambro container or pot with water using an adjustable clamp and preheat the water to 172°F. Lightly grease four canning or mason jars with oil or cooking spray and set aside.

2. Add the milk and eggs to a bowl and whisk until well combined. Set aside.

3. Add a slice of bacon on the bottom of each jar, divide the egg mixture into four equal portions, and pour into the jars. Sprinkle with jalapeño and top with cheese.

4. Cover with lids or seal the jars and immerse into the water bath. Set the cooking time to 1½ hours. Remove the jars when ready and let rest for about 5 minutes before removing the egg cups from the jars.

5. Transfer onto a serving platter and serve immediately

OVERNIGHT BACON

Preparation Time: 10 mins
Cooking Time: 8 to 48 hours
Cooking Temperature: 145°F
Servings: 4

INGREDIENTS:

1 pound thick-cut bacon, still in its package

DIRECTIONS:

1. Attach the sous vide immersion circulator to a Cambro container or pot with water using an adjustable clamp and preheat the water to 145°F.

2. Immerse the packaged bacon into the water bath and set the cooking time for at least

3. Remove from water bath and let rest for 5 minutes before opening.

4. While the bacon is cooling, preheat a large skillet over medium-high heat. Add one slice of bacon one at a time and cook for about 3 minutes on each side, or until nicely browned and crisp. 5. Turn to cook the other side and transfer onto a plate lined with paper towels. Let rest for about five minutes to drain excess oil from the bacon.

5. Transfer onto a serving platter and serve immediately.

Parmesan Omelette

Preparation Time: 5 mins
Cooking Time: 20 mins
Cooking Temperature: 165°F
Servings: 2

Ingredients:

4 large eggs

2 tablespoon minced scallion greens

2 tablespoon finely grated Parmesan cheese

1 tablespoon unsalted butter, diced

salt and pepper

fresh parsley, chopped, for serving

Directions:

1. Attach the sous vide immersion circulator to a Cambro container or pot with water using an adjustable clamp and preheat the water to 165°F.

2. In a large bowl, add all ingredients except parsley, season with salt and pepper, and whisk until well combined.

3. Pour the mixture into a cooking pouch, remove excess air and seal the bag. Immerse the bag in the water bath and set the cooking time to 10 minutes. Remove the bag and carefully press down to form a flat round. Return to the water bath and set the cooking time to an additional 10 minutes.

4. Remove the bag from the water bath and let cool for 5 minutes before opening.

5. Transfer onto a serving platter, cut into two portions, and serve immediately with minced parsley on top.

FRENCH SCRAMBLED EGGS

Preparation Time: 10 mins
Cooking Time: 30 mins
Cooking Temperature: 165°F
Servings: 4 to 6

INGREDIENTS:

6 large eggs

4½ tablespoons unsalted butter, melted and slightly cooled

¼ cup heavy cream

1 teaspoon kosher salt, or to taste

1 teaspoon ground pepper, or to taste

DIRECTIONS:

1. Attach the sous vide immersion circulator to a Cambro container or pot with water using an adjustable clamp and preheat the water to 165°F.

2. Add all ingredients to a large bowl and whisk until well combined. Transfer to a cooking pouch, remove excess air and seal the bag before submerging into the water bath.

3. Set the cooking time to 30 minutes. After 20 minutes, remove the bag and gently massage the mixture to thoroughly mix the ingredients and return the bag to the water bath to continue cooking.

4. Remove the bag from the water bath, briefly massage the egg mixture, and transfer the scrambled egg onto a large plate before serving.

Scotch Eggs

Preparation Time: 15 mins
Cooking Time: 1¼ hours
Cooking Temperature: 147°F
Servings: 4 to 6

Ingredients:

4 to 6 large eggs

1 cup of flour

salt and pepper

1 large pinch of Italian seasoning

1 cup of panko bread crumbs.

4 to 6 links of smoked sausage, casings removed

oil, for deep frying

Directions:

1. Attach the sous vide immersion circulator to a Cambro container or pot with water using an adjustable clamp and preheat the water to 147°F. Gently drop in the eggs and set the cooking time to 1 hr.

2. Prepare an ice bath and immerse the cooked eggs immediately after boiling to stop further cooking. Let cool completely and freeze for 4 to 8 hours.

3. While freezing the eggs, prepare the rest of the ingredients. In a bowl, mix the flour, salt, pepper, and Italian seasoning and place the crumbs into separate bowl. Divide the sausage into 6 to 8 equal portions and press down to form into flat rounds. You will need two sausage rounds for every egg you've prepared.

4. Add the oil to a deep pan or skillet over high heat. Preheat oven to 300°F.

5. Remove the eggs from the freezer and rinse with running water (room temperature). Crack the eggs and remove the shells. Coat each egg entirely with flour and shake to remove excess. Place one egg on top of one flattened sausage round, place another sausage round on top and gently press onto the egg surface to fully cover. Coat the egg and sausage ball in the Panko crumbs. Roll to make a smooth surface. Repeat the procedure with the remaining eggs. and fry for about 3 to 3½ minutes, or until golden brown. Remove from pan and transfer to a plate lined with paper towels to drain excess fat.

6. Finish the scotch eggs in the preheated oven for about 10 minutes. Remove from the oven, transfer to a wire rack, and let rest for about 5 minutes before serving.

7. Transfer onto a serving platter and serve whole or sliced into halves.

BRIOCHE BUNS WITH CHEESY EGG TOPPING

Preparation Time: 10 mins
Cooking Time: 45 mins
Cooking Temperature: 149°F
Servings: 4

INGREDIENTS:

4 large eggs

4 brioche buns

½ cup grated Cheddar cheese

½ cup grated Parmesan cheese

2 scallions, green parts only, thinly sliced

DIRECTIONS:

1. Attach the sous vide immersion circulator to a Cambro container or pot with water using an adjustable clamp and preheat the water to 149°F. Carefully immerse the eggs into the water bath and set the cooking time to 45 minutes. Remove from the water bath and set aside.

2. While cooking the eggs, pinch out or remove the center part of the each bun to fit the size of an egg. Repeat with the rest of the bread and set aside. Preheat oven broiler to high, line a baking sheet with foil, and set aside.

3. Carefully crack an egg on each brioche bun and add 2 tablespoons each of Cheddar and Parmesan cheese. Transfer onto the prepared baking sheet and broil for about 3 to 5 minutes, or until the cheese starts to melt and the top is lightly golden. Remove from the oven, transfer to a wire rack, and let rest for a couple of minutes before serving.

4. Transfer onto a serving platter, garnish with sliced scallions, and serve immediately.

OVERNIGHT OATMEAL WITH STEWED FRUIT COMPOTE

Preparation Time: 15 mins
Cooking Time: 6-10 hours
Cooking Temperature: 155°F
Servings: 2

INGREDIENTS:

For the Oatmeal:

1 cup oatmeal (quick-cooking rolled oats)

3 cups water

pinch of salt

pinch of cinnamon

For the Stewed Fruit Compote:

¾ of a cup dried fruit (any mix of the following – cherries, blueberries, golden raisins, apricots, cranberries)

2 tablespoons white sugar

½ cup water

2 drops vanilla extract

zest of half a lemon, finely grated

zest of half an orange, finely grated

DIRECTIONS:

1. Attach the sous vide immersion circulator to a Cambro container or pot with water using an adjustable clamp and preheat the water to 155°F.

2.   Add all ingredients for the oatmeal mixture to a bowl and stir until well combined. Transfer into a cooking pouch, remove excess air and seal the pouch. In a separate bowl, add all ingredients for the compote and mix until well combined. Transfer into a separate pouch, remove air and seal.

3.   Immerse the bags into the water bath and set the cooking time for 6 to 10 hours. Remove bags from the water bath and gently massage to distribute the ingredients properly. Let rest for about 5 minutes before opening and serving.

4.   Divide the oatmeal into two portions, place in serving bowls and serve with fruit compote on top.

TOASTED BREAD PUDDING

Preparation Time: 20 mins
Cooking Time: 2 hours
Cooking Temperature: 170°F
Servings: 4

INGREDIENTS:

3 cups brioche cubes, toasted

2 large eggs

¼ cup sugar

1 tsp vanilla extract or paste

1 tablespoon butter

2 cups whole milk

dash of cinnamon

For the Toppings:

sugar, as needed, for brûlée topping

maple syrup

½ cup heavy cream, whipped

berries

DIRECTIONS:

1. Preheat oven to 350 degrees.

2. Attach the sous vide immersion circulator to a Cambro container or pot with water using an adjustable clamp and preheat the water to 170°F.

3. Place the cubed brioche breads on a greased baking sheet and toast for about 6 to 8 minutes, or until golden brown. Remove from the oven and set aside.

4. In a mixing bowl, add eggs, sugar, and vanilla and stir until well combined. Set aside.

5. Combine the butter, milk, and cinnamon in a medium saucepan over medium heat and cook until the mixture starts to form steam and bubbles, stirring occasionally. Remove the saucepan from heat.

6. Gradually pour in the egg mixture into the milk mixture while stirring constantly, until the ingredients are well incorporated. Add the toasted brioche slowly while stirring regularly until the brioche is evenly coated with the milk mixture. Let stand for about 2 minutes for the bread to absorb the liquid.

7. While soaking the bread, grease four canning or mason jars with oil or cooking spray. Divide the soaked bread into four equal portions and transfer into the greased jars. Seal the jars, immerse into the water bath and set the cooking time to 2 hours.

8. Carefully remove the jars from the water bath and let rest for about 5 minutes before opening and serving.

9. Transfer the bread pudding to separate serving bowls or plates and sprinkle sugar on top.

10. Blowtorch the sugar until caramelized and drizzle with maple syrup. Add a dollop of cream and serve with berries on top.

FRENCH TOAST

Preparation Time: 5 mins
Cooking Time: 1 hour
Cooking Temperature: 147°F
Servings: 2

INGREDIENTS:

2 large eggs
125 mL (½ cup) milk
½ tsp ground cinnamon
4 slices of stale bread
butter, for frying
sugar, for serving

DIRECTIONS:

1. Attach the sous vide immersion circulator to a Cambro container or pot with water using an adjustable clamp and preheat the water to 147°F.

2. Add the milk, eggs, and cinnamon to a mixing bowl and whisk until well combined.

3. Dip the bread slices into the milk-egg mixture until fully coated. Place a slice of bread in a small cooking pouch and repeat the procedure with rest of the bread slices, placing each piece of bread in a separate bag. Vacuum seal the bags and set the cooking time to 1 hour. Remove bread from the bags and carefully transfer to a plate.

4. While waiting, preheat a skillet over medium-high heat and lightly grease the bottom with butter. In batches, fry the bread slices for 2 to 3 minutes or until lightly golden on each side.

5. Remove from heat, transfer to a serving plate, and sprinkle with sugar before serving.

EGG AND CHORIZO TOAST

Preparation Time: 10 mins
Cooking Time: 20 mins
Cooking Temperature: 167°F
Servings: 2 to 4

INGREDIENTS:

2 tablespoons of cream

2 tablespoons of milk

2 tablespoons of melted butter

6 large eggs

salt and pepper

For Serving:

2 medium links of precooked chorizo or pork sausage, sliced into rounds

4 slices of precooked French toast

sliced green onions

DIRECTIONS:

1. Attach the sous vide immersion circulator to a Cambro container or pot with water using an adjustable clamp and preheat the water to 167°F.

2. Add the cream, milk, and melted butter to a large mixing bowl, and whisk until well combined. Whisk in the eggs, season with salt and pepper, and stir until the ingredients are well incorporated.

3. Pour the mixture into a cooking pouch, remove excess air and seal the pouch. Immerse the bag into the water bath and set the cooking time to 15 minutes. Gently massage the bag every 5 minutes to evenly distribute the ingredients and prevent the formation of clumps. Remove from the water bath and gently massage the egg mixture to break into smaller pieces.

4. While cooking the eggs, reheat the sausage and French toast in a skillet and set aside.

5. Place a slice of toast on one serving plate, add a layer of sliced chorizo, and top with eggs. Garnish with green onions and serve immediately.

YOGURT

Preparation Time: 30 mins

Cooking Time: 24 hours

Cooking Temperature: 115°F

Servings: 4

INGREDIENTS:

2 to 2½ cups of whole milk

40 g live-culture yogurt

DIRECTIONS:

1. Attach the sous vide immersion circulator to a Cambro container or pot with water using an adjustable clamp and preheat the water to 115°F.

2. In a medium pot, add the milk and heat to 180°F. Cook until the milk is just heated through while stirring and scraping the bottom of the pot to prevent scalding or burning.

3. While heating the milk, prepare an ice bath and immerse the pot to stop further cooking until it cools to 110°F.

4. Place the yogurt in a large mixing bowl, add half of the milk and stir until well combined. Add the rest of the milk and stir until smooth.

5. Transfer the mixture into a large mason or canning jar and seal properly. Immerse into the water bath and set cooking for 24 hours. Remove the jar from the water bath. Strain the yogurt using a few layers of cheesecloth into a mixing bowl in the refrigerator for at least 4-12 hours.

6. Serve yogurt with your favorite fruits, vegetables, or other flavorings.

2

POULTRY

WHOLE CHICKEN

Preparation Time: 15 minutes
Cooking Time: 6 hours
Cooking Temperature: 150°F

INGREDIENTS:

4-pound whole chicken, trussed

4 cups chicken broth

2 cups celery stalk, chopped

2 cups carrots, peeled and chopped

2 cups leeks, chopped

1 dried bay leaf

1 teaspoon kosher salt

1 teaspoon whole black peppercorns

DIRECTIONS:

1. Attach the sous vide immersion circulator to a Cambro container or pot with water using an adjustable clamp and preheat water to 150°F.

2. In a large cooking pouch, mix together all ingredients. Seal the pouch tightly after removing the excess air. Place pouch in sous vide bath and set the cooking time to 6 hours. Cover the sous vide bath with plastic wrap to minimize water evaporation. Add water intermittently to properly maintain the water level.

3. Preheat the oven broiler to high and line a baking sheet with a piece of foil.

4. After 6 hours, remove pouch from the sous vide bath and open carefully. Remove the chicken from pouch and pat dry chicken completely with paper towels.

5. Arrange chicken on the prepared baking sheet. Broil for 5-7 minutes.

6. Remove from oven and allow to sit for 10 minutes. Cut into desired pieces and serve.

CHICKEN CORDON BLEU

Preparation Time: 20 minutes
Cooking Time: 1 hour 35 minutes
Cooking Temperature: 140°F

INGREDIENTS:

2 (8-10 ounce) boneless, skinless chicken breasts, butterflied

Salt and freshly ground black pepper, to taste

4 slices of honey deli ham

2 ounces white sharp cheddar, cut into 2 batons

Vegetable oil, for frying

½ cup all-purpose flour

½ cup heavy cream

1 cup panko bread crumbs

Chopped fresh parsley, for garnishing

DIRECTIONS:

1. Attach the sous vide immersion circulator to a Cambro container or pot with water using an adjustable clamp and preheat water to 140°F.

2. Season chicken breasts evenly with salt and black pepper.

3. Wrap 2 slices of ham around each cheese baton. Place 1 ham-wrapped cheese piece in the center of each chicken breast. Fold chicken breasts around the ham-wrapped cheese.

4. Place stuffed chicken breasts in a large cooking pouch. Seal pouch tightly after removing excess air. Place sealed pouch in sous vide bath and set the cooking time for 1½ hours.

5. In a shallow dish, mix together flour, salt, and pepper. In a second shallow dish, place heavy cream. In a third shallow dish, place panko crumbs.

6. Remove the pouch from the sous vide bath and open carefully. Remove chicken breasts from pouch and pat dry chicken breasts completely with paper towels.

7. Lightly coat chicken breasts with the flour mixture, dip into the heavy cream, then coat each chicken breast evenly with panko crumbs.

8. In a large Dutch oven, heat 2 inches of oil on medium-high heat until the temperature reaches 375 ºF. Fry chicken breasts in oil for 2-3 minutes or until golden brown on both sides.

9. Transfer chicken breasts to a paper towel-lined plate to drain excess oil. Top with parsley for garnish and serve.

Chicken Breast with Mushroom Sauce

Preparation Time: 15 minutes
Cooking Time: 4 hours
Cooking Temperature: 140°F

INGREDIENTS:

For Chicken:

    2 boneless, skinless chicken breasts

    ⅛ teaspoon salt

    1 teaspoon vegetable oil

For Mushroom Sauce:

    1 teaspoon olive oil

    3 French shallots, finely chopped

    2 tablespoons butter

    2 large garlic cloves, finely chopped

    1 cup button mushrooms, sliced

    2 tablespoons port wine

    ½ cup chicken broth

    1 cup cream

    Salt, to taste

    ¼ teaspoon cracked black pepper

DIRECTIONS:

1. Attach the sous vide immersion circulator to a Cambro container or pot with water using an adjustable clamp and preheat water to 140°F.

2. Season chicken breasts lightly with salt.

3. Place chicken breasts in a large cooking pouch. Seal pouch tightly after removing the excess air. Place pouch in sous vide bath and set the cooking time for 1½-4 hours.

4. For the mushroom sauce: heat olive oil in a skillet over medium heat and sauté shallots for 2-3 minutes. Stir in butter and garlic and sauté for 1 minute.

5. Increase the heat to medium-high. Stir in mushrooms and cook until all liquid is absorbed.

6. Add wine. Cook until all liquid is absorbed then add broth and cook for 2 minutes.

7. Stir in cream and reduce heat back to medium. Once the sauce becomes thick, stir in the black pepper and desired amount of salt and remove from heat.

8. Remove pouch from the sous vide bath and open carefully. Remove chicken breasts from pouch and pat dry chicken breasts completely with paper towels. Coat chicken breasts evenly with vegetable oil.

9. Heat a grill pan over high heat and cook chicken breasts for 1 minute per side.

10. Divide onto serving plates once cooked, top with mushroom sauce, and serve.

Coq au Vin

Preparation Time: 20 minutes
Cooking Time: 12 hours 30 minutes
Cooking Temperature: 151°F

INGREDIENTS:

1 bottle red wine, reserving 1 glass

1/2 cup bacon, crumbled

3 large carrots, peeled and chopped

3 celery stalks, finely chopped

4 garlic cloves, pressed

4 bay leaves

7 tbsp unsalted butter, divided

10 shallots or small onions

1 chicken, jointed into 2 breasts on the bone with wings and 2 legs attached

Sea salt and freshly ground black pepper, to taste

A few thyme sprigs

2 tablespoons all-purpose flour

Vegetable oil*

7 ounces button mushrooms

Finely chopped fresh parsley, for garnishing

DIRECTIONS:

1. Add wine, bacon, carrots, celery, garlic, and bay leaves to a pan and bring to a gentle boil. Cook for 25 minutes, stirring occasionally. Remove from heat and allow to cool completely.

2. Meanwhile in another pan, melt 1 tbsp butter and sauté onions for 4-5 minutes. Remove from heat and set aside.

3. Attach the sous vide immersion circulator to a Cambro container or pot with water using an adjustable clamp and preheat water to 151°F.

4. Season the jointed chickens evenly with salt and black pepper.

5. Divide chicken pieces, sautéed onions, and thyme sprigs between two cooking pouches. Seal pouches tightly after removing excess air. Place pouches in sous vide bath and set the cooking time for 12 hours.

6. Preheat the oven to 355°F.

7. Remove pouches from the sous vide bath and open carefully. Remove chicken pieces from pouches, reserving cooking liquid in a pan. Pat dry chicken pieces with paper towels.

8. Season chicken lightly with salt and pepper.

9. In a large frying pan, heat oil and 2 tablespoons butter. Add chicken, skin side down, and fry for 6-8 minutes on each side.

10. Move chicken pieces to a baking sheet, skin side up, and bake for 10 minutes.

11. While the chicken is baking, remove thyme sprigs from cooking liquid and bring liquid to a gentle boil, adding reserved wine.

12. In a bowl, combine flour and 2 tablespoons unsalted butter and mix well. Add flour mixture to pan with cooking liquid, stirring continuously. Stir in salt and black pepper and simmer until desired consistency is reached.

13. Move baked chicken pieces to a different pan on the stove. Add 2 tablespoons of butter and stir fry with mushrooms for 6-7 minutes or until browned on both sides.

14. Place chicken on a serving platter and top with sauce, followed by mushrooms. Garnish with parsley and serve.

SIMPLE CHICKEN BREAST

Preparation Time: 10 minutes
Cooking Time: 4 hours
Cooking Temperature: 146°F

INGREDIENTS:

1 chicken breast

Salt and freshly ground black pepper, to taste

1 teaspoon olive oil

DIRECTIONS:

1. Attach the sous vide immersion circulator to a Cambro container or pot with water using an adjustable clamp and preheat water to 146°F.

2. Season chicken breasts lightly with salt and black pepper.

3. Place chicken breasts in a cooking pouch. Seal pouch tightly after removing the excess air. Place pouch in sous vide bath and set the cooking time for 1-4 hours.

4. Remove pouch from the sous vide bath and open carefully. Remove chicken breasts from pouch and set aside for 10-15 minutes to cool. Cut into desired sizes pieces and serve.

Orange Balsamic Chicken

Preparation Time: 15 minutes
Cooking Time: 1 hour 35 minutes
Cooking Temperature: 146°F

Ingredients:

1 large, whole, boneless chicken breast

Salt and freshly ground black pepper, to taste

1 orange

1 small sprig fresh oregano or rosemary

3 tablespoons balsamic vinegar

Directions:

1. Attach the sous vide immersion circulator to a Cambro container or pot with water using an adjustable clamp and preheat water to 146°F.

2. Season chicken breasts lightly with salt and black pepper. Cut 2 (¼-inch) slices from orange. Extract juice from remaining orange into a small bowl. Add vinegar and mix together with the juice of the orange.

3. Place chicken breast in a cooking pouch and top breast with orange slices and herb sprig. Carefully pour vinegar mixture into pouch. Seal pouch tightly after removing the excess air. Place pouch in sous vide bath and set the cooking time for 1½ hours.

4. Remove pouch from the sous vide bath and open carefully. Remove chicken breast from the pouch, reserving the cooking liquid.

5. Add the cooking liquid to a small pan and cook until slightly thickened.

6. Serve chicken with sauce.

Chicken Parmigiana

Preparation Time: 20 minutes
Cooking Time: 12 hours
Cooking Temperature: 141°F

Ingredients:

For Chicken:

4 chicken breasts

½ teaspoon garlic powder

Salt and freshly ground black pepper, to taste

4 fresh rosemary sprigs

4 fresh thyme sprigs

For Coating:

¾ cup flour

2 teaspoons salt

1 teaspoon ground black pepper

2 eggs

¼ cup Parmesan cheese, grated

¾ cup dried Italian breadcrumbs

2 tablespoons fresh parsley, chopped

For Cooking:

Oil, as required

For Topping:

½ cup fresh basil, chopped

1 cup fresh mozzarella cheese, shredded

¼ cup Parmesan cheese, grated

DIRECTIONS:

1. Season chicken breasts with garlic powder, salt, and black pepper evenly.

2. Divide chicken breasts and herb sprigs into two cooking pouches. Seal pouches tightly after removing the excess air. Refrigerate pouches for up to 2 days.

3. Attach the sous vide immersion circulator to a Cambro container or pot with water using an adjustable clamp and preheat water to 141°F.

4. Place pouches in sous vide bath and set the cooking time for 2-12 hours.

5. Preheat the oven broiler.

6. Remove the pouches from the sous vide bath and open carefully. Remove the chicken breasts and pat dry chicken breasts completely with paper towels.

7. In a shallow dish, mix together flour, salt, and black pepper for coating. In a second shallow dish, beat eggs. In a third shallow dish, mix together Parmesan cheese, breadcrumbs, and parsley.

8. Coat chicken breasts evenly with flour mixture, then dip in egg mixture before coating with parmesan mixture.

9. In a deep skillet, heat ½-inch of oil to 350°F and sear chicken breasts until crust is golden brown then turn and repeat on other side.

10. Transfer chicken breasts to a sheet pan. Top each breast with the basil, Parmesan, and mozzarella cheese for topping. Broil until cheese is bubbly.

11. Serve immediately.

CHICKEN TIKKA

Preparation Time: 15 minutes
Cooking Time: 2 hours
Cooking Temperature: 146°F

INGREDIENTS:

4 boneless, skinless chicken breasts

Salt and freshly ground black pepper, to taste

2 tablespoons butter

2 cups half-and-half

2 cups canned crushed tomatoes

4 garlic cloves, peeled

1 (1-inch) piece fresh ginger, cut into chunks

1½ tablespoons honey

1 tablespoon ground turmeric

1 tablespoon paprika

1 tablespoon ground cumin

2 teaspoons ground coriander

½ teaspoons salt

2 cups cooked rice

Chopped fresh cilantro, for garnishing

DIRECTIONS:

1. Attach the sous vide immersion circulator to a Cambro container or pot with water using an adjustable clamp and preheat water to 146°F.
2. Season chicken breasts evenly with salt and black pepper.

3. In a food processor, add half-and-half, tomatoes, garlic, ginger, honey, and spices and pulse until smooth.

4. Divide chicken and butter into two cooking pouches with two chicken breasts and one tablespoon butter in each pouch. Add mixture from food processor into a third, large pouch. Seal pouches tightly after removing the excess air. Place all pouches in the sous vide bath and set the cooking time for 2 hours.

5. Remove the pouches from the sous vide bath and open carefully. Remove chicken breasts from pouches and cut into slices of the desired size.

6. Divide cooked rice onto serving plates. Top with chicken slices and drizzle with sauce. Garnish with cilantro and serve.

BBQ Chicken Breasts

Preparation Time: 15 minutes
Cooking Time: 2 hours 30 minutes
Cooking Temperature: 165°F

Ingredients:

For BBQ Sauce:

3 dried ancho chile peppers, stemmed and seeded

1 dried New Mexico chile pepper, stemmed and seeded

¼ cup sunflower oil

1 small yellow onion, chopped

2 garlic cloves, minced

4½ ounces tomato paste

½ cup apple cider vinegar

¼ cup brown sugar

¼ cup molasses

3 tablespoons cocoa powder

1½ teaspoons ground cumin

1 teaspoon ground coriander

1 tablespoon sea salt

2 teaspoons ground black pepper

1 teaspoon fresh lemon zest, grated

¼ cup fresh lemon juice

¼ cup fresh lime juice, divided

1 teaspoon fresh lime zest, grated

For Chicken:

4 skin-on, bone-in chicken breasts

Sea salt and freshly ground black pepper, to taste

For Garnishing:

1 orange, cut into 8 wedges

Fresh cilantro, chopped

DIRECTIONS:

1. In a heatproof bowl, add both types of chile peppers. Add enough hot water to cover and set aside for 15 minutes.

2. Drain chile peppers, reserving ½ cup of the soaking water. In a blender, add chile peppers and reserved soaking water and pulse until a smooth paste is formed.

3. Heat oil in a medium pan over medium heat. Add and sauté onion and garlic for 10 minutes.

4. Add chile paste and remaining BBQ sauce ingredients except for 2 tablespoons of lime juice and the lime zest and bring to a boil. Reduce heat to low and simmer for 20-30 minutes.

5. Remove from heat and set aside to cool completely. Stir in remaining lime juice and lime zest. Transfer to a container and refrigerate before using.

6. Attach the sous vide immersion circulator to a Cambro container or pot with water using an adjustable clamp and preheat water to 165°F.

7. Season chicken breasts evenly with salt and black pepper.

8. Divide the chicken breasts into two large pouches. Seal pouches tightly after removing the excess air. Place pouches in sous vide bath and set the cooking time for 2½ hours.

9. Preheat grill to high heat. Grease grill grate.

10. Remove pouches from the sous vide bath and open carefully. Remove chicken breasts and coat each breast with BBQ sauce. Grill chicken breasts for 1 minute per side.

11. Serve with orange wedges and cilantro.

SPINACH STUFFED CHICKEN BREASTS

Preparation Time: 20 minutes
Cooking Time: 1 hour 5 minutes
Cooking Temperature: 145°F

INGREDIENTS:

2 chicken breasts, pounded thinly

2 tablespoons olive oil, divided

½ shallot, minced

2 garlic cloves, minced

2 cups fresh spinach

1 teaspoon red pepper flakes, crushed

Salt and freshly ground black pepper, to taste

3 tablespoons heavy cream

¼ cup Parmesan cheese, grated

DIRECTIONS:

1. Attach the sous vide immersion circulator to a Cambro container or pot with water using an adjustable clamp and preheat water to 145°F.

2. In a skillet, heat 1 tablespoon of oil and sauté shallot and garlic until fragrant. Stir in spinach, red pepper flakes, salt, and black pepper and cook until spinach is wilted. Add heavy cream and simmer for 1-2 minutes. Remove from the heat and stir in Parmesan cheese. Set aside to cool.

3. Place half of spinach mixture on one chicken breast and roll chicken from top to bottom. Secure with toothpicks. Repeat with remaining filling and chicken breast. Season both breast rolls with salt and black pepper.

4. Place chicken rolls in one large cooking pouch. Seal pouch tightly after removing the excess air. Place pouch in sous vide bath and set the cooking time for 1 hour.

5. Remove pouch from the sous vide bath and open carefully. Remove the chicken rolls from pouch and pat dry the chicken rolls completely with paper towels.

6. In a large skillet, heat remaining tablespoon of oil and sear chicken rolls until golden brown on both sides.

7. Remove from skillet, cut each roll into desired slices, and serve.

CHICKEN MARSALA

Preparation Time: 20 minutes
Cooking Time: 2 hours 20 minutes
Cooking Temperature: 141°F

INGREDIENTS:

4 chicken breasts

Salt and freshly ground black pepper, to taste

1-2 fresh thyme sprigs

1 cup all-purpose flour

Olive oil, as required

3 tablespoons butter, divided

3 cups fresh mushrooms (baby bella, cremini, oyster, or porcini), sliced

¾ cup Marsala wine

¾ cup chicken broth

4 tablespoons fresh Italian parsley, chopped

DIRECTIONS:

1. Attach the sous vide immersion circulator to a Cambro container or pot with water using an adjustable clamp and preheat water to 141°F.

2. Season chicken breasts generously with salt and black pepper.

3. Place chicken breasts in a cooking pouch and add thyme sprigs. Seal pouch tightly after removing the excess air. Place pouch in sous vide bath and set the cooking time for 1½-2 hours.

4. Remove the pouch from the sous vide bath and open carefully. Remove chicken breasts from pouch and pat dry chicken breasts completely with paper towels. Evenly coat chicken breasts with flour.

5. In a sauté pan, heat olive oil over high heat and sear chicken breasts for 1 minute per side. Transfer chicken breasts onto a plate and cover with a piece of foil to keep warm.

6. In the same pan, melt 1 tablespoon of butter over medium-high heat and sauté mushrooms for 4-6 minutes. Reduce heat to medium and stir in wine. Simmer for 1 minute, scraping the browned bits from bottom. Add the chicken broth and simmer for 5-10 minutes. Remove from heat and immediately stir in remaining butter.

7. Divide chicken breasts onto serving plates. Evenly top with mushroom sauce. Garnish with parsley and serve.

PROSCIUTTO WRAPPED CHICKEN

Preparation Time: 15 minutes
Cooking Time: 1 hour 5 minutes
Cooking Temperature: 145°F

INGREDIENTS:

2 (6-ounce) boneless, skinless chicken breasts, sliced in half lengthwise

Kosher salt and freshly ground black pepper, to taste

2 thin prosciutto slices

1 tablespoon extra-virgin olive oil

DIRECTIONS:

1. Attach the sous vide immersion circulator to a Cambro container or pot with water using an adjustable clamp and preheat water to 145°F.

2. Season chicken breasts evenly with salt and black pepper.

3. Arrange a piece of plastic wrap onto a cutting board. Place one prosciutto slice in the center of the plastic wrap. Arrange two of the strips of chicken in the center of prosciutto, side-by-side to form an even rectangle. Roll prosciutto around the chicken so that it creates a uniform cylinder. Wrap the cylinder tightly in the plastic wrap and tie off the ends with butcher's twine. Repeat with remaining prosciutto and chicken.

4. Place the chicken cylinders in a large cooking pouch. Seal pouch tightly after removing the excess air. Place the pouch in the sous vide bath and set the cooking time for 1 hour.

5. Remove pouch from the sous vide bath and open carefully. Remove the chicken cylinders from the pouch and take off the plastic wrap, patting dry the chicken cylinders. Season each cylinder with salt and black pepper.

6. In a large, non-stick skillet, heat olive oil over medium-high heat and sear chicken cylinders for 5 minutes or until golden brown.

7. Remove from heat and allow to cool for 10 minutes. Cut into desired slices and serve.

Hawaiian Chicken

Preparation Time: 15 minutes
Cooking Time: 3 hours 5 minutes
Cooking Temperature: 147°F

Ingredients:

For Glaze:

2 cups chicken broth

1½ cups soy sauce

¾ cup light brown sugar

½ cup plus 1 tablespoon water, divided

½ cup mirin

1 tablespoon fish sauce

3 tablespoons cornstarch

1 tablespoon water

For Chicken:

6 pounds boneless, skinless chicken thighs

1 (3-inch) piece fresh ginger, peeled and cut into three pieces

6 large garlic cloves, minced

For Garnishing:

1 cup scallions, thinly sliced

DIRECTIONS:

1. Attach the sous vide immersion circulator to a Cambro container or pot with water using an adjustable clamp and preheat water to 147°F.

2. In a large bowl, add chicken broth, soy sauce, brown sugar, ½ cup water, mirin, and fish sauce and beat until well combined for the glaze.

3. Divide the glaze, chicken, ginger, and garlic into three cooking pouches. Seal the pouches tightly after removing the excess air. Place pouches in sous vide bath and set the cooking time for 3 hours.

4. Remove the pouches from the sous vide bath and open carefully. Strain half of the cooking liquid into a pan. Transfer all chicken into a new cooking pouch and seal it. Return pouch to sous vide bath with the sous vide turned off.

5. Place pan of reserved cooking liquid on stove and bring to a boil. In a small bowl, dissolve cornstarch into 1 tablespoon of water. Add the cornstarch mixture to the cooking liquid, stirring continuously. Cook until the glaze becomes thick.

6. Place chicken on a platter and top with glaze. Garnish with scallions and serve.

CHICKEN THIGHS WITH GARLIC MUSTARD SAUCE

Preparation Time: 15 minutes
Cooking Time: 4 hours 10 minutes
Cooking Temperature: 165°F

INGREDIENTS:

1½ pound skin-on chicken thighs

Salt and freshly ground black pepper, to taste

2 tablespoons canola oil

1 tablespoon butter

1 teaspoon champagne or white wine vinegar

1 large garlic clove, mashed into a paste

1 teaspoon whole-grain Dijon mustard

DIRECTIONS:

1. Attach the sous vide immersion circulator to a Cambro container or pot with water using an adjustable clamp and preheat water to 165°F.

2. Season chicken generously with salt and pepper.

3. Place chicken in a cooking pouch and seal pouch tightly after removing the excess air. Place pouch in sous vide bath and set the cooking time for 1-4 hours.

4. Remove pouch from the sous vide bath and open carefully. Transfer chicken to a plate, reserving the cooking liquid from the pouch.

5. In a large non-stick skillet, heat oil over high heat. Place chicken skin side down and cook for 2-3 minutes. Transfer chicken to a plate and set aside.

6. Wipe out skillet with paper towels then melt butter over low heat. Add reserved cooking liquid and remaining ingredients and simmer until sauce becomes thick.

7. Place sauce over chicken and serve.

CHICKEN THIGHS WITH MUSTARD WINE SAUCE

Preparation Time: 15 minutes
Cooking Time: 4 hours
Cooking Temperature: 165°F

INGREDIENTS:

4 bone-in, skin-on chicken thighs

Kosher salt and freshly ground black pepper, to taste

4 thyme or rosemary sprigs

1 tablespoon canola oil

1 small shallot, minced

1 cup dry white wine

1 tablespoon whole-grain mustard

2 tablespoons unsalted butter

1 tablespoon fresh parsley leaves, minced

½ teaspoon fresh lemon juice

DIRECTIONS:

1. Attach the sous vide immersion circulator to a Cambro container or pot with water using an adjustable clamp and preheat water to 165°F.

2. Season chicken generously with salt and pepper.

3. Place chicken and herbs sprigs in a cooking pouch. Seal pouch tightly after removing the excess air. Place pouch in sous vide bath and set the cooking time for 1-4 hours.

4. Remove pouch from the sous vide bath and open carefully. Take out the chicken thighs, reserving the cooking liquid, and pat dry the chicken thighs with paper towels.

5. Arrange chicken thighs on a cutting board, skin side down. With your hands, press down firmly on each thigh to flatten the skin against the board.

6. In a non-stick skillet, heat oil over medium heat. Place chicken skin side down and cook for 8 minutes. Flip chicken and cook for another 2 minutes then transfer to a paper towel-lined plate.

7. In the same skillet, add the shallot over medium-high heat and sauté for 30 seconds. Add wine and cook for another 2 minutes. Stir in reserved cooking liquid and mustard then remove the skillet from heat. Immediately add butter, parsley, lemon juice, salt, and black pepper and beat until well combined.

8. Serve the chicken with the wine sauce.

CHICKEN THIGHS WITH YOGURT MARINADE

Preparation Time: 15 minutes
Cooking Time: 3 hours
Cooking Temperature: 140°F

INGREDIENTS:

¾ cup plain Greek yogurt

1 garlic clove, minced finely

1 teaspoon fresh ginger, grated

Fresh juice of ½ lemon

1 teaspoon ground cardamom

1 teaspoon ground coriander

1 teaspoon ground cumin

1 teaspoon red chili powder

Salt and freshly ground black pepper, to taste

2 pounds boneless, skinless chicken thighs

Chopped fresh cilantro, for garnishing

Lemon slices, for serving

DIRECTIONS:

1. In a bowl, add yogurt, garlic, ginger, lemon juice, spices, salt, and black pepper and mix until well combined. Add chicken to the yogurt mixture and coat generously.

2. Pour the chicken thighs with all yogurt mixture into a cooking pouch. Seal pouch tightly after removing the excess air. Refrigerate for at least 2 hours.

3. Attach the sous vide immersion circulator to a Cambro container or pot with water using an adjustable clamp and preheat water to 140°F.

4. Remove pouch from the refrigerator 30 minutes before cooking.

5. Place pouch in sous vide bath and set the cooking time for 2½-3 hours.

6. Preheat grill to high heat.

7. Remove pouch from the sous vide bath and open carefully. Remove chicken thighs from pouch and discard any remaining marinade.

8. Grill chicken thighs for 2 minutes per side.

9. Garnish with cilantro and serve alongside lemon slices.

CHICKEN ADOBO

Preparation Time: 15 minutes
Cooking Time: 8 hours
Cooking Temperature: 160°F

INGREDIENTS:

2 whole chicken legs, leg and thigh attached

4-5 garlic cloves, smashed

¼ cup cane vinegar or apple cider vinegar

2 tablespoons soy sauce

1 bay leaf

¼ teaspoon whole black peppercorns

DIRECTIONS:

1. Attach the sous vide immersion circulator to a Cambro container or pot with water using an adjustable clamp and preheat water to 160°F.

2. Mix all ingredients together in a large cooking pouch. Seal pouch tightly after removing the excess air. Place pouch in sous vide bath and set the cooking time for 8 hours.

3. Preheat the oven broiler to high. Line a baking sheet with a piece of foil.

4. Remove pouch from the sous vide bath and open carefully. Remove the chicken legs from the pouch, reserving the cooking liquid in the pouch, and pat dry the chicken legs with paper towels.

5. Arrange chicken legs onto prepared baking sheet in a single layer. Broil for 3-6 minutes.

6. Add reserved cooking liquid to a small pan and bring to a gentle boil. Cook for 5 minutes.

7. Arrange chicken legs onto a serving platter and drizzle with sauce. Serve immediately.

KOREAN CHICKEN WINGS

Preparation Time: 15 minutes
Cooking Time: 2 hours 10 minutes
Cooking Temperature: 147°F

INGREDIENTS:

8 whole chicken wings

Salt and freshly ground black pepper, to taste

2 tablespoons light brown sugar

2 tablespoons rice vinegar

2 tablespoons low-sodium soy sauce

1 tablespoon chili sauce

½ teaspoon sesame oil

½ teaspoon ground ginger

Pinch of ground white pepper

1 scallion, finely chopped

1 tablespoon unsalted peanuts, toasted and chopped

DIRECTIONS:

1. Attach the sous vide immersion circulator to a Cambro container or pot with water using an adjustable clamp and preheat water to 147°F.

2. Season the chicken wings with salt and pepper.

3. In a large cooking pouch, mix together all ingredients. Seal pouch tightly after removing the excess air. Place pouch in sous vide bath and set the cooking time for 2 hours.

4. In a medium pan, mix together brown sugar, vinegar, soy sauce, chili sauce, sesame oil, ground ginger, and white pepper over medium heat and bring to a boil. Simmer until sauce reduces to half. Transfer sauce to a large bowl and set aside.

5. Preheat the oven broiler to high. Line a rimmed baking sheet with a piece of foil.

6. Remove pouch from the sous vide bath and open carefully. Remove chicken wings from pouch and pat dry chicken wings with paper towels.

7. Place chicken wings into the bowl of sauce and toss to coat well. Arrange wings and remaining sauce onto prepared baking sheet. Broil for 10 minutes.

8. Serve with the garnishing of scallion and peanuts.

Chicken with White Wine & Lemon Sauce

Preparation Time: 15 minutes
Cooking Time: 1 hour 10 minutes
Cooking Temperature: 140°F

Ingredients:

2 chicken breasts

Salt and freshly ground black pepper, to taste

1 lemon, sliced

Butter, as required

¼ cup Madeira wine

¼ cup chicken broth

1 teaspoon mustard

Chopped fresh parsley, for garnishing

Directions:

1. Attach the sous vide immersion circulator to a Cambro container or pot with water using an adjustable clamp and preheat water to 140°F.

2. Season chicken breasts evenly with salt and black pepper.

3. Place chicken breasts in a cooking pouch with 1-2 lemon slices. Seal pouch tightly after removing the excess air. Place pouch in sous vide bath and set the cooking time for 1 hour.

4. Remove the pouch from the sous vide bath and open carefully, removing chicken wings from pouch.

5. In a medium skillet, melt butter and sear the chicken breasts for 2-3 minutes or until browned on both sides. Transfer chicken to a plate and set aside.

6. Squeeze the juice from ½ of the lemon into the skillet used to sear the chicken breast. Add wine and scrape browned bits from the bottom of the skillet. Cook until wine is reduced by half. Add chicken broth and mustard and cook until sauce reaches desired thickness. Stir in salt and black pepper and remove from heat.

7. Cut chicken breasts into desired slices and divide onto serving plates. Top evenly with the lemon sauce. Garnish with parsley and serve.

GREEK FLAVORED CHICKEN MEATBALLS

Preparation Time: 15 minutes
Cooking Time: 2 hours
Cooking Temperature: 146°F

INGREDIENTS:

1-pound ground chicken

2 garlic cloves, minced

1 teaspoon fresh oregano, minced

½ teaspoon fresh lemon zest, finely grated

1 teaspoon kosher salt

½ teaspoon freshly ground black pepper

1 tablespoon extra-virgin olive oil

¼ cup panko breadcrumbs

Lemon wedges, for serving

DIRECTIONS:

1. Attach the sous vide immersion circulator to a Cambro container or pot with water using an adjustable clamp and preheat water to 146°F.

2. In a bowl, add all ingredients except for the breadcrumbs and lemon wedges and mix with your hands until well combined. Add breadcrumbs and gently mix. Make 12-14 equal-sized meatballs from the mixture.

3. Place the meatballs in a cooking pouch. Seal pouch tightly after removing the excess air. Place pouch in sous vide bath and set the cooking time for 2 hours.

4. Preheat the oven broiler to high. Line a rimmed baking sheet with a piece of foil.

5. Remove the pouch from the sous vide bath and open carefully, removing the meatballs from pouch.

6. Arrange meatballs onto the prepared baking sheet. Broil meatballs for 5-7 minutes, flipping once halfway through cooking time. Serve alongside lemon wedges.

DUCK BREAST A LA ORANGE

Preparation Time: 15 minutes
Cooking Time: 3 hours 40 minutes
Cooking Temperature: 135°F

INGREDIENTS:

2 (6-ounce) duck breasts

1 shallot, quartered

4 garlic cloves, crushed

4 fresh thyme sprigs

Juice and zest of 1 orange

1 tablespoon black peppercorns

Salt and freshly ground black pepper, to taste

1 tablespoon sherry vinegar

1 cup chicken broth

2 tablespoons cold, unsalted butter

DIRECTIONS:

1. Attach the sous vide immersion circulator to a Cambro container or pot with water using an adjustable clamp and preheat water to 135°F.

2. Place duck breasts, shallot, garlic, thyme, orange zest, juice from orange, and the peppercorns in a cooking pouch. Seal pouch tightly after removing the excess air. Place pouch in sous vide bath and set the cooking time for 3½ hours.

3. Remove pouch from the sous vide bath and open carefully. Remove the duck breasts from pouch, reserving the remaining pouch ingredients and liquid.

4. Pat dry the duck breasts with paper towels. Using a sharp knife, score a wide crisscross pattern on the top skin of both breasts. Season breasts evenly with salt and pepper.

5. Heat a non-stick sauté pan over medium heat and sear breasts for 5 minutes. Transfer the duck breasts to a plate, discarding the duck fat left in the pan.

6. For sauce: in the same pan, add vinegar over medium-high heat and scrape browned bits from bottom of pan. Add the broth and the reserved orange mixture from pouch and simmer until sauce reduces to ¼ cup. Add cold butter and beat until well combined. Stir in desired amount of salt and black pepper and remove from heat.

7. Cut duck breasts into desired slices and serve alongside orange sauce.

TERIYAKI CHICKEN

Preparation Time: 20 minutes
Cooking Time: 56 minutes
Cooking Temperature: 145°F

INGREDIENTS:

For Chicken Bowl:

1 teaspoon garlic, minced

1 teaspoon fresh ginger, minced

4 tablespoons sake

4 tablespoons soy sauce

2 tablespoons rice wine vinegar

1 tablespoon brown sugar

¼ teaspoon chili powder

Freshly ground black pepper, to taste

4 medium chicken thighs

Salt, to taste

1 tablespoon corn flour

1 tablespoon water

4 eggs

2 cups white rice

For Pickled Veggies:

3 cups veggies (2-parts carrot and cucumber, 1-part red onion and daikon), sliced finely

1 cup water

1 cup vinegar

2 tablespoons brown sugar

1 tablespoon salt

DIRECTIONS:

1. Attach the sous vide immersion circulator to a Cambro container or pot with water using an adjustable clamp and preheat water to 145°F.

2. In a bowl, add garlic, ginger, sake, soy sauce, vinegar, brown sugar, chili powder, and black pepper and mix until well combined.

3. Place chicken thighs in a cooking pouch with the ginger mixture. Seal pouch tightly after removing the excess air. Place pouch in sous vide bath and set the cooking time for 50 minutes.

4. Gently place the eggs in the same sous vide bath for 50 minutes.

5. Prepare white rice according to the package's directions

6. For pickled veggies: add all ingredients in a pan over high heat and bring to a boil. Remove from heat and set aside until chicken cooks, keeping the pan covered.

7. Remove pouch and eggs from the sous vide bath. Carefully open pouch and remove chicken thighs, reserving the cooking liquid in a bowl. Pat dry chicken thighs with paper towels. Lightly season chicken thighs with salt.

8. In a small bowl, dissolve corn flour into water. Add the flour mixture to the bowl of reserved cooking liquid and stir to combine.

9. Heat a non-stick skillet over medium heat and sear chicken thighs for 2 minutes on each side. Add reserved liquid mixture to the skillet for the last minute of cooking and toss chicken thighs to coat.

10. With a slotted spoon, transfer chicken thighs to a platter. Continue cooking sauce in the skillet, stirring continuously, until it reaches desired thickness. Remove sauce from heat.

11. Drain pickled veggies and cut chicken thighs into desired slices.

12. Divide cooked rice into serving bowls and top with chicken slices. Pour sauce over chicken slices and place pickled veggies on the side. Crack the egg over rice and chicken. Season with salt and pepper and serve.

LEMON THYME CHICKEN BREASTS

Preparation Time: 10 minutes
Cooking Time: 2 hours
Cooking Temperature: 141°F

INGREDIENTS:

Leaves of 6-7 fresh thyme sprigs

2-3 garlic cloves, finely chopped

1½ tablespoons olive oil

Salt and freshly ground black pepper, to taste

2 chicken breasts

1 lemon, thinly sliced

Chopped fresh thyme, for garnishing

1 lemon, halved

DIRECTIONS:

1. In a bowl, mix together thyme leaves, garlic, oil, salt, and black pepper. Add chicken breasts and coat generously with mixture. Cover and refrigerate for 2 hours.

2. Attach the sous vide immersion circulator to a Cambro container or pot with water using an adjustable clamp and preheat water to 141°F.

3. Place chicken breasts in a large cooking pouch. Place lemon slices over chicken breasts. Seal pouch tightly after removing the excess air. Place pouch in sous vide bath and set the cooking time for 2 hours.

4. Remove pouch from the sous vide bath and open carefully. Remove chicken breasts from pouch and pat dry with paper towels.

5. Heat a cast iron skillet and sear chicken breasts until golden brown on both sides.

6. Serve hot, garnishing with chopped thyme and lemon halves.

TANDOORI CHICKEN

Preparation Time: 15 minutes
Cooking Time: 1 hour 40 minutes
Cooking Temperature: 140°F

INGREDIENTS:

7 tablespoons tandoori paste, divided

3 teaspoons ghee

5 boneless, skinless chicken thighs, sliced into bite-sized pieces

2 tablespoons plain yogurt

1 teaspoon cumin seeds

Vegetable oil, as required

Metal skewers or soaked wooden skewers, for grilling

Your favorite dipping sauce, for serving

DIRECTIONS:

1. Attach the sous vide immersion circulator to a Cambro container or pot with water using an adjustable clamp and preheat water to 140°F.

2. In a small bowl, mix 5 tablespoons of tandoori paste and ghee. Coat chicken thighs evenly with ghee mixture.

3. Place chicken thighs in a cooking pouch. Seal pouch tightly after removing the excess air. Place pouch in sous vide bath and set the cooking time for 1½ hours.

4. For sauce: in a large bowl, add remaining 2 tablespoons tandoori paste, yogurt, and cumin seeds and mix until well combined. Cover the bowl and set aside.

5. Grease a grill pan with oil and heat over high heat.

6. Remove pouch from the sous vide bath and open carefully. Remove chicken thighs from pouch into the bowl with the sauce and toss to coat.

7. Thread the chicken onto skewers and sear on grill pan for 30 seconds on each side.

8. Remove chicken from skewers and divide onto serving plates. Serve with your favorite dipping sauce.

Honey Garlic Chicken Wings

Preparation Time: 15 minutes
Cooking Time: 4 hours 15 minutes
Cooking Temperature: 160°F

Ingredients:

For Sauce:

1 ½-inch piece fresh ginger, chopped

3 garlic cloves, chopped

2 tablespoons honey

1 tablespoon soy sauce

Salt and freshly ground black pepper, to taste

For Wings:

40 split chicken wings

Salt and freshly ground black pepper, to taste

DIRECTIONS:

1. Attach the sous vide immersion circulator to a Cambro container or pot with water using an adjustable clamp and preheat water to 160°F.

2. For sauce: in a bowl, add all sauce ingredients and mix until well combined. Reserve 1 tablespoon of sauce in a separate bowl.

3. Season chicken wings lightly with salt and black pepper.

4. Place chicken wings and all but the 1 tablespoon reserved sauce into a cooking pouch. Seal pouch tightly after removing the excess air. Place pouch in sous vide bath and set the cooking time for 4 hours.

5. Preheat the oven broiler to high. Line a baking sheet with parchment paper.

6. Remove pouch from the sous vide bath and open carefully, removing chicken wings from pouch.

7. Arrange chicken wings onto prepared baking sheet in a single layer. Broil for 10-15 minutes, flipping once halfway through the cooking time.

8. Remove from oven and transfer into bowl of reserved sauce. Toss to coat well and serve immediately.

Aji Amarillo Chicken Wings

Preparation Time: 15 minutes
Cooking Time: 4 hours 15 minutes
Cooking Temperature: 160°F

INGREDIENTS:

For Sauce:

1 teaspoon olive oil

½ white onion, chopped

3 Aji Amarillo peppers, seeded and roughly chopped

2 garlic cloves, chopped

2 tablespoons white vinegar

Salt and freshly ground black pepper, to taste

For Wings:

40 split chicken wings

Salt and freshly ground black pepper, to taste

DIRECTIONS:

1. Attach the sous vide immersion circulator to a Cambro container or pot with water using an adjustable clamp and preheat water to 160°F.

2. For sauce: in a pan, heat oil over medium heat and sauté onion, peppers, and garlic until onion is translucent and peppers softened.

3. Transfer mixture to a blender, add vinegar, salt, and black pepper, and pulse until smooth. Reserve 1 tablespoon of sauce in a bowl.

4. Season chicken wings lightly with salt and black pepper.

5. Place chicken wings and all but the 1 tablespoon of reserved sauce in a cooking pouch. Seal pouch tightly after removing the excess air. Place pouch in sous vide bath and set the cooking time for 4 hours.

6. Preheat the oven broiler to high. Line a baking sheet with parchment paper.

7. Remove pouch from the sous vide bath and open carefully, removing chicken wings from pouch.

8. Arrange chicken wings onto the prepared baking sheet in a single layer. Broil for 10-15 minutes, flipping once halfway through the cooking time.

9. Remove from oven and transfer into bowl of reserved sauce. Toss to coat well and serve immediately.

Extra Spicy Habanero Chicken Wings

Preparation Time: 15 minutes
Cooking Time: 4 hours 15 minutes
Cooking Temperature: 160°F

Ingredients:

For Sauce:

6 habanero peppers

3 tablespoons white vinegar

1 teaspoon butter or oil

For Wings:

40 split chicken wings

Salt and freshly ground black pepper, to taste

DIRECTIONS:

1. Attach the sous vide immersion circulator to a Cambro container or pot with water using an adjustable clamp and preheat water to 160°F.

2. For sauce: add all sauce ingredients in a blender and pulse until smooth. Reserve 1 tablespoon of sauce in a bowl.

3. Season chicken wings lightly with salt and black pepper.

4. In a cooking pouch, place chicken wings and all but the 1 tablespoon of reserved sauce. Seal pouch tightly after removing the excess air. Place pouch in sous vide bath and set the cooking time for 4 hours.

5. Preheat the oven broiler to high. Line a baking sheet with parchment paper.

6. Remove pouch from the sous vide bath and open carefully, removing chicken wings from pouch.

7. Arrange chicken wings onto the prepared baking sheet in a single layer. Broil for 10-15 minutes, flipping once halfway through the cooking time.

8. Remove from oven and transfer into bowl of reserved sauce. Toss to coat well and serve immediately.

CLASSIC CHICKEN WINGS

Preparation Time: 15 minutes
Cooking Time: 4 hours 15 minutes
Cooking Temperature: 160°F

INGREDIENTS:

For Sauce:

> 4 tablespoons hot sauce
>
> 2 tablespoons butter

For Wings:

> 40 split chicken wings
>
> Salt and freshly ground black pepper, to taste

DIRECTIONS:

1. Attach the sous vide immersion circulator to a Cambro container or pot with water using an adjustable clamp and preheat water to 160°F.

2. For sauce: add hot sauce and butter to a bowl and mix until well combined. Reserve 1 tablespoon of all but the 1 tablespoon of reserved sauce in a separate bowl.

3. Season chicken wings lightly with salt and black pepper.

4. Place chicken wings and sauce in a cooking pouch. Seal pouch tightly after removing the excess air. Place pouch in sous vide bath and set the cooking time for 4 hours.

5. Preheat the oven broiler to high. Line a baking sheet with parchment paper.

6. Remove pouch from the sous vide bath and open carefully, removing the chicken wings from pouch.

7. Arrange chicken wings onto the prepared baking sheet in a single layer. Broil for 10-15 minutes, flipping once halfway through the cooking time.

8. Remove from oven and transfer into bowl of reserved sauce. Toss to coat well and serve immediately.

CHICKEN SALAD

Preparation Time: 20 minutes
Cooking Time: 2 hours
Cooking Temperature: 150°F

INGREDIENTS:

2 pounds chicken breast

2 tarragon sprigs

2 garlic cloves, smashed

Zest and juice of 1 lemon

Kosher salt and freshly ground black pepper, to taste

½ cup mayonnaise

1 tablespoon honey

1 celery stalk, minced

1 garlic clove, minced

½ Serrano Chile, stemmed, seeded, and minced

2 tablespoons fresh tarragon leaves, minced

DIRECTIONS:

1. Attach the sous vide immersion circulator to a Cambro container or pot with water using an adjustable clamp and preheat water to 150°F.

2. Place chicken breasts, tarragon sprigs, smashed garlic cloves, lemon zest, salt, and pepper in a cooking pouch. Seal pouch tightly after removing the excess air. Place pouch in sous vide bath and set the cooking time for 2 hours.

3. Remove pouch from the sous vide bath and immediately plunge into a large bowl of ice water.

4. Once cooled completely, remove chicken breasts from pouch and transfer to a cutting board, discarding the tarragon sprigs, garlic, and lemon zest.

5. Roughly chop chicken and transfer place in a bowl. Add remaining ingredients and a little salt and black pepper and stir to combine. Serve immediately.

WHOLE TURKEY

Preparation Time: 20 minutes
Cooking Time: 7 hours 30 minutes
Cooking Temperature: 185°F & 168°F

INGREDIENTS:

8-10 pound whole turkey, rinsed

Olive oil, as required

4 chicken breasts

4 fresh rosemary sprigs, divided

64 ounces chicken broth

2 fresh thyme sprigs

Salt and freshly ground black pepper, to taste

DIRECTIONS:

1. Before use, remove neck and giblets from turkey, reserving the turkey neck. Cover turkey & refrigerate until use.

2. Cut turkey neck and chicken breasts into pieces.

3. In a large pan, heat a little oil over medium heat and sear turkey neck and chicken breasts until browned. Add 2 rosemary sprigs and the chicken broth and bring to a boil. Skim the foam from the surface of the mixture. Reduce heat to low and simmer for 1 hour. Using a strainer, strain the liquid from the pan into a bowl, discarding the turkey neck and chicken pieces. Refrigerate the broth to chill it completely.

4. Attach the sous vide immersion circulator to a Cambro container or pot with water using an adjustable clamp and preheat water to 185°F.

5. Season turkey evenly with salt and pepper then cover both legs and neck bones with aluminum foil pieces.

6. Place turkey neck side down in a large cooking pouch. Place chilled broth and 2 thyme sprigs into the turkey cavity. Arrange 2 rosemary sprigs on the top side of the turkey. Seal pouch tightly after removing the excess air. Place pouch in sous vide bath and set the cooking time for 1 hour.

7. After 1 hour, set sous vide bath temperature to 168°F and set the cooking time for 5 hours.

8. Remove pouch from the sous vide bath and immediately plunge the pouch into a large bowl of ice water. Set aside for 30 minutes to cool.

9. Preheat conventional oven to 350°F.

10. Remove turkey from pouch, reserving cooking liquid in a pan. Transfer turkey to a roasting pan with a raised grill. Roast for 1½ hours.

11. For gravy: place the pan of reserved cooking liquid over medium heat and simmer until desired thickness.

12. Remove turkey from oven and allow to cool on cutting board for 15-20 minutes before carving.

13. Cut turkey into pieces of the desired size and serve alongside gravy.

TURKEY BREAST WITH ORANGE ROSEMARY BUTTER

Preparation Time: 20 minutes
Cooking Time: 2 hours 35 minutes
Cooking Temperature: 145°F

INGREDIENTS:

For Butter Mixture:

¼ cup unsalted butter, softened

1 tablespoon honey

Zest of navel orange

1 teaspoon fresh rosemary, chopped

½ teaspoon salt

⅛ teaspoon ground black pepper

⅛ teaspoon red pepper flakes, crushed

For Turkey Breast:

2 (1½-2-pound) skin-on, boneless turkey breast halves

1½ teaspoons kosher salt

2 fresh rosemary sprigs

DIRECTIONS:

1. Attach the sous vide immersion circulator to a Cambro container or pot with water using an adjustable clamp and preheat water to 145.

2. For butter mixture: add all butter mixture ingredients to a small bowl and mix until well combined.

3. Gently separate skin from each turkey breast half, leaving one side of skin attached to the breast. Sprinkle each exposed breast half with kosher salt. Evenly rub butter mixture under and on top of the skin .

4. Place turkey breast halves and rosemary sprigs in a large cooking pouch. Seal pouch tightly after removing the excess air. Place pouch in sous vide bath and set the cooking time for 2½ hours.

5. Preheat the oven broiler to high.

6. Remove pouch from the sous vide bath and open carefully. Remove turkey breast halves from pouch and pat dry with paper towels. Place on a roasting tray.

7. Broil for 5 minutes.

8. Remove turkey breast halves from the oven. Cut into desired slices and serve.

Turkey Breast with Spiced Sage Rub

Preparation Time: 15 minutes
Cooking Time: 4 hours 5 minutes
Cooking Temperature: 133°F

Ingredients:

For Brine:

> 8 cups water
>
> 2 tablespoons light brown sugar
>
> ¼ cup kosher salt
>
> 1 teaspoon black peppercorns
>
> ½ teaspoon allspice berries

For Turkey:

> 1 whole skin-on, boneless turkey breast, about 4 pounds

For Rub:

> 2 tablespoons fresh sage leaves, minced
>
> 2 garlic cloves, minced
>
> 1½ teaspoon fennel seeds, crushed
>
> ¼ teaspoon red pepper flakes, crushed

For Searing:

> Olive oil, as required

DIRECTIONS:

1. For brine: add all brine ingredients to a large bowl and mix until brown sugar and salt dissolve. Place turkey breast in the bowl and refrigerate, covered, for 6-8 hours.

2. For rub: add all rub ingredients in a bowl and mix until well combined.

3. Attach the sous vide immersion circulator to a Cambro container or pot with water using an adjustable clamp and preheat water to 133°F.

4. Remove turkey breast from brine and pat dry with paper towels.

5. Arrange turkey breast on a smooth surface so that it is flat. Spread rub mixture evenly over breast. Roll up breast into a cylinder and tie with kitchen twine at 1-inch intervals.

6. Place turkey roll in a cooking pouch. Seal pouch tightly after removing the excess air. Place pouch in sous vide bath and set the cooking time for 4 hours.

7. Remove pouch from the sous vide bath and open carefully. Remove turkey roll from pouch and pat dry with paper towels.

8. Heat oil in a skillet. Place turkey roll skin side down in skillet and sear until browned completely.

9. Remove from heat and carefully remove kitchen twine. Cut into slices of the desired size and serve immediately.

Turkey Breast with Crispy Skin

Preparation Time: 15 minutes
Cooking Time: 3 hours 30 minutes
Cooking Temperature: 145°F

Ingredients:

For Turkey Breast:

> 5-pound whole skin-on, bone-in turkey breast
>
> Kosher salt and freshly ground black pepper, to taste

For Gravy:

> 1 tablespoon vegetable oil
>
> 2 celery ribs, roughly chopped
>
> 1 large carrot, peeled and roughly chopped
>
> 1 large onion, roughly chopped
>
> 4 cups low-sodium chicken broth
>
> 1 teaspoon soy sauce
>
> 2 bay leaves
>
> 3 tablespoons butter
>
> ¼ cup flour

Directions:

1. Attach the sous vide immersion circulator to a Cambro container or pot with water using an adjustable clamp and preheat water to 145°F.

2. Carefully remove turkey skin in a single piece and set aside. With a sharp boning knife, carefully remove meat from breastbone and set breastbone aside after chopping it into 1-inch chunks.

3. Season turkey breast generously with salt and black pepper. Place 1 breast half onto a smooth surface with the cut side facing up. Place second breast half with the cut side facing down and the fat end aligning with the skinny end of the first breast half. Gently roll up breast halves into an even cylinder and tie at 1-inch intervals with kitchen twine.

4. Place turkey roll in a cooking pouch. Seal pouch tightly after removing the excess air. Place pouch in sous vide bath and set the cooking time for 2½ hours.

5. Preheat oven to 400°F. Arrange a rack in the center position of the oven. Line a rimmed baking sheet with parchment paper.

6. For crispy skin: spread skin evenly onto prepared baking sheet. Season generously with salt and black pepper. Arrange a second parchment paper over the turkey skin and carefully squeeze out any air bubbles with the side of your hand. Place another rimmed baking sheet on top of the parchment paper.

7. Roast for 30-45 minutes. Remove from oven and set aside to cool in room temperature.

8. For gravy: heat oil over high heat in a medium pan. Add chopped breastbone, celery, carrot, and onion and cook for 10 minutes, stirring occasionally.

9. Add broth, soy sauce, and bay leaves and bring to a boil. Reduce heat and simmer for 1 hour. Through a fine-mesh strainer, strain mixture. The broth should be a little over 4 cups. Discard solids from mixture and keep broth, setting aside.

10. in another medium pan, melt butter over medium heat. Add flour and cook for 3 minutes, stirring continuously. Slowly add broth, beating continuously, and bring to a boil. Reduce heat and simmer until mixture reduces to 3 cups. Season with salt and pepper.

11. Remove pouch from the sous vide bath and open carefully. Remove turkey roll from pouch and carefully remove kitchen twine.

12. Cut roll into ¼-½ inch slices. Break skin into serving-sized pieces. Place turkey slices onto a warmed serving platter with skin pieces arranged around and serve alongside gravy.

Moroccan Turkey Burgers

Preparation Time: 20 minutes
Cooking Time: 1 hour
Cooking Temperature: 146°F

Ingredients:

For Burgers:

½ pound ground turkey breast

2 garlic cloves, crushed

1 tablespoon fresh parsley, chopped

1 teaspoon ground coriander

1 teaspoon ground cumin

¼ teaspoon paprika

¼ teaspoon salt

Freshly ground black pepper, to taste

1 teaspoon peanut oil

For Serving:

2 whole wheat burger buns

Fresh baby spinach leaves, as required

2 beefsteak tomato slices

2 feta cheese slices

Directions:

1. Attach the sous vide immersion circulator to a Cambro container or pot with water using an adjustable clamp and preheat water to 146°F.

2. For burgers: in a bowl, add all burger ingredients except peanut oil and mix until well combined. Divide turkey mixture into 2 equal-sized portions. Press each portion into chefs' rings.

3. Place filled chef rings in a cooking pouch. Seal pouch tightly after removing the excess air. Place pouch in sous vide bath and set the cooking time for 1 hour.

4. Preheat grill to high heat.

5. Remove pouch from the sous vide bath and open carefully. Remove rings from pouch. Carefully push burgers out of the rings and pat dry burgers with paper towels. Coat burgers evenly with peanut oil.

6. Grill burgers until golden brown on both sides.

7. Place 1 burger on each burger bun. Top with baby spinach, followed by tomato, then feta cheese. Serve immediately.

TURKEY MEATBALLS

Preparation Time: 20 minutes
Cooking Time: 1 hour
Cooking Temperature: 145°F

INGREDIENTS:

1 pound ground turkey

¼ cup fresh basil, finely chopped

3 garlic cloves, minced

Zest of 1 lemon

2 tablespoons extra-virgin olive oil

¼ cup mozzarella cheese, cut into small cubes

Salt and freshly ground black pepper, to taste

Grapeseed oil, as required

DIRECTIONS:

1. Attach the sous vide immersion circulator to a Cambro container or pot with water using an adjustable clamp and preheat water to 145°F.

2. In a large bowl, add ground turkey, basil, garlic, lemon zest, and olive oil and mix until well combined. Form mixture into half-spheres. Place a mozzarella cube in the center of a half-sphere then add another half-sphere on top. Roll each sphere into a 1½-inch wide ball.

3. Place meatballs in a cooking pouch. Seal pouch tightly after removing the excess air. Place pouch in sous vide bath and set the cooking time for 1 hour.

4. Remove pouch from the sous vide bath and open carefully. Remove meatballs from pouch and season generously with salt and black pepper.

5. In a cast iron skillet, heat a little grapeseed oil over high heat and sear meatballs until completely golden brown.

6. Serve hot.

Pheasant with Mushrooms

Preparation Time: 20 minutes
Cooking Time: 1 hour
Cooking Temperature: 145°F

Ingredients:

For Pheasant:

2 pheasant breasts, trimmed

Kosher salt and freshly ground black pepper, to taste

2 tablespoons unsalted sweet butter

1 tablespoon extra-virgin olive oil

For Mushrooms:

2 tablespoons extra-virgin olive oil

4 ounces of Beech mushrooms, trimmed

½ cup red onion, finely chopped

2 tablespoons fresh sage leaves, chopped

2 tablespoons unsalted butter

Kosher salt and freshly ground black pepper, to taste

White truffle oil, to taste

Directions:

1. Attach the sous vide immersion circulator to a Cambro container or pot with water using an adjustable clamp and preheat water to 145°F.
2. Season pheasant breasts evenly with salt and black pepper.

3. Place pheasant breasts and butter in a cooking pouch. Seal pouch tightly after removing the excess air. Place pouch in sous vide bath and set the cooking time for 45-60 minutes.

4. Remove pouch from the sous vide bath and open carefully. Remove pheasant breasts from pouch, reserving cooking liquid, and pat dry pheasant breasts with paper towels.

5. In a large, non-stick skillet, heat oil over medium heat. Place pheasant breasts skin side down and sear for 1 minute per side. Transfer pheasant breasts to a plate and set aside.

6. For mushrooms: in the same skillet, heat oil over medium-high heat and sauté mushrooms and onion for 3-5 minutes. Stir in sage, butter, and reserved cooking liquid and bring to a boil. Season with salt and pepper then remove from heat.

7. Place pheasant breasts onto a serving platter and top with the mushroom sauce. Drizzle with truffle oil and serve immediately.

Honey Thyme Duck Breasts

Preparation Time: 10 minutes
Cooking Time: 2 hours 40 minutes
Cooking Temperature: 140°F

Ingredients:

2 medium duck breasts

Salt and freshly ground black pepper, to taste

2 tablespoons balsamic vinegar

1 handful fresh thyme, finely chopped

1 tablespoon honey

DIRECTIONS:

1. Attach the sous vide immersion circulator to a Cambro container or pot with water using an adjustable clamp and preheat water to 140°F.

2. Pat dry duck breasts with paper towels. Season skin side of duck breasts evenly with salt and black pepper. Rub thyme over meat side of breasts.

3. Place duck breasts in a cooking pouch. Seal pouch tightly after removing the excess air. Place pouch in sous vide bath and set the cooking time for 2½ hours.

4. Remove pouch from the sous vide bath and open carefully. Remove duck breasts from pouch, reserving cooking liquid. Pat dry duck breasts with paper towels.

5. Heat a heavy frying pan over medium-high heat. Place duck breasts skin side down in pan and cook for 5 minutes, pressing with a wooden spoon. Flip and cook for 1 minute. Transfer duck breasts to a plate and cover with a piece of foil to keep warm. Leave 1 tablespoon of excess grease in pan, draining the rest.

6. For glaze: in the same pan, add reserved cooking liquid, vinegar, thyme, and honey and cook until desired thickness, stirring occasionally.

7. Cut duck breast into slices of the desired size. Top with glaze and serve.

BBQ Chicken

Preparation Time: 15 minutes
Cooking Time: 2 hours
Cooking Temperature: 141°F

Ingredients:

4 chicken breasts

½ teaspoon ground ancho pepper

Salt and freshly ground black pepper, to taste

1-2 sprigs fresh rosemary

1-2 sprigs fresh thyme

BBQ sauce, as required

Directions:

1. Attach the sous vide immersion circulator to a Cambro container or pot with water using an adjustable clamp and preheat water to 141°F.

2. Rub chicken breasts with ancho pepper then lightly season with salt and black pepper.

3. Place the chicken breast and herb sprigs in a cooking pouch. Seal pouch tightly after removing the excess air. Place pouch in sous vide bath and set the cooking time for 1½-2 hours.

4. Preheat grill to high heat. Grease grill grate.

5. Remove pouch from the sous vide bath and open carefully. Remove chicken breasts from pouch and pat dry chicken breasts with paper towels.

6. Coat each chicken breast evenly with BBQ sauce. Grill chicken breasts for 1 minute per side.

7. Serve alongside rice and fresh salad.

PESTO & MOZZARELLA CHICKEN ROULADE

Preparation Time: 15 minutes
Cooking Time: 1 hour 20 minutes
Cooking Temperature: 141°F

INGREDIENTS:

4 small boneless, skinless chicken breast, butterflied

¼ cup prepared pesto

4 mozzarella cheese slices

1 tablespoon extra-virgin olive oil

Fresh salad, for serving

DIRECTIONS:

1. Attach the sous vide immersion circulator to a Cambro container or pot with water using an adjustable clamp and preheat water to 141°F.

2. With a meat mallet, flatten chicken breast into ¼-⅓ inch thickness. Spread pesto evenly across the breast and top with mozzarella slices. Roll chicken breast tightly into the shape of a cylinder.

3. Place the chicken breast roll in a cooking pouch. Seal pouch tightly after removing the excess air. Place pouch in sous vide bath and set the cooking time for 1¼ hours.

4. Remove pouch from the sous vide bath and open carefully. Remove chicken roll from pouch and pat dry chicken roll with paper towels.

5. In a medium skillet, heat oil over high heat and sear chicken roll for 2-3 minutes or until browned on both sides.

6. Remove from heat and place on a cutting board for 5 minutes before slicing. Cut into desired slices and serve alongside salad.

BREADED CHICKEN SANDWICH

Preparation Time: 25 minutes
Cooking Time: 3 hours
Cooking Temperature: 155°F

INGREDIENTS:

- 4 boneless chicken thighs
- 1 jar dill pickles with juice
- 2 cups plus 3 tablespoons all-purpose flour
- 3 tablespoons paprika
- 2¾ tablespoons onion powder
- 2 teaspoons garlic powder
- 1 cup buttermilk
- Canola oil, for frying
- Sriracha, as required
- Mayonnaise, as required
- 8 Hawaiian rolls, halved and toasted

DIRECTIONS:

1. Attach the sous vide immersion circulator to a Cambro container or pot with water using an adjustable clamp and preheat water to 155°F.
2. With a meat mallet, lightly pound chicken thighs into an even thickness.
3. Place chicken thighs and the pickle juice from the jar of dill pickles in a cooking pouch. Seal pouch tightly after removing the excess air. Place pouch in sous vide bath and set the cooking time for 3 hours.

4. Remove pouch from the sous vide bath and open carefully. Remove chicken thighs from pouch and pat dry chicken thighs with paper towels. Cut each chicken thigh in half lengthwise.

5. In a shallow bowl, mix together flour and spices. In another shallow bowl, mix together buttermilk and a dash of Sriracha.

6. Coat chicken pieces evenly with flour mixture and then dip into buttermilk mixture. Return chicken pieces to the flour mixture to coat a second time.

7. Heat oil to 400°F in a large skillet and fry chicken in batches for 2-3 minutes or until golden brown.

8. Mix together mayonnaise and Sriracha in a bowl. Spread the mayonnaise mixture generously over the top half of each roll. Place a chicken piece on the bottom half of each roll and top with a dill pickle slice. Cover with top halves and serve.

FRIED CHICKEN

Preparation Time: 20 minutes
Cooking Time: 3 hours
Cooking Temperature: 155°F

INGREDIENTS:

4 pound skin-on whole chicken, cut into 6 pieces

4½ teaspoons salt, divided

6 cups pastry flour

3 tablespoons paprika

2¾ tablespoons onion powder

2 teaspoons garlic powder

Freshly ground black pepper, to taste

2 cups buttermilk

4 cups oil

DIRECTIONS:

1. Attach the sous vide immersion circulator to a Cambro container or pot with water using an adjustable clamp and preheat water to 155°F.

2. Evenly season chicken pieces with 2 teaspoons of salt. Place the chicken legs and thighs in one cooking pouch and the breast pieces in another cooking pouch. Seal pouches tightly after removing the excess air. Refrigerate the pouch of breasts to chill.

3. Place pouch of chicken legs and thighs in sous vide bath and set the cooking time for 2 hours. After the 2 hours is complete, add the pouch of chicken breasts to the sous vide bath and set the cooking time for 1 hour.

4. Remove the pouches from the sous vide bath and open carefully. Remove chicken pieces from the pouches and pat dry chicken pieces with paper towels.

5. In a shallow bowl, mix together flour, spices, remaining salt, and black pepper. In another shallow bowl, place buttermilk.

6. Coat chicken pieces evenly with flour mixture then dip into buttermilk mixture. Return chicken pieces to the flour mixture to coat a second time.

7. Heat oil to 400°F in a deep fryer and fry chicken pieces in batches for 2-3 minutes or until golden brown.

QUAIL WITH PANCETTA, LIME, & THYME

Preparation Time: 15 minutes
Cooking Time: 1 hour 45 minutes
Cooking Temperature: 140°F

INGREDIENTS:

For Marinade:

1 tablespoon roasted garlic puree

1 tablespoon fresh thyme leaves

1 tablespoon fresh lemon zest, finely grated

¼ cup extra-virgin olive oil

2 tablespoons fresh lemon juice

Kosher salt and freshly ground black pepper, to taste

For Quail:

4 semi-boneless whole quail

4 slices pancetta rounds, thinly sliced

8 fresh thyme sprigs, divided

DIRECTIONS:

1. Attach the sous vide immersion circulator to a Cambro container or pot with water using an adjustable clamp and preheat water to 140°F.

2. Add all marinade ingredients to a bowl and mix with a wire whisk until well combined.

3. Place 1 quail flat in a cooking pouch. Place 1 pancetta round and 1 thyme sprig over quail. Top with a few tablespoons of the marinade. Repeat with remaining quail, pancetta slices, thyme sprigs, and

marinade so that you have 4 cooking pouches. Reserve the remaining marinade for serving.

4. Seal pouches tightly after removing the excess air. Place pouches in sous vide bath and set the cooking time for 1½ hours.

5. Remove pouches from the sous vide bath and open carefully. Remove quail from the pouches and transfer the pancetta slices onto a plate. Discard thyme sprigs. Pat dry quail with paper towels.

6. Heat a cast iron grill pan over high heat and sear quail, one at a time, for 1 minute per side or until golden brown. Transfer quail to a serving platter.

7. In the same grill pan, sear the pancetta slices for 1-2 minutes per side or until browned.

8. Top each quail with a pancetta slice and one of the remaining thyme sprigs. Drizzle with reserved marinade and serve.

PHEASANT CONFIT

Preparation Time: 15 minutes
Cooking Time: 4-8 hours 45 minutes
Cooking Temperature: 170-180°F

INGREDIENTS:

2 teaspoons fresh lemon zest, minced

1 tablespoon dried thyme, crushed

¼ cup kosher salt

1 tablespoon freshly ground black pepper

6 pheasant legs with thighs

2 bay leaves

6 tablespoons olive oil or melted butter

DIRECTIONS:

1. In a large bowl, mix together lemon zest, thyme, salt, and black pepper. Add pheasant legs and toss to coat with mixture. Refrigerate for 6-24 hours.

2. Attach the sous vide immersion circulator to a Cambro container or pot with water using an adjustable clamp and preheat water to 170-180°F.

3. Remove pheasant legs from the refrigerator and rinse under cold running water. Pat dry each leg with paper towels.

4. Place 3 legs, 1 bay leaf, and 2-3 tablespoons of oil or butter in a cooking pouch. Repeat with remaining legs, bay leaf, and oil or butter so that you have 2 cooking pouches.

5. Seal pouches tightly after removing the excess air. Place pouches in sous vide bath and set the cooking time for 4-8 hours, flipping every 30 minutes. Young, tender pheasant will only need 4 hours cooking time, but older pheasant will need 8 hours.

6. Prepare a greased baking sheet.

7. Remove pouches from the sous vide bath and immediately plunge into a large bowl of ice water. Remove pheasant legs from the pouches and pat dry with paper towels.

8. Set the oven temperature to 400°F. Preheating isn't required.

9. Place pheasant legs onto greased baking sheet, skin side up, and roast for 15-45 minutes or until legs reach desired crispness.

3

PORK

BBQ Ribs with Spiced Rub

Preparation Time: 15 minutes
Cooking Time: 48 hours
Cooking Temperature: 138°F

INGREDIENTS:

1 tablespoon dried oregano, crushed

1 tablespoon ground cumin

1 tablespoon paprika

1 tablespoon red chili powder

1 tablespoon onion powder

1 tablespoon garlic powder

1 tablespoon kosher salt

1 tablespoon freshly ground black pepper

2 pork rib racks, trimmed and each cut into 3-4 bone sections

2 cups barbecue sauce (of your choice)

DIRECTIONS:

1. Attach the sous vide immersion circulator to a Cambro container or pot with water using an adjustable clamp and preheat water to 138°F.

2. In a bowl, mix together oregano, spices, salt, and black pepper. Rub ribs with spice mixture.

3. Place each rib section into a cooking pouch. Seal pouches tightly after removing the excess air. Place pouches in sous vide bath and set the cooking time for 24-48 hours. Cover the sous vide bath with plastic wrap to minimize water evaporation. Add water intermittently to keep the water level up.

4. Preheat the oven broiler.

5. Remove pouches from the sous vide bath and open carefully. Remove rib sections from pouches and pat dry with paper towels.

6. Coat each rib section with BBQ sauce and broil for 1-2 minutes on each side.

7. Serve immediately.

BRINED BBQ RIBS

Preparation Time: 15 minutes
Cooking Time: 24 hours
Cooking Temperature: 155°F

INGREDIENTS:

For Brine:

3-4 pounds Pork spare ribs

6 cups water

1/2 cup brown sugar

1/2 cup salt

For Spice Rub:

3 teaspoons dried basil

2 teaspoons brown sugar

2 teaspoons white sugar

3 teaspoons garlic powder

3 teaspoons paprika

3 teaspoons ancho chiles

2 teaspoons salt

1 teaspoon cumin seeds

Freshly ground black pepper, to taste

For Serving:

BBQ sauce (of your choice)

DIRECTIONS:

1. Cut each rib into 3-4 rib portions.

2. For brine: add water, sugar, and salt to a large bowl and stir until sugar and salt dissolve completely. Add pork ribs, cover, and refrigerate for 24 hours.

3. Attach the sous vide immersion circulator to a Cambro container or pot with water using an adjustable clamp and preheat water to 155°F.

4. For spice rub: mix all spice rub ingredients together in a bowl.

5. Drain ribs and rinse under cold running water then pat dry ribs with paper towels. Season all ribs generously with spice rub.

6. Place each rib portion into a cooking pouch. Seal pouches tightly after removing the excess air. Place pouches in sous vide bath and set the cooking time for 24 hours. During cooking, cover the sous vide bath with plastic wrap to minimize water evaporation. Add water intermittently to keep the water level up.

7. Remove pouches from the sous vide bath and open carefully. Remove rib portions from pouches and pat dry ribs completely with paper towels.

8. Preheat grill to high heat.

9. Grill each rib portion until browned on both sides.

10. Serve immediately with your favorite BBQ sauce.

Chipotle Baby Back Ribs

Preparation Time: 15 minutes
Cooking Time: 48 hours
Cooking Temperature: 143°F

Ingredients:

For BBQ Sauce:

   3 dried ancho chiles, stemmed and seeded

   1 dried New Mexico chile, stemmed and seeded

   ¼ cup sunflower oil

   1 small yellow onion, chopped

   2 garlic cloves, minced

   4½ ounces tomato paste

   ½ cup apple cider vinegar

   ¼ cup brown sugar

   ¼ cup molasses

   3 tablespoons cocoa powder

   1½ teaspoons ground cumin

   1 teaspoon ground coriander

   1 tablespoon sea salt

   2 teaspoons ground black pepper

   1 teaspoon fresh lemon zest, grated

   ¼ cup fresh lemon juice

   ¼ cup fresh lime juice, divided

   1 teaspoon fresh lime zest, grated

For Ribs:

2 racks baby back pork ribs, each rack cut in half

Sea salt and freshly ground black pepper, to taste

For Garnishing:

1-2 limes, cut into wedges

Scallions, chopped

Fresh cilantro, chopped

DIRECTIONS:

1. Add chiles to a heatproof bowl. Add enough hot water to cover and set aside for 15 minutes.

2. Drain chiles, reserving ½ cup of soaking water. Add chiles and reserved soaking water to a blender and pulse until a smooth paste is formed.

3. In a medium pan, heat oil over medium heat and sauté onion and garlic for 10 minutes.

4. Add tomato paste and remaining BBQ sauce ingredients except lime zest and 2 tablespoons of lime juice and bring to a boil. Reduce heat to low and simmer for 20-30 minutes.

5. Remove from heat and set aside to cool completely. Once cool, stir in remaining lime juice and the lime zest. Transfer to a container and refrigerate before use.

6. For ribs: Attach the sous vide immersion circulator to a Cambro container or pot with water using an adjustable clamp and preheat water to 143°F.

7. Season rib racks with salt and black pepper.

8. Divide rib racks into 2 cooking pouches. Seal pouches tightly after removing the excess air. Place pouches in sous vide bath and set the cooking time for 12-48 hours. Cover the sous vide bath with plastic wrap to minimize water evaporation. Add water intermittently to keep the water level up.

9. Preheat grill to high heat and grease grill grate.

10. Remove pouches from the sous vide bath and open carefully. Remove ribs from pouches.

11. Coat each rib rack with BBQ sauce. Grill for 1 minute per side.

12. Serve, garnishing with lime wedges, scallions, and cilantro.

Smokey Baby Back Ribs

Preparation Time: 15 minutes
Cooking Time: 9 hours 15 minutes
Cooking Temperature: 165°F

Ingredients:

¼ cup liquid smoke

¼ cup yellow mustard

A rack of ribs, cut into 3-4 portions

BBQ rub of your choice*

BBQ sauce of your choice*

Directions:

1. Attach the sous vide immersion circulator to a Cambro container or pot with water using an adjustable clamp and preheat water to 165°F.

2. Mix liquid smoke and mustard in a small bowl. Coat ribs with mustard mixture then coat with BBQ rub.

3. Place ribs in a large cooking pouch. Seal pouch tightly after removing the excess air. Place pouch in sous vide bath and set the cooking time for 9 hours.

4. Preheat charcoal grill with a two-zone fire. Place all charcoal on one side of grill.

5. Remove pouch from the sous vide bath and open carefully. Remove pork ribs from pouch.

6. Arrange ribs on a cooler zone and grill meat side up with the cover on for 5 minutes.

7. Remove the lid, coat ribs with BBQ sauce, and grill for 5 more minutes. Repeat a second time, coating ribs with BBQ sauce and grill for 5 minutes.

PORK CHOP WITH CORN, PEPPERS, & TOMATOES

Preparation Time: 10 minutes
Cooking Time: 1 hour
Cooking Temperature: 144°F

INGREDIENTS:

2 bone-in pork chop

½ teaspoon ground ginger

Salt and freshly ground black pepper, to taste

1 handful cherry tomatoes

1 ear of corn, kernels removed and cob discarded

1 bell pepper, peeled, seeded, and sliced into strips

1 garlic clove, minced

2 tablespoons sesame oil

DIRECTIONS:

1. Attach the sous vide immersion circulator to a Cambro container or pot with water using an adjustable clamp and preheat water to 144°F.

2. Season pork chops generously with ground ginger, salt, and pepper.

3. Place pork chops and remaining ingredients in a large cooking pouch. Seal pouch tightly after removing the excess air. Place pouch in sous vide bath and set the cooking time for 1 hour.

4. Remove pouch from the sous vide bath and open carefully. Transfer the pork chops to a serving plate, reserving the vegetables.

5. Heat a cast iron skillet and sear reserved vegetables for 1 minute. Transfer vegetables onto plate with pork chops and serve.

PORK BELLY

Preparation Time: 10 minutes
Cooking Time: 8 hours 15 minutes
Cooking Temperature: 158°F

INGREDIENTS:

2 pounds pork belly

1 teaspoon Chinese five-spice powder

2 teaspoons salt

1 teaspoon ground white pepper

3 tablespoons white vinegar

DIRECTIONS:

1. Attach the sous vide immersion circulator to a Cambro container or pot with water using an adjustable clamp and preheat water to 158°F.

2. Using a sharp paring knife, slide cuts through the pork belly skin 1 inch apart horizontally. Be careful to only cut through the skin and not too deep into the underlying fatty layer.

3. Insert 2 skewers, crisscrossed, into the pork belly.

4. In a small bowl, mix together Chinese five-spice powder, salt, and white pepper. Rub the underside of the pork belly generously with half of the salt mixture.

5. Place pork belly in a large cooking pouch. Seal pouch tightly after removing the excess air. Place pouch in sous vide bath and set the cooking time for 6-8 hours.

6. Preheat the oven broiler to high. Arrange a rack on a baking sheet.

7. Remove pouch from the sous vide bath and open carefully. Remove pork belly from pouch and pat dry pork belly with paper towels.

8. Generously sprinkle underside of pork belly with remaining salt mixture. Flip the belly over and coat with a very thin layer of vinegar.

9. Place pork belly on the rack that is on the baking sheet. Broil for 10-15 minutes, rotating baking sheet occasionally.

10. Transfer pork belly to a cutting board and cut into bite-sized pieces with a large knife. Serve immediately.

BRINED PORK BELLY

Preparation Time: 10 minutes
Cooking Time: 12 hours 10 minutes
Cooking Temperature: 158°F

INGREDIENTS:

4 cups water

½ cup light brown sugar

½ cup kosher salt

2 tablespoons whole black peppercorns

6 fresh thyme sprigs

1 pound skinless pork belly

1 tablespoon vegetable oil

DIRECTIONS:

1. Add water, brown sugar, salt, peppercorns, and thyme to a large pan and bring to a boil. Remove from heat and refrigerate for at least 5 hours. After 5 hours, place pork belly in brine, cover, and refrigerate again for 24 hours.

2. Attach the sous vide immersion circulator to a Cambro container or pot with water using an adjustable clamp and preheat water to 158°F.

3. Remove pork belly from brine and place in a large cooking pouch. Seal pouch tightly after removing the excess air. Place pouch in sous vide bath and set the cooking time for 12 hours. Cover the sous vide bath with plastic wrap to minimize water evaporation. Add water intermittently to keep the water level up.

4. Remove pouch from the sous vide bath and immediately plunge into a large bowl of ice water. Set aside to cool completely. Transfer the pouch to the refrigerator for at least 4 hours.

5. After 4 hours, remove pork belly from pouch and cut into ¾-inch thick slices.

6. In a large, non-stick skillet, heat oil over medium heat and sear pork pieces for 10 minutes. Serve immediately.

SZECHUAN PORK BELLY BITES

Preparation Time: 15 minutes
Cooking Time: 10 hours 5 minutes
Cooking Temperature: 158°F

INGREDIENTS:

1¼ pound pork belly strips, rind removed and cut into 1-inch pieces

1 tablespoon clear honey

Pinch of freshly ground white pepper

Peel of 1 Mandarin orange

1 star anise pod

Pinch of sea salt

2 tablespoons Szechuan peppercorns, ground with a pestle and mortar

1 bottle BBQ sauce (of your choice)

DIRECTIONS:

1. Attach the sous vide immersion circulator to a Cambro container or pot with water using an adjustable clamp and preheat water to 158°F.

2. Place pork belly strips, honey, and a pinch of white pepper in a large cooking pouch. Squish the pouch to coat the pork well. Add orange peel and star anise pod. Seal pouch tightly after removing the excess air. Place pouch in sous vide bath and set the cooking time for 6-10 hours.

3. Preheat conventional oven to 400°F.

4. Mix salt and ground Szechuan peppercorns together in a small bowl.

5. Remove pouch from the sous vide bath and open carefully. Remove pork pieces from pouch and pat dry pork pieces with paper towels.

6. Coat the fatty side of each pork piece with the salt mixture. Arrange pork pieces on a baking sheet and coat pieces with BBQ sauce. Bake for 5 minutes.

7. Insert a cocktail stick into each piece and serve immediately.

PORK TENDERLOIN

Preparation Time: 10 minutes
Cooking Time: 2 hours
Cooking Temperature: 140°F

INGREDIENTS:

1-pound pork tenderloins

1½ tablespoons dry rub of your choice

1½ tablespoons kosher salt

Freshly ground black pepper, to taste

2 tablespoons butter

DIRECTIONS:

1. Attach the sous vide immersion circulator to a Cambro container or pot with water using an adjustable clamp and preheat water to 140°F.

2. Season pork tenderloin with dry rub, salt, and black pepper generously.

3. Divide pork tenderloins and butter into 2 cooking pouches. Seal pouches tightly after removing the excess air. Place pouches in sous vide bath and set the cooking time for 2 hours.

4. Remove pouches from the sous vide bath and open carefully. Remove pork tenderloins from pouches and pat dry pork tenderloins with paper towels.

5. Heat a cast iron skillet and sear pork tenderloin until browned. Serve immediately.

PORK CARNITAS

Preparation Time: 15 minutes
Cooking Time: 24 hours 10 minutes
Cooking Temperature: 145°F

INGREDIENTS:

1 tablespoon red chili powder

1 teaspoon garlic powder

1 teaspoon ground cumin

1 teaspoon salt

1 teaspoon ground black pepper

2 pounds of pork shoulder

DIRECTIONS:

1. Attach the sous vide immersion circulator to a Cambro container or pot with water using an adjustable clamp and preheat water to 145°F.

2. Mix all spices together in a small bowl. Rub pork shoulder generously with spice rub.

3. Place pork shoulder in a large cooking pouch. Seal pouch tightly after removing the excess air. Place pouch in sous vide bath and set the cooking time for 24 hours. Cover the sous vide bath with plastic wrap to minimize water evaporation. Add water intermittently to keep the water level up.

4. Remove pouch from the sous vide bath and open carefully. Remove pork shoulder from pouch and place in a bowl, setting aside to cool slightly.

5. Pull the pork meat from pork shoulder, discarding any fatty pieces.

6. Heat a cast iron skillet and sear meat until crisp.

7. Serve over corn tortillas with your favorite toppings.

COUNTRY PORK RIBS WITH DIJON

Preparation Time: 15 minutes
Cooking Time: 24 hours
Cooking Temperature: 165°F

INGREDIENTS:

1 tablespoon ground rosemary

1 tablespoon garlic powder

1 tablespoon onion powder

2 tablespoons kosher salt

1 tablespoon ground black pepper

3 pounds country style pork ribs

1 tablespoon cornstarch

2 tablespoons water

3 tablespoons Dijon mustard

1 tablespoon vegetable oil

DIRECTIONS:

1. Attach the sous vide immersion circulator to a Cambro container or pot with water using an adjustable clamp and preheat water to 165°F.

2. Mix rosemary, spices, salt, and black pepper together in a small bowl. Rub pork ribs generously with spice mixture.

3. Place ribs in a cooking pouch. Seal pouch tightly after removing the excess air. Place pouch in sous vide bath and set the cooking time for 24 hours. Cover the sous vide bath with plastic wrap to minimize water evaporation. Add water intermittently to keep the water level up.

4. In a small bowl, dissolve cornstarch into water. Set aside.

5. Remove pouch from the sous vide bath and open carefully. Remove ribs from pouch, reserving cooking liquid in pan, pat dry ribs with paper towels.

6. Place the pan of cooking liquid on medium-high heat. Add cornstarch mixture and Dijon mustard to pan and beat until well combined. Cook until desired thickness is reached.

7. Heat oil in a skillet over high heat and sear ribs until browned on both sides.

8. Serve ribs topped with sauce.

SIMPLE PORK CHOPS

Preparation Time: 15 minutes
Cooking Time: 4 hours
Cooking Temperature: 140°F

INGREDIENTS:

4 (1½-inch thick) bone-in pork rib chops

Kosher salt and freshly ground black pepper, to taste

2 tablespoons vegetable oil

2 tablespoons butter, divided

2 garlic cloves

4 thyme or rosemary sprigs

2 shallots, thinly sliced

DIRECTIONS:

1. Attach the sous vide immersion circulator to a Cambro container or pot with water using an adjustable clamp and preheat water to 140°F.

2. Season pork chops generously with salt and black pepper.

3. Place pork chops in a cooking pouch. Seal pouch tightly after removing the excess air. Place pouch in sous vide bath and set the cooking time for 1-4 hours.

4. Remove pouch from the sous vide bath and open carefully. Remove chops from pouch and pat dry with paper towels.

5. In a heavy, large cast iron skillet, heat oil and 1 tablespoon of butter over high heat and sear chops for 45 seconds. Flip pork chops and add remaining butter, garlic, herb sprigs, and shallots to the skillet. Cook for 45 seconds, occasionally pouring the butter over the chops.

6. Serve pork chops topped with sauce left in skillet.

GARLIC & HERB RUBBED PORK CHOPS

Preparation Time: 20 minutes
Cooking Time: 2 hours 10 minutes
Cooking Temperature: 140°F

INGREDIENTS:

¼ cup fresh chives

¼ cup fresh rosemary, stems removed

¼ cup fresh parsley

6 fresh thyme sprigs, stems removed

10 large basil leaves

2 garlic cloves, minced

Zest of 1 lemon

¼ cup extra-virgin olive oil

1 tablespoon white balsamic vinegar

½ teaspoon salt

1 teaspoon freshly cracked black pepper

4 (1½-inch thick) large bone-in pork chops

DIRECTIONS:

1. Attach the sous vide immersion circulator to a Cambro container or pot with water using an adjustable clamp and preheat water to 140°F.

2. In a food processor, add herbs and pulse until finely chopped. Add garlic, lemon zest, olive oil, vinegar, salt, and black pepper and pulse until a smooth paste is formed. Rub chops evenly with herb mixture.

3. Place chops in a cooking pouch. Seal pouch tightly after removing the excess air. Place pouch in sous vide bath and set the cooking time for 2 hours.

4. Preheat the oven broiler to high. Grease a baking sheet.

5. Remove pouch from the sous vide bath and open carefully. Remove chops from pouch.

6. Transfer chops onto prepared baking sheet and broil for 3-4 minutes per side. Serve immediately.

THAI PORK CHOPS WITH GREEN CURRY

Preparation Time: 15 minutes
Cooking Time: 2 hours
Cooking Temperature: 135°F

INGREDIENTS:

4 boneless pork loin chops

2 Thai green chili peppers, minced

2 tablespoons fresh ginger, minced

3 garlic cloves, minced

4 tablespoons oil

1 teaspoon salt

1 can coconut milk

3 tablespoons green curry paste

2 tomatoes, chopped

4 tablespoons fresh Thai basil, minced

Vegetable oil, as required

DIRECTIONS:

1. In a large bowl, add Thai chilies, ginger, garlic, ginger, 4 tablespoons oil, and salt. Add pork chops and toss to coat well. Let sit for 1-2 hours.

2. Attach the sous vide immersion circulator to a Cambro container or pot with water using an adjustable clamp and preheat water to 135°F.

3. In a cooking pouch, place chops with some of marinade. Seal pouch tightly after removing the excess air. Place pouch in sous vide bath and set the cooking time for 2 hours.

4. For green curry sauce: while pork chops are in sous vide bath, add coconut milk and green curry paste to a small pan and cook until just starting to boil. Reduce heat to low and simmer for 10 minutes.

5. In a bowl, mix together tomatoes and basil. Set aside.

6. Remove pouch from the sous vide bath and open carefully. Remove chops from pouch and pat dry chops with paper towels.

7. In a cast iron skillet, heat a little vegetable oil over high heat and sear pork chops for 30-60 seconds per side.

8. Divide chops onto serving plates and top with tomato mixture. Drizzle with green curry sauce and serve.

PORK CHOPS WITH APPLE CIDER SAUCE

Preparation Time: 20 minutes
Cooking Time: 12 hours
Cooking Temperature: 140°F

INGREDIENTS:

4 extra-thick pork chops

Salt and freshly ground black pepper, to taste

5 tablespoons butter, divided

8 thyme sprigs

2 apples, cored and sliced

2 garlic cloves, finely chopped

⅔ cup hard apple cider

1 tablespoon whole grain mustard

1 teaspoon cider vinegar

1 teaspoon sugar

DIRECTIONS:

1. Attach the sous vide immersion circulator to a Cambro container or pot with water using an adjustable clamp and preheat water to 140°F.

2. Season pork chops lightly with salt and black pepper.

3. Divide chops, 4 tablespoons of butter, and thyme sprigs into 4 cooking pouches with each pouch containing 1 pork chop, 1 tablespoon of butter, and 2 thyme sprigs. Seal pouches tightly after removing the excess air. Place pouches in sous vide bath and set the cooking time for 12 hours.

4. For sauce: add apples and remaining tablespoon of butter to a pan and cook over medium-high heat until apples just begin to soften.

5. Remove pouches from the sous vide bath and open carefully. Remove the chops from the pouches, reserving the cooking liquid.

6. Heat a grill pan over high heat and sear chops until browned on both sides.

7. Add garlic, apple cider, mustard, cider vinegar, sugar, and ½ cup of reserved cooking liquid to pan of apples and simmer for a few minutes or until desired sauce thickness is reached.

8. Divide chops onto serving plates and top evenly with the apple sauce. Serve immediately.

CHAR SUI (CHINESE PORK)

Preparation Time: 15 minutes
Cooking Time: 15 hours 5 minutes
Cooking Temperature: 155°F

INGREDIENTS:

For Pork Shoulder:

2 tablespoons caster sugar

2 cubes Chinese red fermented bean curd

2 teaspoons Chinese rose wine

1 tablespoon mild honey

1 tablespoon oyster sauce

1 tablespoon hoisin sauce

1 teaspoon soy sauce

1 teaspoon Chinese five spice powder

¼ teaspoon ground white pepper

large pork shoulder

For Glaze:

1 tablespoon honey

DIRECTIONS:

1. Attach the sous vide immersion circulator to a Cambro container or pot with water using an adjustable clamp and preheat water to 155°F.

2. For pork shoulder: in a large bowl, add all ingredients for pork shoulder except the meat and mix until well combined. Add pork shoulder and coat generously with marinade.

3. Place the pork shoulder in a cooking pouch with the marinade. Seal pouch tightly after removing the excess air. Place pouch in sous vide bath and set the cooking time for 15 hours. Cover the sous vide bath with plastic wrap to minimize water evaporation. Add water intermittently to keep the water level up.

4. Preheat the oven broiler to high.

5. Remove pouch from the sous vide bath and open carefully. Remove pork shoulder from pouch, reserving 1-2 tablespoons of the cooking liquid.

6. For glaze: in a small bowl, mix together reserved cooking liquid and honey. Coat pork shoulder with glaze mixture.

7. Transfer pork shoulder onto a roasting pan. Broil until charred on both sides.

8. Remove from oven. Cut into slices of the desired size and serve.

SMOKEY PULLED PORK SHOULDER

Preparation Time: 20 minutes
Cooking Time: 25 hours 30 minutes
Cooking Temperature: 165°F

INGREDIENTS:

For Spice Rub:

¼ cup dark brown sugar

¼ cup paprika

3 tablespoons kosher salt

2 tablespoons granulated garlic powder

1 tablespoon whole yellow mustard seed

1 tablespoon whole coriander seed

1 tablespoon dried oregano

1 teaspoon freshly ground black pepper

1 teaspoon red pepper flakes

½ teaspoon Prague Powder

For Pork:

1 (5-7 pound) boneless pork shoulder

½ teaspoon liquid smoke

Kosher salt, to taste

DIRECTIONS:

1. Attach the sous vide immersion circulator to a Cambro container or pot with water using an adjustable clamp and preheat water to 165°F.

129

2. For Spice Rub: in a spice grinder, add all ingredients for spice rub in batches and grind until a fine powder is formed.

3. Rub pork evenly with half of spice mixture.

4. Place pork shoulder and liquid smoke in a large cooking pouch. Seal pouch tightly after removing the excess air. Place pouch in sous vide bath and set the cooking time for 18-24 hours. Cover the sous vide bath with plastic wrap to minimize water evaporation. Add water intermittently to keep the water level up.

5. Preheat oven to 300°F. In the oven, arrange a rack in the lower-middle position. Arrange another rack on a rimmed baking sheet.

6. Remove pouch from the sous vide bath and open carefully. Remove pork shoulder from pouch.

7. Rub remaining spice mixture evenly onto the surface of the pork. Place pork on the wire rack that is on the rimmed baking sheet. Roast for 1½ hours.

8. Remove pork from oven and transfer to a cutting board. With 2 forks, shred meat into bite-size pieces.

9. Season pulled pork with salt and serve immediately.

Pulled Pork Shoulder

Preparation Time: 25 minutes
Cooking Time: 36 hours
Cooking Temperature: 149°F

Ingredients:

For Pork:

4-pound bone-in pork shoulder, trimmed of large fat pieces

Salt and freshly ground black pepper, to taste

3 whole garlic cloves, peeled

1 bay leaf

1 teaspoon dried thyme, crushed

¼ teaspoon celery salt

For Barbecue Sauce:

1 cup ketchup

¼ cup red onion, finely chopped

1 garlic clove, minced

¼ cup fresh orange juice

1 tablespoon fresh lemon juice

2 tablespoons molasses

2 tablespoons apple cider vinegar

1 tablespoon tomato paste

1 teaspoon yellow mustard

1 teaspoon liquid smoke

1 teaspoon Worcestershire sauce

¼ teaspoon celery salt

For Pickled Onion:

½ red onion, thinly sliced

1 tablespoon apple cider vinegar

1½ teaspoons raw (turbinado) sugar

¼ teaspoon salt

1½ tablespoons boiling water

For Serving:

4 dinner rolls, halved

DIRECTIONS:

1. Attach the sous vide immersion circulator to a Cambro container or pot with water using an adjustable clamp and preheat water to 149°F.
2. Season pork shoulder evenly with salt and pepper.
3. Place pork shoulder, whole garlic cloves, bay leaf, thyme, and celery salt in a large cooking pouch. Roll the pork around in the bag to coat with seasonings.
4. Seal pouch tightly after removing the excess air. Place pouch in sous vide bath and set the cooking time for 36 hours. Cover the sous vide bath with plastic wrap to minimize water evaporation. Add water intermittently to keep the water level up.
5. For barbecue sauce: add all barbecue sauce ingredients to a pan over medium-high heat and bring to a boil. Reduce heat to low and simmer for 30 minutes, stirring occasionally. Remove from heat and set aside to cool at room temperature. Transfer sauce into a bowl and refrigerate until serving.
6. Remove pouch from the sous vide bath and open carefully. Remove pork shoulder from pouch, reserving cooking liquid in a large bowl.

7. With 2 forks, shred pork into small pieces. Discard all large fat pieces and bones. Transfer pork into a bowl with reserved cooking liquid and refrigerate overnight.

8. For pickled onion: in a small bowl, mix together sliced onion, vinegar, sugar, and salt. Add boiling water and stir to combine. Set aside at room temperature to cool. Refrigerate before serving.

9. For sandwiches: Add sauce to a medium pan over medium-high heat and cook for 2-3 minutes or until warmed. Add 1 pound of shredded pork and stir to combine. Reduce heat to low and simmer for 4-5 minutes or until heated completely.

10. Place pork mixture over each roll evenly. Top with pickled onion and serve.

MISO PORK MEATBALLS

Preparation Time: 20 minutes
Cooking Time: 2 hours
Cooking Temperature: 150°F

INGREDIENTS:

1 pound ground pork

⅓ cup mushrooms, minced finely

⅓ cup fresh cilantro, chopped

⅓ cup scallions, minced finely

1 lemongrass stalk (white, tender, inner part), minced finely

2 garlic cloves, finely chopped

1 tablespoon fish sauce

1 tablespoon miso

1½ teaspoons cornstarch

1 teaspoon kosher salt

Few grinds of black pepper

3-4 tablespoons sesame seeds

DIRECTIONS:

1. In a large bowl, add all ingredients except sesame seeds and mix until well combined. Refrigerate mixture for at least 1 hour.

2. With slightly damp hands, make golf-ball sized meatballs from pork mixture. Arrange meatballs onto a baking sheet lined with parchment and freeze for at least 1½-2 hours.

3. Attach the sous vide immersion circulator to a Cambro container or pot with water using an adjustable clamp and preheat water to 150°F.

4. Place meatballs in a large cooking pouch with space around each meatball. Seal pouch tightly after removing the excess air. Place pouch in sous vide bath and set the cooking time for 2-3 hours.

5. Remove pouch from the sous vide bath and open carefully. Remove meatballs from pouch and pat dry with paper towels. Evenly coat meatballs with sesame seeds.

6. Heat a non-stick skillet over medium-high heat and fry meatballs until browned on both sides.

7. Serve immediately.

PORK SAUSAGE

Preparation Time: 10 minutes
Cooking Time: 4 hours
Cooking Temperature: 171°F

INGREDIENTS:

3 pounds raw, natural casing sausages

6-ounces beer

2-6 teaspoons kosher salt

1 tablespoon butter

DIRECTIONS:

1. Attach the sous vide immersion circulator to a Cambro container or pot with water using an adjustable clamp and preheat water to 171°F.

2. Place sausages in a single layer in cooking pouches. Add a few tablespoons of beer and 2 teaspoons of salt to each pouch. Seal pouches tightly after removing the excess air. Place pouches in sous vide bath and set the cooking time for 4 hours.

3. Remove pouches from the sous vide bath and open carefully. Remove sausages from pouch and pat dry with paper towels.

4. In a skillet, melt butter over medium heat and cook sausages for 3 minutes, flipping occasionally.

5. Serve immediately.

ITALIAN SAUSAGE WITH PEPPERS & ONION

Preparation Time: 20 minutes
Cooking Time: 3 hours
Cooking Temperature: 140°F

INGREDIENTS:

For Sausage:

8 Italian sausage links

For Vegetables:

1 orange bell pepper

1 red bell pepper

1 poblano pepper

2 onions, cut into ½-¾-inch thick slices

Salt and freshly ground black pepper, to taste

Canola oil, as required

DIRECTIONS:

1. Attach the sous vide immersion circulator to a Cambro container or pot with water using an adjustable clamp and preheat water to 140°F.

2. Place sausages in cooking pouches in a single layer. Seal pouches tightly after removing the excess air. Place pouches in sous vide bath and set the cooking time for 2-3 hours.

3. Preheat the grill to high heat.

4. While the sausages are in the sous vide bath, cut into the sides of each pepper, leaving them whole. Sprinkle each of the peppers and onion with salt and pepper and drizzle with oil.

5. Grill peppers and onions until they begin to brown.

6. Remove from grill and set aside to cool slightly. After cooling, cut peppers into ½-inch strips.

7. Remove pouches from the sous vide bath and open carefully. Remove sausages from pouch and pat dry with paper towels.

8. Sear sausages over high heat on the grill for 1-2 minutes per side.

9. Divide peppers and onions onto serving plates and top with sausages.

ROSEMARY PORK CHOPS

Preparation Time: 15 minutes
Cooking Time: 2 hours 5 minutes
Cooking Temperature: 140°F

INGREDIENTS:

1-pound bone-in, double-cut pork chop

Kosher salt and freshly ground black pepper, to taste

1 garlic clove, finely chopped

1 fresh rosemary sprig, finely chopped

1 cup hard cider, divided

1 tablespoon vegetable oil

1 tablespoon dark brown sugar

Sautéed apples, for serving

Sautéed cabbage, for serving

DIRECTIONS:

1. Attach the sous vide immersion circulator to a Cambro container or pot with water using an adjustable clamp and preheat water to 140°F.

2. Season pork chop generously with salt and pepper then rub with garlic and rosemary.

3. Place pork chop and ½ cup of hard cider in a cooking pouch. Seal pouch tightly after removing the excess air. Place pouch in sous vide bath and set the cooking time for 45-120 minutes.

4. Remove pouch from the sous vide bath and open carefully. Remove pork chop from pouch, reserving the cooking liquid. Pat dry the pork chop with paper towels.

5. In a cast iron skillet, heat oil over medium-high heat and sear pork chop for 30-45 seconds per side. Transfer pork chop to a serving platter.

6. In the same skillet used for the pork chop, add reserved cooking liquid, remaining hard cider, and sugar and bring to a rapid simmer for 1 minute, stirring continuously.

7. Place sauce over pork chop and serve alongside sautéed apples and cabbage.

HOISIN GLAZED PORK TENDERLOIN

Preparation Time: 10 minutes
Cooking Time: 3 hours 5 minutes
Cooking Temperature: 145°F

INGREDIENTS:

1-pound pork tenderloin, trimmed

1 teaspoon kosher salt

½ teaspoon freshly ground black pepper

3 tablespoons hoisin sauce

DIRECTIONS:

1. Attach the sous vide immersion circulator to a Cambro container or pot with water using an adjustable clamp and preheat water to 145°F.

2. Season pork tenderloin generously with salt and pepper.

3. Place pork tenderloin in a cooking pouch. Seal pouch tightly after removing the excess air. Place pouch in sous vide bath and set the cooking time for 3 hours.

4. Preheat grill to high heat.

5. Remove pouch from the sous vide bath and open carefully. Remove pork tenderloin from pouch and pat dry with paper towels.

6. Coat pork tenderloin with hoisin sauce. Grill for 5 minutes, flipping once halfway through cooking time.

7. Remove from grill, transfer to a cutting board, and set aside for 5 minutes. Cut tenderloin into small medallions and serve immediately.

PORK CHOPS WITH MIXED MUSHROOMS

Preparation Time: 10 minutes
Cooking Time: 55 minutes
Cooking Temperature: 140°F

INGREDIENTS:

8-ounce thick-cut, bone-in pork chops

Salt and freshly ground black pepper, to taste

2 tablespoons cold unsalted butter, divided

4 ounces mixed wild mushrooms

¼ cup sherry

1 tablespoon steak marinade

½ cup beef broth

Chopped garlic chives, for garnishing

DIRECTIONS:

1. Attach the sous vide immersion circulator to a Cambro container or pot with water using an adjustable clamp and preheat water to 140°F.

2. Season pork chops generously with salt and pepper.

3. Place pork chops in a cooking pouch. Seal pouch tightly after removing the excess air. Place pouch in sous vide bath and set the cooking time for 45 minutes.

4. Remove pouch from the sous vide bath and open carefully. Remove pork chops from pouch and pat dry with paper towels.

5. In a large skillet, melt 1 tablespoon of butter over medium-high heat and sear pork chops for 1 minute on each side. Transfer chops to a plate and cover with foil to keep warm.

6. In the same skillet used for the pork chops, add the mushrooms and cook for 2-3 minutes, stirring occasionally. Add sherry and bring to a boil, scraping up browned bits from the bottom of skillet.

7. Stir in steak marinade and broth and bring to a boil. Reduce heat to medium and simmer until sauce becomes slightly thick, stirring occasionally.

8. Remove from heat and immediately stir in remaining butter, ½ tablespoon at a time until sauce becomes smooth. Add salt and black pepper.

9. Divide pork chops on serving plates and top with mushroom sauce. Garnish with garlic chives and serve.

PORK STEAKS WITH CREAMY SLAW

Preparation Time: 15 minutes
Cooking Time: 24 hours
Cooking Temperature: 160°F

INGREDIENTS:

For Pork Steaks:

2 (1-inch thick) pork shoulder steaks

1 teaspoon kosher salt

½ teaspoon freshly ground black pepper

1 teaspoon vegetable oil

For Creamy Slaw:

½ small, purple cabbage head, cored and thinly sliced

¼ teaspoon fine sea salt

½ teaspoon freshly ground black pepper

2 tablespoons olive oil

2 tablespoons mayonnaise

Fresh juice of 1 lemon

1 teaspoon Dijon mustard

DIRECTIONS:

1. Attach the sous vide immersion circulator to a Cambro container or pot with water using an adjustable clamp and preheat water to 160°F.

2. For pork steaks: season pork steaks evenly with salt and black pepper.

3. Divide pork steaks into two cooking pouches. Seal pouches tightly after removing the Cover the sous vide bath with plastic wrap to minimize water evaporation. Add water intermittently to keep the water level up.

4. For slaw: in a large bowl, place cabbage, sea salt, and black pepper and toss to coat well.

5. In a small bowl, add remaining slaw ingredients and beat until well combined. Pour mustard mixture over cabbage and toss to coat well.

6. Remove pouches from the sous vide bath and open carefully. Remove pork steaks from pouches and pat dry with paper towels.

7. In a cast iron skillet, heat oil over medium heat and sear pork steaks for 1 minute on each side.

8. Cut each steak into 2 pieces of equal size. Divide pork pieces onto serving plates and serve alongside creamy slaw.

HAM WITH BALSAMIC BROWN SUGAR GLAZE

Preparation Time: 15 minutes
Cooking Time: 8 hours
Cooking Temperature: 140°F

INGREDIENTS:

7-10-pound bone-in half ham, packing intact

1 cup brown sugar

1 cup balsamic vinegar

DIRECTIONS:

1. Attach the sous vide immersion circulator to a Cambro container or pot with water using an adjustable clamp and preheat water to 140°F.

2. Place ham in a cooking pouch. Seal pouch tightly after removing the excess air. Place pouch in sous vide bath and set the cooking time for 3-8 hours.

3. In a small pan, add brown sugar over medium-high heat and cook until melted. Continue cooking until sugar becomes deep brown.

4. Immediately add vinegar and cook until the sugar dissolves, stirring occasionally.

5. Reduce heat and simmer for 5 minutes, continuing to stir. Remove from heat and set aside.

6. Preheat the oven to 500°F. Arrange a rack in the lower position of the oven. Arrange another rack on a foil-lined, rimmed baking sheet.

7. Remove pouch from the sous vide bath and open carefully. Remove packaging and pat dry ham with paper towels.

8. Place ham on rack arranged on the baking sheet, cut-side down. Coat ham with glaze. Roast for 5 minutes.

9. Remove the ham from the oven and coat with glaze. Set aside for 5 minutes.

10. Place ham on a cutting board, cut-side down. Divide ham into 2 pieces by making a single slice right next to the bone.

11. Place boneless side with the newly-cut side facing down and cut into thin slices. Repeat with remaining ham.

CREAM POACHED PORK LOIN

Preparation Time: 15 minutes
Cooking Time: 4 hours 10 minutes
Cooking Temperature: 145°F

INGREDIENTS:

3-pound boneless pork loin roast

Kosher salt and freshly ground black pepper, to taste

2 onions, thinly sliced

¼ cup cognac

1 cup heavy cream

1 cup whole milk

DIRECTIONS:

1. Attach the sous vide immersion circulator to a Cambro container or pot with water using an adjustable clamp and preheat water to 145°F.

2. Season pork roast evenly with salt and black pepper. Heat a large cast iron skillet over medium-high heat and sear pork roast for 15 minutes or until golden brown on both sides. Transfer pork roast to a platter, leaving grease in the pan.

3. In the same pan, add onions and sauté. After 5 minutes, add cognac and bring to a boil. Reduce heat and simmer for 1 minute. Remove from heat and set aside to cool for at least 10 minutes.

4. Place pork, onions, cream, and milk in a cooking pouch. Seal pouch tightly after removing the excess air. Place pouch in sous vide bath and set the cooking time for 4 hours.

5. Remove pouch from the sous vide bath and open carefully. Remove pork roast from pouch and transfer to a cutting board, reserving cooking liquid. Cover pork roast with a piece of foil to keep warm.

6. Place cream mixture from pouch in a large skillet over medium heat and bring to a boil. Cook for 10 minutes, stirring occasionally. Stir in salt and black pepper and remove from heat.

7. Cut pork roast into slices of the desired size and serve alongside cream sauce.

HAWAIIAN PORK SLIDERS

Preparation Time: 25 minutes
Cooking Time: 24 hours
Cooking Temperature: 150°F

INGREDIENTS:

3 tablespoons light brown sugar

3 tablespoons ground Hawaiian sea salt

2 tablespoons garlic powder

Freshly ground black pepper, to taste

3 pounds bone-in pork shoulder

1 tablespoon vegetable oil

3 tablespoons liquid smoke

1 cup pineapple juice

½ cup mayonnaise

¼ cup white wine vinegar

1 cup pineapple, diced finely

14-ounce bag coleslaw mix

2 tablespoons scallions, thinly sliced

Kosher salt, to taste

24 King's Hawaiian rolls

DIRECTIONS:

1. Mix sugar, Hawaiian salt, garlic powder, and 2 tablespoons of black pepper together in a large bowl. Add pork shoulder and coat with sugar mixture. Cover and refrigerate for at least 12 hours.

2. Attach the sous vide immersion circulator to a Cambro container or pot with water using an adjustable clamp and preheat water to 150°F.

3. Remove pork shoulder from refrigerator and pat dry with paper towels. Discard any accumulated liquid.

4. In a large skillet, heat oil over medium-high heat and sear pork shoulder for 5 minutes or until golden brown on both sides. Transfer pork shoulder to a plate and set aside to cool for 10 minutes.

5. Place pork shoulder, liquid smoke, and pineapple juice in a cooking pouch.

6. Seal pouch tightly after removing the excess air. Place pouch in sous vide bath and set the cooking time for 24 hours.

7. Remove pouch from the sous vide bath and open carefully. Remove pork roast from pouch and place into a bowl. Set aside to cool for 20 minutes. Reserve cooking liquid in a large bowl.

8. With 2 forks, shred pork shoulder into bite-sized pieces. Discard any large fat pieces and bones. Add the shredded pork to the bowl of reserved cooking liquid and toss to coat.

9. In another large bowl, add mayonnaise and vinegar and beat until well combined. Add pineapple, coleslaw mix, scallions, kosher salt, and black pepper and mix until well combined.

10. Place pulled pork and coleslaw mixture on each roll and serve.

SWEET & SPICY PORK LOIN

Preparation Time: 15 minutes
Cooking Time: 6 hours
Cooking Temperature: 153°F

INGREDIENTS:

2-pound pork loin roast

1 teaspoon garlic powder

½ teaspoon chipotle powder

1 teaspoon salt

1 teaspoon freshly ground black pepper

2 tablespoons sweet & sour duck sauce or sweet glaze of your choice

DIRECTIONS:

1. Attach the sous vide immersion circulator to a Cambro container or pot with water using an adjustable clamp and preheat water to 153°F.

2. In a small bowl, mix together garlic powder, chipotle powder, salt, and black pepper. Rub pork loin generously with spice mixture.

3. Place pork loin in a cooking pouch. Seal pouch tightly after removing the excess air. Place pouch in sous vide bath and set the cooking time for 4-6 hours.

4. Preheat the oven broiler to high.

5. Remove pouch from the sous vide bath and open carefully. Remove pork loin from pouch and pat dry with paper towels.

6. Coat each rib section evenly with BBQ sauce and broil for 5 minutes per side.

7. Serve immediately.

PORK ROAST WITH MILK GRAVY

Preparation Time: 20 minutes
Cooking Time: 6 hours
Cooking Temperature: 150°F

INGREDIENTS:

For Pork Roast:

¼ cup olive oil

½ teaspoon dried parsley, crushed

½ teaspoon dried oregano, crushed

Onion powder, to taste

Garlic salt, to taste

Salt and freshly ground black pepper, to taste

1½-2-pound pork sirloin roast

For Milk Gravy:

½ cup butter

⅓ cup flour

3 cups milk, either 2% or whole

Cooking liquid from pork roast

½ teaspoon beef "better than bouillon" stock (optional)

Salt and freshly ground black pepper, to taste

DIRECTIONS:

1. Attach the sous vide immersion circulator to a Cambro container or pot with water using an adjustable clamp and preheat water to 150°F.

2. For pork roast: in a small bowl, mix together all ingredients for pork roast except for the roast. Rub the oil mixture generously over the pork roast.

3. Place pork roast in a cooking pouch. Seal pouch tightly after removing the excess air. Place pouch in sous vide bath and set the cooking time for 4-6 hours.

4. Remove pouch from the sous vide bath and open carefully. Remove pork roast from pouch, reserving cooking liquid into a large bowl.

1. For milk gravy: melt butter over medium-low heat in a medium pan. Slowly add flour, beating continuously. Cook for 2-3 minutes, continuing to beat.

2. While beating, slowly add milk and reserved cooking liquid. Increase heat to medium and cook until gravy becomes thick, stirring continuously. Stir in bouillon, salt, and black pepper and remove from heat.

5. Heat a cast iron grill pan over high heat and sear pork roast for 2-3 minutes or until completely golden brown and serve with gravy.

6. Beef

RIBEYE WITH PEPPER SAUCE

Preparation Time: 15 minutes
Cooking Time: 7 hours
Cooking Temperature: 131°F

INGREDIENTS:

For Steak:

> 4-pounds bone-in ribeye steaks
>
> Dry spice rub of your choice
>
> Kosher salt, to taste
>
> Sunflower oil, as required

For Sauce:

> ½ teaspoon Sichuan peppercorns
>
> 1 tablespoon butter
>
> 1 tablespoon plain flour
>
> 2 tablespoons Brandy
>
> 5 tablespoons heavy cream
>
> Milk, as required
>
> Salt, to taste

DIRECTIONS:

1. Attach the sous vide immersion circulator to a Cambro container or pot with water using an adjustable clamp and preheat water to 131°F.
2. Season steak generously with dry rub and salt.

3. Place steak in a large cooking pouch. Seal pouch tightly after removing the excess air. Place pouch in sous vide bath and set the cooking time for 7 hours.

4. For sauce: in a pestle and mortar, crush peppercorns lightly. Heat a dry frying pan and toast crushed peppercorns until fragrant.

5. In the same frying pan, melt butter and stir in the flour. Add brandy and stir until a paste is formed. Add cream and stir until smooth to remove any lumps. Stir in a little milk and cook until desired thickness of sauce is reached. Stir in salt and remove from heat.

6. Remove pouch from the sous vide bath and open carefully. Remove steak from pouch and pat dry with paper towels.

7. Lightly grease a cast iron frying pan with oil and heat. Add steak and cook for 1 minute on each side.

8. Remove from heat and transfer onto a cutting board. Cut steak into slices, going against the grain of the meat. Serve immediately with sauce.

BEEF SHORT RIBS

Preparation Time: 15 minutes
Cooking Time: 72 hours
Cooking Temperature: 131°F

INGREDIENTS:

¾ cup unsweetened pineapple juice

⅓ cup soy sauce

¼ cup molasses

½ cup peanut oil

1 teaspoon ground ginger

1 pound short ribs

Salt and freshly ground black pepper, to taste

DIRECTIONS:

1. In a large bowl, combine pineapple juice, soy sauce, molasses, peanut oil, and ginger.

2. Add ribs and coat generously with mixture. Cover and refrigerate overnight.

3. Attach the sous vide immersion circulator to a Cambro container or pot with water using an adjustable clamp and preheat water to 131°F.

4. Place ribs and sauce in a cooking pouch. Vacuum seal the pouch.

5. Place pouch in sous vide bath and set the cooking time for 72 hours.

6. Remove from sous vide bath when cooking time is complete. Ribs will be falling off the bone tender. Serve with the sauce.

MISO GLAZED BEEF STEAK

Preparation Time: 15 minutes
Cooking Time: 18 hours
Cooking Temperature: 150°F

INGREDIENTS:

¼ cup brown sugar

¼ cup miso paste

¼ cup mirin

¼ cup soy sauce

2 pounds beef BBQ steaks

Salt, to taste

DIRECTIONS:

1. In a food processor, combine brown sugar, miso paste, mirin, and soy sauce and pulse until smooth.

2. Transfer mirin mixture to a large bowl. Add steaks, coat with mixture, and refrigerate to marinate overnight.

3. Attach the sous vide immersion circulator to a Cambro container or pot with water using an adjustable clamp and preheat water to 150°F.

4. Place steaks with marinade in a cooking pouch. Seal pouch tightly after removing the excess air. Place pouch in sous vide bath and set the cooking time for 18 hours. Cover the sous vide bath with plastic wrap to minimize water evaporation. Add water intermittently to keep the water level up.

5. Remove pouch from the sous vide bath and open carefully. Remove steaks from pouch, reserving cooking liquid in a pan.

6. Place pan over stove and cook until the liquid reduces by half.

7. Preheat grill to high heat.

8. Season steaks with salt. Coat with reduced sauce and grill until desired doneness is reached.

PORTERHOUSE STEAK

Preparation Time: 15 minutes
Cooking Time: 1 hour
Cooking Temperature: 126°F

INGREDIENTS:

2 tablespoons organic butter

8 fresh thyme sprigs, divided

1 fresh rosemary sprig, split in half

2 bay leaves

2 (1-inch thick) porterhouse steaks

Kosher salt and cracker black pepper, to taste

DIRECTIONS:

1. Attach the sous vide immersion circulator to a Cambro container or pot with water using an adjustable clamp and preheat water to 126°F.

2. In a small pan, melt butter over medium heat and cook herb sprigs and bay leaves for 3 minutes. Remove from heat and set aside to cool.

3. Season porterhouse steaks with salt and fresh cracked black pepper.

4. In 2 large cooking pouches, evenly divide steaks and butter mixture so each pouch contains 1 steak, 4 thyme sprigs, ½ rosemary sprig, and 1 bay leaf. Seal pouches tightly after removing the excess air. Place pouch in sous vide bath and set the cooking time for 1 hour.

5. Preheat grill to high heat.

6. Remove pouches from the sous vide bath and open carefully. Remove steaks from pouches, reserving cooking liquid in a baking tray. Pat dry steaks with paper towels.

7. Place steaks on the grill for 15 seconds then rotate 90 degrees and grill for another 15 seconds. Flip and repeat the process.

8. Remove steaks from grill and transfer to the baking tray of reserved cooking liquid. Coat steaks evenly with cooking liquid.

9. Serve immediately.

BUTTER BASTED PORTERHOUSE STEAK

Preparation Time: 15 minutes
Cooking Time: 6 hours
Cooking Temperature: 125°F

INGREDIENTS:

2-pound (1½-inch thick) porterhouse steak

1½ teaspoons kosher salt

½ teaspoon freshly ground black pepper

2 tablespoons butter

DIRECTIONS:

1. Season porterhouse steak evenly with salt and black pepper. Place steak in a large cooking pouch. Seal pouch tightly after removing the excess air. Refrigerate for up to 3 days.

2. Attach the sous vide immersion circulator to a Cambro container or pot with water using an adjustable clamp and preheat water to 125°F.

3. Seal pouch tightly after removing the excess air. Place pouch in sous vide bath and set the cooking time for 1½-6 hours.

4. Remove pouch from the sous vide bath and open carefully. Remove porterhouse steak from pouch and pat dry with paper towels.

5. Heat a cast iron pan in a 425°F oven for at least 20 minutes. Transfer pan to the stove top over medium-high heat and melt butter. Add the steak and sear for 1 minute on each side, basting with butter occasionally.

6. Remove from heat and transfer porterhouse steak to a cutting board. Cut into desired slices and serve.

BEEF TENDERLOIN WITH LEMON PARSLEY BUTTER

Preparation Time: 15 minutes
Cooking Time: 1-4 hours
Cooking Temperature: 140°F

INGREDIENTS:

1½-pound center cut beef tenderloin, trimmed

Kosher salt and freshly cracked black pepper, to taste

4 thyme sprigs

7 tablespoons unsalted butter, softened and divided

1 garlic clove, minced

2 tablespoons fresh parsley leaves, chopped

1 teaspoon fresh lemon zest

1 teaspoon fresh lemon juice

1 tablespoon vegetable oil

DIRECTIONS:

1. Attach the sous vide immersion circulator to a Cambro container or pot with water using an adjustable clamp and preheat water to 140°F.

2. With a sharp knife, cut tenderloin into 4 6-ounce portions. Place each portion onto a cutting board, cut-side down and flatten gently with your hand until the portion reaches 2-inch thickness. Season tenderloin generously with salt and black pepper.

3. Place beef tenderloin and thyme sprigs in a cooking pouch. Seal pouch tightly after removing the excess air. Place pouch in sous vide bath and set the cooking time for a minimum of 1 hour and a maximum time of 4 hours.

4. While tenderloin cooks, combine 6 tablespoons of butter, garlic, parsley, lemon zest, lemon juice, salt, and black pepper in a bowl. Set aside.

5. Remove pouch from the sous vide bath and open carefully. Remove tenderloin pieces from pouch and pat dry with paper towels.

6. In a heavy-bottomed 12-inch skillet, heat oil and remaining butter over high heat and sear tenderloin pieces for 1 minute on each side.

7. Divide tenderloin pieces onto serving plates. Top with parsley butter and serve immediately.

Santa Maria Tri-Tip

Preparation Time: 15 minutes
Cooking Time: 2 hours
Cooking Temperature: 135°F

INGREDIENTS:

1½ tablespoons garlic salt with dried parsley

1 tablespoon freshly ground black pepper

2½-pound (2-inch thick) tri-tip

1 teaspoon liquid smoke

1 tablespoon extra-virgin olive oil

DIRECTIONS:

1. Attach the sous vide immersion circulator to a Cambro container or pot with water using an adjustable clamp and preheat water to 135°F.

2. In a bowl, combine garlic salt and black pepper. Sprinkle tri-tip with garlic salt mixture generously.

3. Place tri-tip, liquid smoke, and oil in a cooking pouch. Seal pouch tightly after removing the excess air. Place pouch in sous vide bath and set the cooking time for 2 hours.

4. Preheat grill to high heat.

5. Remove pouch from the sous vide bath and open carefully. Remove tri-tip from pouch and pat dry with paper towels.

6. Grill tri-tip for 1 minute on each side.

7. Remove from grill and cut into desired slices. Serve immediately.

MARINATED TRI-TIP

Preparation Time: 15 minutes
Cooking Time: 4 hours
Cooking Temperature: 135°F

INGREDIENTS:

3 tablespoons low-sodium soy sauce

1 tablespoon honey

1 tablespoon red miso

1-2 teaspoons chili paste with fermented soy bean

1 teaspoon onion powder

1 teaspoon garlic powder

1 teaspoon ginger powder

1 teaspoon sesame oil (optional)

3-pound tri-tip roast

DIRECTIONS:

1. Attach the sous vide immersion circulator to a Cambro container or pot with water using an adjustable clamp and preheat water to 135°F.

2. Mix all ingredients in a large bowl except tri-tip. Add tri-tip and coat generously with mixture.

3. Place tri-tip in a cooking pouch. Seal pouch tightly after removing the excess air. Place pouch in sous vide bath and set the cooking time for 4 hours.

4. Preheat grill to high heat.

5. Remove pouch from the sous vide bath and open carefully. Remove tri-tip from pouch and pat dry with paper towels.

6. Grill tri-tip for 1 minute on each side.

7. Remove from grill and cut into desired slices. Serve immediately.

SMOKEY BRISKET

Preparation Time: 10 minutes
Cooking Time: 24 hours
Cooking Temperature: 135°F

INGREDIENTS:

2½-pound grass-fed beef brisket

½ tablespoon salt

2 teaspoons ground black pepper

DIRECTIONS:

1. Attach the sous vide immersion circulator to a Cambro container or pot with water using an adjustable clamp and preheat water to 135°F.

2. Season brisket with salt and black pepper generously.

3. Place brisket in a cooking pouch. Seal pouch tightly after removing the excess air. Place pouch in sous vide bath and set the cooking time for 24 hours. Cover the sous vide bath with plastic wrap to minimize water evaporation. Add water intermittently to keep the water level up.

4. Remove pouch from the sous vide bath and open carefully. Remove brisket from pouch and pat dry completely with paper towels. Season brisket once again with salt and black pepper.

5. Heat a cast iron skillet over medium-high heat and sear brisket for 2-3 minutes on each side.

6. Remove from heat and transfer to a cutting board for 5-10 minutes. Cut into desired slices and serve.

TERIYAKI BEEF RIBS

Preparation Time: 20 minutes
Cooking Time: 72 hours
Cooking Temperature: 132°F

INGREDIENTS:

For Ribs:

3-4 pound beef ribs, cut into three portions

½ cup sugar

½ cup salt

Vegetable oil, as required

For Teriyaki Glaze:

1 cup mirin

⅔ cup sake

½ cup dark soy sauce

For Chili Oil:

3 tablespoons vegetable oil

4 tablespoons garlic, chopped

4 tablespoons fresh ginger, grated

1 green chili, finely chopped

DIRECTIONS:

1. In a large bowl of water, dissolve sugar and salt. Add beef ribs and set aside for 1-2 hours. Remove ribs from brine and pat dry with paper towels.

2. Attach the sous vide immersion circulator to a Cambro container or pot with water using an adjustable clamp and preheat water to 132°F.

3. Divide ribs into two large cooking pouches. Seal pouches tightly after removing the excess air. Place pouches in sous vide bath and set the cooking time for 72 hours. Cover the sous vide bath with plastic wrap to minimize water evaporation. Add water intermittently to keep the water level up.

4. For teriyaki glaze: while ribs cook, add mirin, sake, and soy sauce to a pan and bring to a boil. Reduce heat and simmer for 10 minutes, stirring occasionally.

5. For chili oil: in another pan, add oil, garlic, ginger, and green chili over low heat and cook until fragrant.

6. Remove pouches from the sous vide bath and open carefully. Remove ribs from pouch and pat dry with paper towels.

7. In a cast iron skillet, heat oil over medium-high heat and sear ribs for 1 minute on each side.

8. Place ribs on a serving platter and top with glaze and chili oil. Serve immediately.

FILET MIGNON

Preparation Time: 15 minutes
Cooking Time: 47 minutes
Cooking Temperature: 129°F

INGREDIENTS:

4 (1-inch thick) filet mignons

Salt and freshly ground black pepper, to taste

Olive oil, as required

Minced garlic clove, to taste

Chopped fresh thyme, to taste

Butter, as required

DIRECTIONS:

1. Attach the sous vide immersion circulator to a Cambro container or pot with water using an adjustable clamp and preheat water to 129°F.

2. Season steaks evenly with salt and pepper.

3. Divide steaks, olive oil, garlic, and thyme into two cooking pouches. Seal pouches tightly after removing the excess air. Place pouches in sous vide bath and set the cooking time for 45 minutes.

4. Remove pouches from the sous vide bath and open carefully. Remove steaks from pouches and pat dry with paper towels.

5. In a non-stick pan, melt butter over medium-high heat and sear steaks until browned.

CRUSTED PRIME RIB ROAST

Preparation Time: 15 minutes
Cooking Time: 5-10 hours
Cooking Temperature: 131°F

INGREDIENTS:

For Rib Roast:

½ tablespoon garlic powder

¼ tablespoon ancho Chile powder

3-4-pound prime rib roast

Salt and freshly ground black pepper, to taste

4 fresh thyme sprigs

2 fresh rosemary sprigs

For Crust:

8 garlic cloves, peeled and root cut off

4 fresh thyme sprigs

4 fresh rosemary sprigs

2-4 tablespoons olive oil

DIRECTIONS:

1. Attach the sous vide immersion circulator to a Cambro container or pot with water using an adjustable clamp and preheat water to 131°F.

2. In a small bowl, mix together garlic powder, ancho Chile powder, salt, and black pepper. Coat prime rib roast generously with spice mixture.

3. Place roast and herb sprigs in a cooking pouch. Seal pouch tightly after removing the excess air. Place pouch in sous vide bath and set the

cooking time for a minimum of 5 and no more than10 hours. Longer cooking times will be required for for more tender results.

4. Preheat oven to 400°F.

5. For crust: place garlic cloves and herb sprigs on a square of tinfoil and drizzle with olive oil. Fold the tin foil around the garlic mixture to make a sealed pouch. Bake for 30 minutes.

6. Remove from oven and mash roasted garlic into a paste with a fork. Set aside.

7. Preheat oven to 450°F.

8. Remove pouch from the sous vide bath and open carefully. Remove roast from pouch and pat dry with paper towels.

9. Coat roast evenly with garlic paste. Arrange roast in a roasting pan and bake for 5 minutes, then serve.

BEEF CHUCK ROAST

Preparation Time: 15 minutes
Cooking Time: 48 hours
Cooking Temperature: 132°F

INGREDIENTS:

3-4-pound chuck roast

Olive oil, as required

4 garlic cloves, minced

Salt and freshly ground black pepper, to taste

Butter, as required

DIRECTIONS:

1. Attach the sous vide immersion circulator to a Cambro container or pot with water using an adjustable clamp and preheat water to 132°F.

2. Coat roast evenly with olive oil and garlic.

3. Place roast in a cooking pouch. Seal pouch tightly after removing the excess air. Place pouch in sous vide bath and set the cooking time for 36-48 hours. Cover the sous vide bath with plastic wrap to minimize water evaporation. Add water intermittently to keep the water level up.

4. Remove pouch from the sous vide bath and open carefully. Remove roast from pouch, reserving cooking liquid. Pat roast dry with paper towels and season evenly with salt and black pepper.

5. Heat a cast iron pan over high heat and sear roast until browned completely. Transfer roast to a cutting board.

6. In the same pan as used for roast, add reserved cooking liquid and scrape the browned bits from the pan. Add butter and cook until sauce reaches desired consistency.

7. Cut roast into strips and serve with the sauce topping.

BEEF MASALA

Preparation Time: 15 minutes
Cooking Time: 10 hours 15 minutes
Cooking Temperature: 180°F

INGREDIENTS:

2 pounds beef, cut into 2-inch cubes

1-2 tablespoons meat curry masala seasoning, divided

Salt, to taste

3 teaspoons ginger garlic paste

2 tablespoons almonds, boiled and skinned

2 tablespoons thick coconut milk

1 onion, chopped

1 cup plain yogurt

1/2 cup tomato puree

Oil, as required

DIRECTIONS:

1. Attach the sous vide immersion circulator to a Cambro container or pot with water using an adjustable clamp and preheat water to 180°F.

2. Rub beef evenly with a little of the curry masala and salt.

3. Place roast in a cooking pouch. Seal pouch tightly after removing the excess air. Place pouch in sous vide bath and set the cooking time for 10 hours.

4. Meanwhile in a food processor, add garlic ginger paste, almonds, and coconut milk and pulse until a paste is formed.

5. Remove pouch from the sous vide bath and open carefully. Remove beef from pouch, reserving cooking liquid.

6. Heat oil in a pan and sauté onion until light golden. Add paste and sauté for 5 minutes. Add remaining masala powder and sauté for 2 minutes. Slowly add yogurt and stir to combine. Add tomato puree and stir for a few minutes more.

7. Add beef along with reserved cooking liquid and bring to a boil. Reduce heat and simmer for 5 minutes. Stir in salt and remove from heat.

8. Serve hot.

BEEF BOURGUIGNON

Preparation Time: 25 minutes
Cooking Time: 25 hours
Cooking Temperature: 180°F

INGREDIENTS:

For Beef:

Vegetable oil, as required

¼ cup small bacon, cubed

2 pounds beef, cubed

1 bottle nice burgundy wine

1 tablespoon butter, divided

1 pound mushrooms, chopped roughly

20 pearl onions

2 celery stalks, finely chopped

2 carrots, peeled and finely chopped

1 white onion, finely chopped

2 garlic cloves, mashed

1 bay leaf

Sugar, to taste

½ tablespoon all-purpose flour

½ tablespoon cold water

Salt and freshly ground black pepper, to taste

1 rosemary sprig

Chopped fresh parsley, for garnishing

For Mashed Potatoes:

2 russet potatoes, peeled and cubed

3 tablespoons heavy cream

Butter, as required

Salt, to taste

DIRECTIONS:

1. In a wide cast iron pan, heat enough vegetable oil to cover the bottom of the pan and cook bacon cubes until just browning. Add beef and sear until browned completely. Transfer beef and bacon to a bowl, reserving fat in a separate small bowl.

2. Add some wine and scrape the brown bits from bottom and sides of the pan. Cook until a thick glaze is formed. Move glaze to a small bowl and set aside to cool.

3. In the same pan as used for glaze, melt ½ tablespoon of butter over medium-high heat. Add mushrooms and cook for 5 minutes. Cover and cook for 1-2 minutes. Transfer mushrooms to a bowl.

4. Add more wine to the now-empty pan and scrape the brown bits from bottom and sides of the pan. Cook until a thick glaze is formed. Add glaze to the bowl of reserved glaze and set aside to cool.

5. Melt remaining ½ tablespoon of butter over medium-high heat in the same pan. Add pearl onions and cook for 5 minutes. Transfer the onions into the bowl of mushrooms.

6. Add some wine to the pan and scrape the brown bits from bottom and sides. Cook until a thick glaze is formed. Transfer glaze into the bowl of reserved glaze and set aside to cool.

7. For wine reduction: In the same pan, cook reserved bacon fat over medium-high heat and add celery, carrot, and white onion for 7-10 minutes. Add 3¼ cups of wine, garlic, bay leaf, some cooked bacon, and reserved glaze and cook for 30 minutes, stirring occasionally.

8. Strain wine reduction through a fine strainer. Return strained sauce to the pan and bring to a gentle boil.

9. In a small bowl, dissolve flour into cold water. Add flour mixture to strained wine reduction and cook for 3 minutes. Remove from heat and stir in sugar, salt, and black pepper. Set aside to cool.

10. Attach the sous vide immersion circulator to a Cambro container or pot with water using an adjustable clamp and preheat water to 180°F.

11. Place beef, bacon, mushrooms, pearl onions, rosemary sprigs, and wine reduction in a large cooking pouch. Seal pouch tightly after removing the excess air. Place pouch in sous vide bath and set the cooking time for 24 hours. Cover the sous vide bath with plastic wrap to minimize water evaporation. Add water intermittently to keep the water level up.

12. For mashed potatoes: cook potatoes in a pan of boiling water for 10 minutes.

13. Remove from heat and drain potatoes. Return potatoes to the pan. Add heavy cream and some butter and mash until well combined. Season with salt.

14. Remove pouch from the sous vide bath and open carefully. Remove beef, mushrooms, and pearl onions from pouch, reserving the cooking liquid in a pan. Discard rosemary sprigs.

15. Place pan with reserved liquid over stove and cook for 5-10 minutes or until desired thickness of sauce is reached. Remove from heat and stir in beef, mushrooms, and pearl onions.

16. Serve with mashed potatoes.

CORNED BEEF AND CABBAGE

Preparation Time: 15 minutes
Cooking Time: 48 hours
Cooking Temperature: 134°F

INGREDIENTS:

4 pounds corned beef

6 bacon slices, cut into ½-inch strips

1 head cabbage, cut into ½-inch strips

2 cups chicken broth

½ cup champagne vinegar

DIRECTIONS:

1. Attach the sous vide immersion circulator to a Cambro container or pot with water using an adjustable clamp and preheat water to 134°F.

2. Place corned beef in a cooking pouch. Seal pouch tightly after removing the excess air. Place pouch in sous vide bath and set the cooking time for 48 hours. Cover the sous vide bath with plastic wrap to minimize water evaporation. Add water intermittently to keep the water level up.

3. Heat a skillet over medium heat and cook bacon until crisp. Remove bacon fat, leaving only 1-2 tablespoons in the skillet.

4. Stir in cabbage and increase heat to medium high. Cook for 5 minutes. Add chicken broth and vinegar and cook until cabbage becomes tender.

5. Remove pouch from the sous vide bath and open carefully. Remove corned beef from pouch and cut into ½-¾-inch slices.

6. Transfer cabbage mixture onto serving plate. Top with corned beef slices and serve.

BACON WRAPPED FILET WITH HORSERADISH CREAM

Preparation Time: 20 minutes
Cooking Time: 6 hours
Cooking Temperature: 131°F

INGREDIENTS:

For Beef Tenderloin:

6-8 pound beef tenderloin

Transglutaminase, as required

Thin bacon strips, as required

Fresh thyme sprigs, as required

Vegetable oil, as required

For Horseradish Cream:

1 cup heavy cream

¼ cup prepared horseradish, drained well

2 tablespoons coarse grain mustard

1 tablespoon Dijon mustard

Salt and freshly ground black pepper, to taste

DIRECTIONS:

1. Attach the sous vide immersion circulator to a Cambro container or pot with water using an adjustable clamp and preheat water to 131°F.

2. Carefully remove silver skin from tenderloin then remove all fats. Cut tenderloin into steaks of the desired size.

3. Arrange a parchment paper on a cutting board. Place bacon strips on parchment paper and dust with the transglutaminase.

4. Arrange 1 tenderloin filet over dusted side of 1 bacon strip. Roll the bacon strip over the filet to wrap and press firmly to adhere. Repeat with remaining fillets. Arrange 1 thyme sprig over each wrapped fillet and sprinkle with salt.

5. Place each filet in an individual cooking pouch. Seal pouches tightly after removing the excess air. Place pouches in sous vide bath and set the cooking time for 2-6 hours.

6. For horseradish cream: in a bowl, add heavy cream and beat with a mixer until thick but not too stiff. Fold in remaining horseradish cream ingredients.

7. Remove pouches from the sous vide bath and open carefully. Remove fillets from pouches and pat dry with paper towels.

8. Heat a cast iron skillet over high heat and sear each fillet until browned on both sides.

9. Serve immediately alongside horseradish cream.

BEEF CARNITAS

Preparation Time: 20 minutes
Cooking Time: 24 hours
Cooking Temperature: 156°F

INGREDIENTS:

For Carnitas:

1 teaspoon dried oregano

2 teaspoons garlic powder

1 teaspoon onion powder

1 teaspoon ground cumin

¼ teaspoon ground cloves

¼ teaspoon ground allspice

2-pound chuck roast

Salt and freshly ground black pepper, to taste

For Sauce:

2 tangerines, seeded and chopped

2-3 chipotle peppers in adobo sauce

1 tablespoon honey

1 tablespoon oregano leaves

½ cup cooking liquid from chuck rust

For Serving:

Corn tortillas

Avocado, peeled, pitted, and cut into slices

DIRECTIONS:

1. Attach the sous vide immersion circulator to a Cambro container or pot with water using an adjustable clamp and preheat water to 156°F.

2. For carnitas: in a small bowl, combine oregano and spices. Season roast with salt and pepper lightly and then coat with spice mixture.

3. Place roast in a cooking pouch. Seal pouch tightly after removing the excess air. Place pouch in sous vide bath and set the cooking time for 18-24 hours. Cover the sous vide bath with plastic wrap to minimize water evaporation. Add water intermittently to keep the water level up.

4. Remove pouch from the sous vide bath and open carefully. Remove roast legs from pouch, reserving ½ cup of cooking liquid.

5. For sauce: in a pan, add all sauce ingredients except cooking liquid and bring to a gentle boil. Cook for 10 minutes, stirring occasionally. Remove from heat and stir in reserved cooking liquid.

6. Shred beef with two forks and set aside.

7. Arrange tortillas on serving plates. Place shredded beef on each tortilla. Top with sauce and avocados and serve.

Cuban Shredded Beef

Preparation Time: 20 minutes
Cooking Time: 24 hours
Cooking Temperature: 140°F

INGREDIENTS:

2-pound center-cut chuck eye roast

Kosher salt and freshly ground black pepper, to taste

4 tablespoons canola oil, divided

1 onion, thinly sliced

2 garlic cloves, minced

2 teaspoons ground cumin

½ teaspoon red pepper flakes, crushed

½ cup orange juice

2 tablespoons fresh lime juice

DIRECTIONS:

1. Attach the sous vide immersion circulator to a Cambro container or pot with water using an adjustable clamp and preheat water to 140°F.

2. Season chuck roast evenly with salt and pepper.

3. Place roast in a cooking pouch. Seal pouch tightly after removing the excess air. Place pouch in sous vide bath and set the cooking time for 24 hours. Cover the sous vide bath with plastic wrap to minimize water evaporation. Add water intermittently to keep the water level up.

4. Remove pouch from the sous vide bath and open carefully. Remove roast legs from pouch and transfer to a cutting board. Shred roast into bite-sized pieces with two forks.

5. In a large skillet, heat 2 tablespoons of oil over medium-high heat and cook onion for 5 minutes, stirring occasionally.

6. Add garlic and spices and cook for 2 minutes. Stir in both juices and cook for 2 minutes. Stir in salt and black pepper and transfer to a bowl.

7. In the same skillet, heat remaining oil and cook shredded beef until browned and crisp, stirring occasionally.

8. Stir in cooked onion mixture, salt, and pepper and serve.

BEEF MEATBALLS

Preparation Time: 20 minutes
Cooking Time: 2 hours
Cooking Temperature: 144°F

INGREDIENTS:

1 pound 85% lean ground beef

½ pound ground sausage

½ cup Parmesan cheese, grated freshly

½ cup onion, finely chopped

⅓ cup quick-cooking oats

1 large egg, beaten lightly

¼ cup milk

½ teaspoon garlic powder

¾ teaspoon salt

¼ teaspoon freshly ground black pepper

Olive oil, as required

Pasta sauce, as required

DIRECTIONS:

1. Combine all ingredients except oil and pasta sauce in a bowl. Make 30-36 equal-sized meatballs from mixture. Arrange meatballs onto baking sheet lined with parchment paper in a single layer. Freeze meatballs on sheet for 1-2 hours or until very firm.

2. Attach the sous vide immersion circulator to a Cambro container or pot with water using an adjustable clamp and preheat water to 144°F.

3. Place meatballs in a cooking pouch. Seal pouch tightly after removing the excess air. Place pouch in sous vide bath and set the cooking time for 2 hours.

4. Remove pouch from the sous vide bath and open carefully. Remove meatballs from pouch and pat dry with paper towels.

5. Heat oil in a skillet and sear meatballs for 1-2 minutes.

6. Add meatballs to a large bowl with the pasta sauce and toss to coat.

7. Serve immediately.

HAMBURGER PATTIES

Preparation Time: 20 minutes
Cooking Time: 4 hours
Cooking Temperature: 138°F

INGREDIENTS:

2 pounds fresh ground beef

Kosher salt and freshly ground black pepper, to taste

1 tablespoon vegetable oil

4 cheese slices

4 soft hamburger buns, toasted lightly

Hamburger toppings, as desired

DIRECTIONS:

1. Attach the sous vide immersion circulator to a Cambro container or pot with water using an adjustable clamp and preheat water to 138°F.

2. Divide beef into 4 equal-sized portions. Make patties that are slightly wider than the buns from each portion. Season each patty generously with salt and black pepper.

3. Divide patties into four cooking pouches. Seal pouches tightly after removing the excess air. Place pouches in sous vide bath and set the cooking time for 40 minutes-4 hours.

4. Remove pouches from the sous vide bath and open carefully. Remove patties from pouches and pat dry with paper towels. Season each patty with salt and black pepper and set aside at room temperature for 10 minutes.

5. In a large cast iron skillet, heat oil over high heat and cook patties for 1 minute. Flip patties and place a cheese slice over each patty. Cook for 45-60 seconds.

6. Place 1 patty over each prepared bun. Top with desired topping and serve immediately.

SUMMER SAUSAGE

Preparation Time: 20 minutes
Cooking Time: 3 hours 30 minutes
Cooking Temperature: 160°F

INGREDIENTS:

1 pound grass-fed, 85% lean ground beef

⅓ teaspoon celery juice powder

1 teaspoon Braggs organic sprinkle seasoning, ground to a powder consistency

1 teaspoon mustard seeds

½ teaspoon mustard powder

½ teaspoon onion powder

½ teaspoon garlic powder

½ teaspoon hot paprika

⅛ teaspoon ground coriander

2 teaspoons canning salt

½ teaspoon freshly ground black pepper

Sausage casings

DIRECTIONS:

1. Add all ingredients to a bowl and combine.
2. Place beef mixture in a cooking pouch and refrigerate for 3-4 days.
3. Attach the sous vide immersion circulator to a Cambro container or pot with water using an adjustable clamp and preheat water to 160°F.

4. Place non-edible, fibrous casing in a bowl of warm water for 30 minutes.

5. Place beef mixture tightly into casing by rolling and pinprick any air pockets. After filling casing, tie off with a knot.

6. Place sausage in a cooking pouch. Seal pouch tightly after removing the excess air. Place pouch in sous vide bath and set the cooking time for 3½ hours.

7. Remove pouch from the sous vide bath and open carefully. Remove sausage from pouch. Untie the knot at the end of sausage stick and pat dry with paper towels.

8. You can preserve this sausage in freezer.

CHUCK ROAST WITH MUSHROOM GRAVY

Preparation Time: 20 minutes
Cooking Time: 48 hours
Cooking Temperature: 160°F

INGREDIENTS:

For Gravy:

2 cups water

1½ cups apple juice

½ cup soy sauce

2 tablespoons mirin

1 tablespoon cider vinegar

1 tablespoon sesame oil

1 onion, chopped

1 carrot, peeled and chopped

2 garlic cloves, minced

Salt and freshly ground black pepper, to taste

¼ cup red wine

For Chuck roast:

2-pound (2-inch thick) beef chuck roast, trimmed and cut into pieces

Butter, as required

For Mushrooms:

Butter, as required

12-ounces mushrooms

DIRECTIONS:

1. Attach the sous vide immersion circulator to a Cambro container or pot with water using an adjustable clamp and preheat water to 160°F.
1. For gravy: add all gravy ingredients except wine to a pan and cook over medium heat for 15 minutes. Strain the gravy through a strainer and set aside to cool.
2. Place roast pieces and ½ of the gravy in a cooking pouch. Seal pouch tightly after removing the excess air. Place pouch in sous vide bath and set the cooking time for 24-48 hours. Cover the sous vide bath with plastic wrap to minimize water evaporation. Add water intermittently to keep the water level up.
3. Transfer remaining gravy to a pan over high heat. Stir in wine and cook until gravy reduces by half.
4. In another pan, melt butter and sauté mushrooms until tender. Transfer mushrooms to the pan of gravy.
5. Remove pouch from the sous vide bath and open carefully. Remove roast pieces from pouch and pat dry with paper towels.
6. In a cast iron skillet, melt butter and sear roast pieces for 1 minute on each side.

7. Serve roast pieces with the mushroom gravy.

LONDON BROIL

Preparation Time: 10 minutes
Cooking Time: 8 hours
Cooking Temperature: 133°F

INGREDIENTS:

2-3 pound London broil, trimmed

3 tbsp Worcestershire sauce

Seasoning of your choice

2 tbsp Butter

DIRECTIONS:

1. Coat meat evenly with Worcestershire sauce then season one side of meat with seasoning.

2. Place meat in a cooking pouch. Seal pouch tightly after removing the excess air. Refrigerate for 1 day.

3. Attach the sous vide immersion circulator to a Cambro container or pot with water using an adjustable clamp and preheat water to 133°F.

4. Place pouch in sous vide bath and set the cooking time for 6-8 hours.

5. Remove pouch from the sous vide bath and open carefully. Remove meat from pouch and pat dry with paper towels.

6. In a cast iron skillet, melt butter and sear meat for 1 minute on each side.

7. Cut into desired slices and serve.

HERB CRUSTED SIRLOIN

Preparation Time: 20 minutes
Cooking Time: 48 hours
Cooking Temperature: 131°F

INGREDIENTS:

For Sirloin Roast:

- ½ tablespoon garlic powder
- ½ tablespoon paprika powder
- ¼ tablespoon ancho Chile powder
- 3-4-pound sirloin roast
- 2 rosemary sprigs
- 2 thyme sprigs

For Crust:

- 8 garlic cloves
- 2-4 tablespoons sweet marjoram
- 4 thyme springs
- 4 rosemary sprigs
- 2-4 tablespoons olive oil

DIRECTIONS:

1. Attach the sous vide immersion circulator to a Cambro container or pot with water using an adjustable clamp and preheat water to 131°F.
2. For sirloin roast: in a bowl, mix together garlic, paprika, and ancho Chile powder. Rub sirloin roast generously with spice mixture.

3. Place sirloin roast and herbs sprigs in a cooking pouch. Seal pouch tightly after removing the excess air. Place pouch in sous vide bath and set the cooking time for 12-48 hours. Cover the sous vide bath with plastic wrap to minimize water evaporation. Add water intermittently to keep the water level up.

4. Preheat oven to 450°F.

5. For crust: add all crust ingredients to a food processor and pulse until a thick paste is formed.

6. Remove pouch from the sous vide bath and open carefully. Remove sirloin roast from pouch and pat dry with paper towels.

7. Evenly coat sirloin roast with paste and arrange on a roasting pan. Roast for 5 minutes.

8. Remove sirloin roast from oven and keep on a cutting board for 5-10 minutes before slicing. Cut into slices of the desired size and serve. Serve with mashed potatoes, a side salad, or mixed vegetables.

FLANK STEAK WITH CHIMICHURRI SAUCE

Preparation Time: 20 minutes
Cooking Time: 36 hours
Cooking Temperature: 134°F

INGREDIENTS:

For Steak:

2-pound flank steak

Salt and freshly ground black pepper, to taste

For Chimichurri Sauce:

¼ medium red onion, chopped

3 garlic cloves, chopped

2 cups fresh parsley leaves

½ cup fresh mint leaves

2 teaspoons fresh lemon zest

½ cup extra-virgin olive oil

2 tablespoons fresh lemon juice

1 tablespoon white vinegar

⅓ teaspoon red pepper flakes

Salt, to taste

DIRECTIONS:

1. Attach the sous vide immersion circulator to a Cambro container or pot with water using an adjustable clamp and preheat water to 134°F.

2. Season flank steak evenly with salt and black pepper.

3. Place flank steak in a cooking pouch. Seal pouch tightly after removing the excess air. Place pouch in sous vide bath and set the cooking time for 30-36 hours. Cover the sous vide bath with plastic wrap to minimize water evaporation. Add water intermittently to keep the water level up.

4. Preheat the grill to high heat.

5. For Chimichurri Sauce: add all sauce ingredients to a food processor and pulse until smooth.

6. Remove pouch from the sous vide bath and open carefully. Remove steak from pouch and pat dry with paper towels.

7. Grill flank steak for 45 seconds on each side. Remove flank steak from grill and set aside for 5 minutes before slicing.

8. Cut into ½-inch slices, across the grain. Serve with a topping of chimichurri sauce.

Rosemary Seasoned Flank Steak

Preparation Time: 15 minutes
Cooking Time: 12 hours
Cooking Temperature: 130°F

Ingredients:

1¼ pound flank steak

½ teaspoon dried rosemary

¼ tablespoon garlic powder

¼ teaspoon onion powder

½ teaspoon kosher salt

¼ teaspoon ground black pepper

Extra-virgin olive oil, for drizzling

2 scallion tops, sliced on the bias

Coarse sea salt, to taste

Directions:

1. Attach the sous vide immersion circulator to a Cambro container or pot with water using an adjustable clamp and preheat water to 130°F.

2. Place flank steak in a cooking pouch. Seal pouch tightly after removing the excess air. Place pouch in sous vide bath and set the cooking time for 12 hours.

3. Preheat grill to high heat.

4. In a coffee grinder, mix together rosemary, garlic powder, onion powder, kosher salt, and black pepper and grind to a fine powder.

5. Remove pouch from the sous vide bath and open carefully. Remove steak from pouch and pat dry with paper towels.

6. Rub steak evenly with rosemary mixture. Grill the steak for 2-3 minutes on each side. Remove flank steak from grill and set aside for 5 minutes before slicing. Cut into thin slices, across the grain.

7. Drizzle steak slices with olive oil and garnish with scallion tops. Sprinkle with coarse sea salt and serve immediately.

BEEF BRISKET

Preparation Time: 15 mins
Cooking Time: 3 days
Cooking Temperature: 135 °F

INGREDIENTS:

1 teaspoon dried oregano, crushed

2 tablespoons ground coriander

2 tablespoons ground cumin

1 teaspoon ground cinnamon

2 tablespoon garlic powder

2 tablespoons paprika

1 teaspoon chipotle powder

1 teaspoon freshly ground black pepper

3-4 pounds beef brisket

1 tablespoon liquid smoke

salt, to taste

DIRECTIONS:

1. In a bowl, mix together the oregano, coriander, spices and black pepper. Generously coat brisket with spice mixture.

2. Into a cooking pouch, add the brisket and the liquid smoke. Seal pouch tightly after squeezing out excess air, and refrigerate for at least 2 days.

3. Attach the sous vide immersion circulator using an adjustable clamp to a Cambro container or pot filled with water and preheat to 135 °F.

4. Place pouch in sous vide bath and set the cooking time for between 1 and 3 days. Grass fed or younger, more tender cuts of meat will require less cooking time to become tender. Cook your cut of meat until it reaches desired level of tenderness.

5. Preheat the grill to a high heat.

6. Remove pouch from sous vide bath and carefully open it. Remove brisket from pouch. With paper towels, pat brisket completely dry.

7. Generously season brisket with salt.

8. Grill brisket for 1-2 minutes per side. Remove from the grill and keep aside for 5 minutes to rest.

9. Cut into 1¼-inch thick slices and serve.

MEATLOAF WITH CHIPOTLE GLAZE

Preparation Time: 15 mins
Cooking Time: 2-6 hours
Cooking Temperature: 140 °F

INGREDIENTS:

For Meatloaf:

2 tablespoons olive oil

1 red bell pepper, seeded and chopped

½ yellow onion, chopped

2 eggs

¼ cup heavy cream

¼ cup breadcrumbs

1 tablespoon soy sauce

½ teaspoon paprika

pinch of cayenne pepper

¼ teaspoon garlic powder

1 teaspoon kosher salt

½ teaspoon freshly ground black pepper

1 pound ground beef

½ pound Italian sausage, casing removed

1 tablespoon canola oil

For Glaze:

½ cup honey

2 tablespoons canola oil

1 tablespoon Dijon mustard

1 tablespoon chipotle in adobo sauce, pureed

1 teaspoon kosher salt

DIRECTIONS:

1. Attach the sous vide immersion circulator using an adjustable clamp to a Cambro container or pot filled with water and preheat to 140 °F.

2. **For the meatloaf:** in a skillet, heat the olive oil over a medium heat.

3. Add bell pepper and onion, and sauté for 4-5 minutes. Remove from heat and keep aside to cool completely.

4. Into a large bowl, add the cooled onion mixture, egg, cream, breadcrumbs, soy sauce, spices, salt and black pepper, and mix until well-combined.

5. Add the beef and sausage and, using your hands, knead until well-combined, then shape beef mixture into a loaf.

6. Place the meatloaf into a cooking pouch, and seal tightly after squeezing out the excess air.

7. Place pouch in sous vide bath and set the cooking time for 2-4 hours.

8. While the meatloaf is cooking:

9. **For the glaze:** in a bowl, add all glaze ingredients and beat until well-combined.

10. Just before the end of the sous vide cooking period:

11. Preheat broiler to a high setting and place a rack into the top position of the oven.

12. Remove pouch from sous vide bath and carefully open it. Remove meatloaf from pouch. With paper towels, pat meatloaf completely dry.

13. In a cast iron skillet, heat the canola oil over a high heat.

14. Add the meatloaf and cook for 1-2 minutes per side, or until browned completely.

15. Remove from heat and coat the top of the meatloaf evenly with the glaze.
16. Broil for 1-2 minutes.

STANDING RIB ROAST

Preparation Time: 15 mins
Cooking Time: 24-36 hours
Cooking Temperature: 130 °F

INGREDIENTS:

1 x 3-rib standing rib roast (6-8 pounds) (a.k.a. prime rib roast)

1-2 ounces dried morel mushrooms

kosher salt and freshly cracked black pepper, to taste

3 ounces garlic-infused olive oil

DIRECTIONS:

1. Attach the sous vide immersion circulator using an adjustable clamp to a Cambro container or pot filled with water and preheat to 130 °F.

2. Into a cooking pouch, add rib roast and mushrooms. Seal pouch tightly after squeezing out the excess air. Place pouch in sous vide bath and set the cooking time for at least 24 and up to 36 hours.

3. Remove pouch from sous vide bath and carefully open it. Transfer rib roast onto a cutting board, reserving mushroom and cooking liquid into a bowl. With paper towels, pat rib roast completely dry.

4. Rub rib roast with salt and black pepper evenly.

5. Heat cast iron pan to medium high heat and place the rib roast in, fat cap down. Sear for 1-2 minutes per side (or until browned on all sides).

6. Meanwhile, season reserved mushroom mixture with garlic oil, a little salt, and black pepper.

7. Transfer rib roast onto a cutting board, bone side down.

8. Carefully, remove rib bones and cut rib roast into ½-inch-thick slices *across* the grain.

9. Serve immediately with mushroom mixture.

BEEF WELLINGTON

Preparation Time: 25 mins
Cooking Time: 4-4½ hours (sous vide) then 1 hour
Cooking Temperature: 130 °F

INGREDIENTS:

2.5 pound beef fillet, trimmed

salt, to taste

7 tablespoons butter

10 Parma ham slices

freshly ground black pepper, to taste

1 pound chestnut mushrooms, finely chopped

1 pound puff pastry

eggs, for egg wash

DIRECTIONS:

1. Attach the sous vide immersion circulator using an adjustable clamp to a Cambro container or pot filled with water and preheat to 130 °F.

2. Season beef fillet evenly with salt.

3. Into a cooking pouch, add beef fillet and some butter. Seal pouch tightly after squeezing out the excess air. Place pouch in sous vide bath and set the cooking time for 4-4½ hours.

4. Remove pouches from sous vide bath and immediately plunge into a large bowl of ice water.

5. Remove beef fillet from pouch. With paper towels, pat beef fillet completely dry.

6. Season fillet with black pepper evenly.

7. Heat a cast iron grill pan over high heat, and sear ribs for 1 minute per side.

8. Remove ribs from pan and keep aside.

9. *For duxelles:* heat a nonstick skillet and sauté mushrooms with salt for 4-5 minutes (or until all liquid is absorbed).

10. Remove mushrooms from the heat and keep aside.

11. Arrange a 24x17-inch double layer of plastic wrap onto a smooth surface.

12. Arrange overlapping ham slices over plastic wrap and top evenly with duxelles.

13. Arrange beef fillets in the center of duxelles.

14. Wrap plastic wrap around fillet, folding in the ham at end.

15. From both ends, twist plastic wrap to create a sausage-like shape.

16. Refrigerate the resulting parcel for 30 minutes.

17. Preheat oven to 450 °F.

18. Remove parcel from refrigerator, carefully remove plastic wrap, and place pastry onto a lightly floured surface.

19. Roll into ⅓- to ½-inch thick rectangle.

20. Wrap pastry around fillet.

21. Fold pastry under each end, then seal ends with egg wash.

22. With a fork, score the pastry.

23. Coat pastry with egg wash.

24. Bake for 10-15 minutes (or until pastry becomes golden brown).

BEST PRIME RIB ROAST

Preparation Time: 15 mins
Cooking Time: 3 days
Cooking Temperature: 135 °F

INGREDIENTS:

1 x 10-pound prime rib roast

prime rib spice rub, to taste

dried rosemary, to taste

dried thyme, to taste

onion powder, to taste

garlic powder, to taste

kosher salt and freshly ground black pepper, to taste

DIRECTIONS:

1. Attach the sous vide immersion circulator using an adjustable clamp to a Cambro container or pot filled with water and preheat to 135 °F.

2. Carefully, cut individual ribs from the roast.

3. In a bowl, mix together spice rub, dried herbs, spices, salt and black pepper.

4. Generously coat roast with spice mixture.

5. Lightly coat ribs with spice mixture.

6. Into a cooking pouch, add the roast. In another cooking pouch, place ribs. Seal pouches tightly after squeezing out the excess air. Place pouches in sous vide bath. Each pouch will cook for a different time to allow for maximum tenderness for each cut of meat.

7. After 5-10 hours, remove roast from sous vide bath and serve. Grass fed or younger, more tender beef will only take 5 hours, while other cuts may take up to 10 hours to become truly tender.

8. The cuts of ribs can remain in the sous vide bath for up to 72 hours before being removed and served.

KOREAN SHORT RIBS

Preparation Time: 15 mins
Cooking Time: 4 hours (sous vide) then 15 mins
Cooking Temperature: 130 °F

INGREDIENTS:

For Barbecue Sauce:

1 scallion, finely chopped

6 garlic cloves, crushed

1 tablespoon fresh ginger, grated

1½ cups soy sauce

1½ cups brown sugar

½ cup mirin

½ cup water plus 2 tablespoons water, divided

3 tablespoons chili paste

2 tablespoons rice wine vinegar

1 tablespoon sesame oil

1 teaspoon black pepper, freshly ground

2 tablespoons cornstarch

2 tablespoons water

For Ribs:

4 x 8-ounce boneless beef short ribs

½ teaspoon salt

½ teaspoon black pepper, freshly ground

DIRECTIONS:

1. Attach the sous vide immersion circulator using an adjustable clamp to a Cambro container or pot filled with water and preheat to 130 °F.

2. *For the barbecue sauce:* in a small bowl, dissolve the cornstarch into 2 tablespoons of water. Keep aside.

3. In a large pan, mix together remaining sauce ingredients and bring to a boil and cook for 5-7 minutes, stirring occasionally.

4. Slowly add cornstarch mixture, beating continuously.

5. Reduce heat to medium and cook for 3-4 minutes.

6. Remove from heat and keep aside.

7. *For the ribs:* lightly season ribs with salt and black pepper.

8. Into a cooking pouch, add 1 short rib and 2 tablespoons of barbecue sauce and toss to coat.

9. Repeat with remaining ribs in separate cooking pouches, and reserve remaining sauce.

10. Seal pouches tightly after squeezing out the excess air. Place pouches in sous vide bath and set the cooking time for 4 hours.

11. Remove pouches from sous vide bath and carefully open them. Remove ribs from pouches. With paper towels, pat ribs completely dry.

12. Heat a cast iron grill pan over high heat, and sear ribs for 10-15 seconds.

13. Remove ribs from pan and keep aside for 5-10 minutes to rest.

14. Cut into thin slices and serve immediately with reserved barbecue sauce.

OTHER MEATS & PROTEINS

ELK STEAK

Preparation Time: 10 mins
Cooking Time: 2 hours
Cooking Temperature: 130 °F

INGREDIENTS:

For Steaks:

> 4 elk steaks
>
> sea salt, to taste
>
> bacon fat, as required

For Brussels Sprouts:

> 3-4 cups brussels sprouts, trimmed
>
> 1-2 tablespoons coconut oil
>
> sea salt, to taste
>
> 1-2 tablespoons balsamic vinegar

DIRECTIONS:

1. Attach the sous vide immersion circulator using an adjustable clamp to a Cambro container or pot filled with water and preheat to 130 °F.
2. Season steaks evenly with salt.
3. Into a cooking pouch, add the steaks. Seal pouch tightly after squeezing out the excess air. Place pouch in sous vide bath and set the cooking time for 1-2 hours.
4. Preheat the oven to 400 °F.
5. For the Brussels sprouts: In a pan of boiling water, cook Brussels sprouts for 3 minutes.

6. Drain well and immediately plunge into a large bowl of ice water to cool.

7. After cooling, cut Brussels sprouts in half.

8. Arrange Brussels sprout onto a baking sheet. Top with some coconut oil and sprinkle with salt.

9. Place baking sheet in oven and bake for 2 minutes.

10. Remove baking sheet from oven and toss sprouts well.

11. Bake for a further 20 minutes, tossing once midway.

12. Remove sprouts from oven and transfer into a bowl with the vinegar, and toss to coat.

13. Remove steak pouch from sous vide bath and carefully open it. Remove steaks from pouch. With paper towels, pat steaks completely dry.

14. In a cast iron skillet, heat bacon fat and sear steaks for 1 minute per side.

15. Serve steaks alongside Brussels sprouts.

LAMB CHOPS

Preparation Time: 15 mins
Cooking Time: 2 hours 30 mins
Cooking Temperature: 140 °F

INGREDIENTS:

4 lamb chops

salt and freshly ground black pepper, to taste

1 teaspoon fresh thyme, minced

1 teaspoon fresh rosemary, minced

2 garlic cloves, sliced

1 tablespoon butter

DIRECTIONS:

1. Attach the sous vide immersion circulator using an adjustable clamp to a Cambro container or pot filled with water and preheat to 140 °F.

2. Season lamb chops evenly with salt and black pepper, and sprinkle with herbs. Place garlic slices over each chop.

3. Into a cooking pouch, add the lamb chops and the butter. Seal pouch tightly after squeezing out the excess air. Place pouch in sous vide bath and set the cooking time for 2½ hours.

4. Remove pouch from sous vide bath and carefully open it. Remove chops from pouch. With paper towels, pat chops completely dry.

5. Heat a cast iron skillet over high heat, and sear chops until browned from both sides.

6. Serve immediately.

LAMB STEAKS

Preparation Time: 10 mins
Cooking Time: 6 hours
Cooking Temperature: 144 °F

INGREDIENTS:

⅔ cup olive oil, divided as ½ cup and the remaining oil

4 garlic cloves, crushed

1 sprig thyme

1 sprig rosemary

1 bay leaf

4 x 7-ounce lamb leg steaks

DIRECTIONS:

1. In a large bowl, mix together ½ cup of oil, garlic, the herbs and the bay leaf.
2. Add steaks to bowl and coat generously with mixture.
3. Refrigerate for 1-4 hours.
4. Attach the sous vide immersion circulator using an adjustable clamp to a Cambro container or pot filled with water and preheat to 144 °F.
5. Into a cooking pouch, add steaks and remaining oil. Seal pouch tightly after squeezing out the excess air. Place pouch in sous vide bath and set the cooking time for 6 hours.
6. Remove pouch from sous vide bath and carefully open it. Remove steaks from pouch. With paper towels, pat steaks completely dry.
7. Heat a cast iron skillet over high heat, and sear steaks until browned from both sides.
8. Serve immediately.

Lamb Sweetbreads

Preparation Time: 15 mins
Cooking Time: 45 mins
Cooking Temperature: 144 °F

INGREDIENTS:

4 cups milk, divided

10 ounces lamb sweetbreads

3 ½ ounces soft flour

1 ounce dried rosemary, crushed

salt and freshly ground black pepper, to taste

oil, as required

DIRECTIONS:

1. Into a large bowl, add 2 cups of milk and the lamb sweetbreads, and allow to soak for 8 hours.
2. Attach the sous vide immersion circulator using an adjustable clamp to a Cambro container or pot filled with water and preheat to 144 °F.
3. Drain lamb sweetbreads.
4. Into a large pan, add 4 cups of water and bring to a boil.
5. Add lamb sweetbreads and cook for 10 seconds.
6. Remove lamb sweetbreads from boiling water and immediately plunge into a large bowl of ice water to cool.
7. After cooling, peel off any excess sinew.
8. Into a cooking pouch, add lamb sweetbreads and the remaining 2 cups of milk. Seal pouch tightly after squeezing out the excess air. Place pouch in sous vide bath and set the cooking time for 40 minutes.

9. Remove pouch from sous vide bath and carefully open it. Remove lamb sweetbreads from pouch. With paper towels, pat lamb sweetbreads completely dry.

10. In a bowl, mix together the flour, rosemary, salt and black pepper.

11. Roll lamb sweetbreads evenly with flour mixture.

12. In a cast iron pan, heat some oil and fry and pan fry lamb sweetbreads until crisp.

13. Serve immediately.

VENISON STEAKS

Preparation Time: 20 mins
Cooking Time: 36 hours
Cooking Temperature: 137 °F

INGREDIENTS:

For Steaks:

1 x 1-pound venison blade steak

2 shallots, roughly chopped

6 cloves garlic, roughly chopped

3 chili peppers, seeded and roughly chopped

salt and freshly ground black pepper, to taste

1 tablespoon avocado oil

For Gravy:

reserved cooking liquid mixture

2 tablespoons butter

1 teaspoon all-purpose flour

1 cup beef broth

For Garnish:

black mustard blossoms

micro green herbs

red amaranth

DIRECTIONS:

1. *For the steak:* to a large bowl, add the steak, shallots, garlic, chili peppers, salt, and pepper, and and toss to coat well.
2. Refrigerate for at least 30 minutes.
3. Attach the sous vide immersion circulator using an adjustable clamp to a Cambro container or pot filled with water and preheat to 137 °F.
4. Into a cooking pouch, add steak mixture. Seal pouch tightly after squeezing out the excess air. Place pouch in sous vide bath and place a weight over pouch. Set the cooking time for 36 hours.
5. Remove pouch from sous vide bath and carefully open it. Remove steak from pouch, reserving cooking liquid mixture. With paper towels, pat steak completely dry and set aside to rest briefly.
6. In a skillet, heat 1 tablespoon of avocado oil and sear steak for 1 minute per side.
7. Transfer steak onto a plate and keep aside.
8. *For the gravy:* in in a food processor, add the reserved cooking liquid mixture and pulse until a smooth paste is formed.
9. In a heavy-bottomed pan, melt butter. Stir in flour and paste cook until browned slightly, stirring continuously.
10. Reduce heat and stir in paste and broth. Bring to a boil and remove from heat.
11. Cut steak into desired slices and decorate with favorite garnish.

12. Serve with gravy.

Rabbit Legs

Preparation Time: 10 mins
Cooking Time: 4 hours
Cooking Temperature: 145 °F

Ingredients:

2 rabbit legs

1 teaspoon kosher salt

½ teaspoon freshly ground black pepper

1 sprig rosemary

2 tablespoons extra-virgin olive oil

Directions:

1. Attach the sous vide immersion circulator using an adjustable clamp to a Cambro container or pot filled with water and preheat to 145 °F.

2. Season rabbit legs with salt and pepper.

3. Into a cooking pouch, add the rabbit legs, rosemary and olive oil. Seal pouch tightly after squeezing out the excess air. Place pouch in sous vide bath and set the cooking time for 4 hours.

4. Preheat broiler to high. Line a rimmed baking sheet with a piece of foil.

5. Remove pouch from sous vide bath and carefully open it. Remove rabbit legs from pouch. With paper towels, pat rabbit legs completely dry.

6. Arrange rabbit legs onto prepare baking sheet. Broil for 5 minutes.

7. Serve immediately.

Osso Buco

Preparation Time: 20 mins
Cooking Time: 72 hours 15 mins
Cooking Temperature: 143 °F

INGREDIENTS:

---

2 veal shanks

salt and freshly ground black pepper, to taste

flour, as required

extra-virgin olive oil, as required

butter, as required

1 onion, chopped

2 ounces pancetta, chopped

1 glass dry white wine

½ cup concentrated veal broth

2 teaspoons tomato paste

For Gremolata:

fresh flat leaf parsley, as required

1 fresh sprig rosemary

2 fresh sage leaves

fresh lemon zest, as required

1 garlic clove

DIRECTIONS:

1. Attach the sous vide immersion circulator using an adjustable clamp to a Cambro container or pot filled with water and preheat to 143 °F.

2. With a sharp knife, make 1-inch cuts in the around the shanks.

3. With paper towels, pat shanks and season with salt and black pepper.

4. Dust each shank with flour evenly.

5. In a frying pan, heat olive oil and sear shanks until browned from both sides.

6. Transfer shanks onto a plate. Discard most of the oil from the pan.

7. In the same pan, melt butter and sauté onion until translucent.

8. Add pancetta and sauté until slightly golden.

9. Stir in wine and cook until half the wine is absorbed.

10. Stir in veal broth and tomato paste, then remove from heat.

11. Into a large cooking ouch, place shanks and wine mixture. Seal pouch tightly after squeezing out the excess air. Place pouch in sous vide bath and set the cooking time for 72 hours.

12. **Meanwhile for gremolata:** in a food processor, add all ingredients listed under gremolata section above, and pulse until minced finely.

13. Remove pouch from sous vide bath and carefully open it. Remove shanks from pouch.

14. Transfer shanks with mixture onto serving platter. Top with gremolata and serve.

RABBIT LOIN

Preparation Time: 20 mins
Cooking Time: 4 hours
Cooking Temperature: 150 °F

INGREDIENTS:

6 tablespoons olive oil, divided 4 + 2

1 ounce fresh flat leaf parsley, chopped

½ ounce fresh dill, chopped

2 tablespoons Dijon mustard

1 teaspoon apple cider vinegar

1 teaspoon garlic, minced

½ teaspoon freshly ground black pepper

¼ teaspoon ground ginger

pinch of salt

4 x 8-ounce rabbit loins

DIRECTIONS:

1. Attach the sous vide immersion circulator using an adjustable clamp to a Cambro container or pot filled with water and preheat to 150 °F.
2. Into a bowl, add all ingredients except 2 tablespoons of oil and the rabbit loins. Mix well.
3. Add rabbit loins and coat generously with mixture.
4. · In 4 separate cooking pouches, divide rabbit loins with marinade. Seal pouches tightly after squeezing out the excess air. Place pouches in sous vide bath and set the cooking time for 4 hours.

5. Remove pouches from sous vide bath and carefully open them. Remove rabbit loins from pouches. With paper towels, pat rabbit loins completely dry.

6. In a skillet, heat remaining oil and sear the loins until golden brown from both sides.

FOIE GRAS

Preparation Time: 10 mins
Cooking Time: 20 mins
Cooking Temperature: 137 °F

INGREDIENTS:

foie gras, cut into 1¼-inch pieces across lobe *

sea salt, to taste

DIRECTIONS:

1. Attach the sous vide immersion circulator using an adjustable clamp to a Cambro container or pot filled with water and preheat to 137 °F.

2. Into a cooking pouch, add foie gras. Seal pouch tightly after squeezing out the excess air. Place pouch in sous vide bath and set the cooking time for 15-20 minutes.

3. Remove pouch from sous vide bath and carefully open it. Remove foie gras from pouch. With paper towels, pat foie gras completely dry.

4. Season with salt and serve immediately.

Frog Legs with Risotto

Preparation Time: 25 mins
Cooking Time: 45 mins
Cooking Temperature: 135 °F

Ingredients:

For Frogs Legs:

4 pounds frog legs

½ cup plus 3 tablespoons butter, divided

5 chicken broth ice cubes

5 fresh thyme sprigs

8 garlic cloves, minced

2 lemon slices

1 bay leaf

½ teaspoon red pepper flakes, crushed

kosher salt and freshly ground black pepper, to taste

3 tablespoons grape seed oil

For Risotto:

4-6 cups vegetable broth

15 ounces pure, unsweetened carrot juice

3 tablespoons grapeseed oil

1½ cups Vialone Nano risotto

1 medium onion, minced

1 cup chardonnay white wine

1 cup bagged frozen carrot/pea mix

½ cup mascarpone cheese

DIRECTIONS:

1. Attach the sous vide immersion circulator using an adjustable clamp to a Cambro container or pot filled with water and preheat to 135 °F.

2. With a sharp knife, cut between the doubled frog legs to separate into two.

3. Into a cooking pouch, add frog leg pieces, ½ cup of butter, thyme, garlic, bay leaf, red pepper flakes, salt and black pepper. Seal pouch tightly after squeezing out the excess air. Place pouch in sous vide bath and set the cooking time for 45 minutes.

4. Remove pouch from sous vide bath and carefully open it. Remove frog pieces from pouch. With paper towels, pat frog pieces completely dry.

5. In a large sauté pan, heat oil and remaining butter over medium-high heat, and sear frog pieces until browned slightly.

6. ***Meanwhile for risotto:*** in a pan, add broth and carrot juice and bring to a boil. Reduce heat to low and allow to simmer.

7. In a large heavy-bottomed pan, heat oil over medium heat and sauté risotto rice and onion for 2 minutes.

8. Add wine and cook until absorbed, stirring continuously.

9. Add hot broth mixture ½ cup at a time, and cook until absorbed, stirring continuously. (This process will take 15 minutes.)

10. Add carrots/peas and cook for 3 minutes, stirring continuously.

11. Remove from heat and stir in mascarpone cheese, salt and black pepper.

12. Divide risotto onto serving plates. Top with frog meat and serve immediately.

Oxtail over Vegetable Mash

Preparation Time: 15 mins
Cooking Time: 21 hours 15 mins
Cooking Temperature: 180 °F

INGREDIENTS:

For Oxtail:

8 medium whole onions, unpeeled

1 full garlic bulb, unpeeled

1 cup white wine

½ cup Demerara sugar

⅛ teaspoon ground cloves

pinch of cayenne pepper

salt and freshly cracked black pepper, to taste

4 pounds oxtail pieces

For Sauce:

2 tablespoons butter

4 medium carrots, peeled and cut into half-moons

2 celery sticks, finely chopped

1 medium leek, thinly sliced

10 closed cup mushrooms, thinly sliced

2 teaspoons English mustard

3 cups cooking liquid from oxtail

4 tablespoons onion puree from oxtail

pinch of cayenne pepper

salt and freshly cracked black pepper, to taste

DIRECTIONS:

1. Preheat oven to 392 °F and line a baking sheet with a piece of foil.

2. Arrange onions and garlic bulb onto prepared baking sheet.

3. Roast for 50 minutes. After 15 minutes, remove garlic bulb from oven and keep aside.

4. Remove onions from oven and keep aside with garlic to cool completely.

5. After cooling, squeeze onion pulp and garlic pulp from the skins and retain.

6. Into a small pan, add wine, sugar, cloves, cayenne pepper, salt, black pepper, onion and garlic pulp and bring to a boil. Simmer for 10-15 minutes.

7. With an immersion blender, blend the onion mixture into a thick paste. Remove from heat and keep aside cool completely.

8. Attach the sous vide immersion circulator using an adjustable clamp to a Cambro container or pot filled with water and preheat to 180 °F.

9. Into a cooking pouch, add oxtail pieces and onion puree and freeze for 15 minutes.

10. Remove from freezer and seal pouch tightly after squeezing out the excess air. Place pouch in sous vide bath and set the cooking time for 20 hours.

11. Remove pouch from sous vide bath and carefully open it. Remove oxtail pieces from pouch.

12. Through a sieve, strain cooking liquid into a bowl and refrigerate to cool. (Reserve 4 tablespoons of this onion puree separately for the sauce.)

13. After cooling, remove solid fat from top.

14. Remove meat from bones and, using 2 forks, shred. Remove any large chunks of fat.

15. *For sauce:* in a large pan, melt butter and sauté carrots, celery and leek until tender.

16. Add oxtail meat, mustard, cooking liquid, and onion puree, and bring to a boil.

17. Reduce heat and simmer, covered, for 10-15 minutes.

18. Add mushrooms and simmer for 5 minutes.

19. Stir in cayenne pepper, salt and black pepper, and remove from heat.

20. This oxtail mixture is great served over mashed potatoes.

BISON RUMP ROAST

Preparation Time: 15 mins
Cooking Time: 14 hours
Cooking Temperature: 130 °F

INGREDIENTS:

1 x 2-pound, 2-inch thick bison rump roast

2 teaspoons dry steak rub (your choice)

DIRECTIONS:

1. Attach the sous vide immersion circulator using an adjustable clamp to a Cambro container or pot filled with water and preheat to 130 °F.

2. Rub bison roast with steak rub evenly.

3. Into a cooking pouch, add bison roast. Seal pouch tightly after squeezing out the excess air. Place pouch in sous vide bath and set the cooking time for 12-14 hours.

4. Remove pouch from sous vide bath and carefully open it. Remove bison roast from pouch, reserving some liquid. With paper towels, pat bison roast completely dry.

5. Heat a cast iron grill pan over high heat, and sear bison roast for 1 minute per side.

6. Remove bison roast from pan and keep aside for 5-10 minutes to rest.

7. Cut into thin slices and serve immediately with reserved cooking liquid.

VENISON LOIN WITH HAZELNUT COFFEE MAPLE BUTTER

Preparation Time: 15 mins
Cooking Time: 2 hours
Cooking Temperature: 140 °F

INGREDIENTS:

For Venison Loin:

1-2 pound venison loin

3 garlic cloves, thinly sliced

kosher salt, to taste

freshly ground black pepper, to taste

1 tablespoon cumin seeds

butter or fat of choice, as required

For Hazelnut Coffee Maple Butter:

¼ cup unsalted butter, chopped

1½ tablespoons cool hazelnut coffee

1 tablespoon maple syrup

DIRECTIONS:

1. Attach the sous vide immersion circulator using an adjustable clamp to a Cambro container or pot filled with water and preheat to 140 °F.

2. Coat venison loin generously with cumin seeds, salt and black pepper. Place garlic slices over loin.

3. Into a cooking pouch, add venison loin. Seal pouch tightly after squeezing out the excess air. Place pouch in sous vide bath and set the cooking time for 2 hours.

4. Into a small food processor, add butter, hazelnut coffee and maple syrup, and pulse until well-combined.

5. Transfer butter mixture onto a wax paper and roll into a cylinder. Refrigerate for at least 1 hour.

6. Remove from the refrigerator and keep aside to come to room temperature. Cut into slices.

7. Remove pouch from sous vide bath and carefully open it. Remove venison loin from pouch. With paper towels, pat venison loin completely dry.

8. In a cast iron skillet, melt butter over medium-high heat, and sear venison loin for 30 seconds per side or until golden brown.

9. Season with salt and pepper, and transfer onto a cutting board.

10. Cut into medallions. Top with coffee butter and serve.

VENISON SHOULDER

Preparation Time: 15 mins
Cooking Time: 8 hours 15 mins
Cooking Temperature: 130 °F

INGREDIENTS:

farmed venison bolar roast *

salt and freshly ground black pepper, to taste

clarified butter *

red wine *

cold butter, cut into small pieces *

DIRECTIONS:

1. Attach the sous vide immersion circulator using an adjustable clamp to a Cambro container or pot filled with water and preheat to 130 °F.

2. Season roast evenly with salt and black pepper.

3. Into a cooking pouch, add roast. Seal pouch tightly after squeezing out the excess air. Place pouch in sous vide bath and set the cooking time for 8 hours.

4. Remove pouch from sous vide bath and carefully open it. Remove venison loin from pouch, reserving pouch juices. With paper towels, pat roast completely dry.

5. In a skillet, melt clarified butter over a very high heat, and sear roast for 1 minute per side.

6. Remove from skillet and transfer onto a cutting board to rest. Cover roast with a piece of foil to keep warm.

7. Add reserved juices into a small pan and bring to a boil.

8. To the skillet used for the roast, add red wine and, using a wooden spatula, scrape the browned pieces from bottom and sides.

9. Strain reserved juices from the sous vide pouch into pan and bring to a boil. Cook until sauce is cooked to taste.

10. Reduce heat to very low. Add cold butter and cook until mixture becomes slightly thick, beating continuously.

11. Cut roast into slices across the grain. Serve roast slices with butter sauce.

VENISON BURGERS

Preparation Time: 20 mins
Cooking Time: 4 hours
Cooking Temperature: 140 °F

INGREDIENTS:

1½ pound ground venison

½ pound high quality ground smoked bacon

6 ounces beer

salt and freshly ground black pepper, to taste

cooking oil, as required

4 artisan hamburger buns, as required

toppings and condiments of your choice

DIRECTIONS:

1. Attach the sous vide immersion circulator using an adjustable clamp to a Cambro container or pot filled with water and preheat to 140 °F.

2. Into a large bowl, add ground venison, ground bacon, beer, salt and black pepper, and gently mix until well-combined.

3. Make 4 patties, using ½ pound of mixture each time.

4. In cooking pouches, gently place the patties. Seal pouch tightly after squeezing out the excess air. Place pouch in sous vide bath and set the cooking time for 1-4 hours, depending on how well done you prefer burgers.

5. Remove pouches from sous vide bath and carefully open them. Remove patties from pouches. With paper towels, pat patties completely dry.

6. Season patties with a little salt and black pepper.

7. In a cast iron skillet, heat oil over high heat, and sear burgers for 45 seconds per side.

8. Place 1 patty in each burger and serve with your desired topping and condiments.

PERSIAN TOFU

Preparation Time: 15 mins
Cooking Time: 2 hours
Cooking Temperature: 180 °F

INGREDIENTS:

1 x 15-ounce package firm tofu, drained, pressed and sliced into ½-inch-thick planks

4 garlic cloves, roughly minced

2 tablespoons extra-virgin olive oil

1 teaspoon ground turmeric

1 teaspoon kosher salt

2 teaspoons freshly ground black pepper

2 limes, cut into wedges

Sumac, for serving

DIRECTIONS:

1. Attach the sous vide immersion circulator using an adjustable clamp to a Cambro container or pot filled with water and preheat to 180 °F.
2. Into a small bowl, add garlic, olive oil, turmeric, salt and black pepper. Rub tofu evenly with the mixture.
3. Into a cooking pouch, add tofu patties. Seal pouch tightly after squeezing out the excess air. Place pouch in sous vide bath and set the cooking time for 2 hours.
4. Preheat broiler to high. Line a baking sheet with a piece of foil.
5. Remove pouch from sous vide bath and carefully open it. Remove tofu from pouch.

6. Arrange tofu slices onto prepared baking sheet in a single layer and drizzle with any remaining oil from pouch. Broil for 2-3 minutes per side.
7. Transfer tofu slices onto a serving plate. Squeeze lime juice from wedges over tofu. Sprinkle with sumac and serve immediately.

TOFU WITH CARAMELIZED ONIONS

Preparation Time: 10 mins
Cooking Time: 2 hours
Cooking Temperature: 180 °F

INGREDIENTS:

1 x 14-ounce package firm or extra-firm tofu, drained, pressed and cut into 6 planks

1 tablespoon extra-virgin olive oil

⅓ cup barbecue sauce

1 tablespoon unsalted butter

1 large yellow onion, thinly sliced

salt and freshly ground black pepper, to taste

DIRECTIONS:

1. Attach the sous vide immersion circulator using an adjustable clamp to a Cambro container or pot filled with water and preheat to 180 °F.
2. Into a cooking pouch, add tofu in a single layer. Add barbecue sauce and seal pouch tightly after squeezing out the excess air. Place pouch in sous vide bath and set the cooking time for 2 hours.
3. ***Meanwhile, for caramelized onions:*** in a sauté pan, heat olive oil and butter over medium heat and cook onion for 20 minutes, stirring occasionally. Season with salt and black pepper.
4. Preheat broiler to high.

5. Remove pouch from sous vide bath and carefully open it. Remove tofu from pouch, reserving cooking liquid.
6. Arrange tofu onto a baking sheet and broil for 4 minutes.

7. Arrange caramelized onion in the center of a serving plate and top with tofu.

8. Drizzle with some reserved cooking liquid and serve.

5

SEAFOOD

JUMBO SHRIMP SCAMPI

Preparation Time: 15 mins
Cooking Time: 35 mins
Cooking Temperature: 135 °F

INGREDIENTS:

4 tablespoons unsalted butter, divided

2 garlic cloves, minced

1 teaspoon fresh lemon zest, grated

2 tablespoons fresh lemon juice

1 teaspoon kosher salt

½ teaspoon freshly ground black pepper

1 pound jumbo shrimp, peeled and deveined, with tails left on

½ cup panko breadcrumbs

1 tablespoon fresh parsley, minced

DIRECTIONS:

1. Attach the sous vide immersion circulator using an adjustable clamp to a Cambro container or pot filled with water and preheat to 135 °F.

2. In a large non-stick skillet, melt 3 tablespoons of butter over medium heat and stir in garlic, lemon zest, lemon juice, salt, and black pepper until well-combined.

3. Immediately remove from heat and keep aside for at least 5 minutes.

4. Into a large cooking pouch, place shrimp and garlic butter mixture. Seal pouch tightly after squeezing out the excess air. Place pouch in sous vide bath and set the cooking time for 30 minutes.

5. Meanwhile, in another skillet, melt remaining butter over medium heat. Add breadcrumbs and toss to coat well. Immediately, remove from heat.

6. Preheat broiler to high.

7. Remove pouch from sous vide bath and carefully open it.

8. Divide shrimp and cooking liquid into 4 broiler-safe baking dishes and top evenly with breadcrumbs. Broil for 2 minutes.

9. Garnish with parsley and serve.

SRIRACHA SHRIMP

Preparation Time: 15 mins
Cooking Time: 30 mins
Cooking Temperature: 135 °F

INGREDIENTS:

- 1 garlic clove, finely minced
- 4 tablespoons Sriracha
- 4 tablespoons unsalted butter, melted
- 1 tablespoon fresh lemon juice
- 1 teaspoon kosher salt
- ½ teaspoon freshly ground black pepper
- 1 pound large shrimp, peeled and deveined
- 2 tablespoons scallions, thinly sliced
- 2 tablespoons sliced almonds, toasted

DIRECTIONS:

1. Attach the sous vide immersion circulator using an adjustable clamp to a Cambro container or pot filled with water and preheat to 135 °F.
2. Into a small bowl, add garlic, Sriracha, butter, lemon juice, salt, and black pepper and beat until well-combined.
3. Into a cooking pouch, add shrimp and butter mixture. Seal pouch tightly after squeezing out the excess air. Place pouch in sous vide bath and set the cooking time for 30 minutes.
4. Remove pouch from sous vide bath and carefully open it.
5. Transfer shrimp with pouch mixture on to a serving bowl. Top with scallions and almonds, and serve.

SESAME COATED TUNA

Preparation Time: 15 mins
Cooking Time: 30 mins
Cooking Temperature: 115 °F

INGREDIENTS:

2½ cups water

¼ cup granulated sugar

¼ cup salt

2 x 5-6 ounce tuna fillets

2 tablespoons extra-virgin olive oil

1 x 1-inch piece fresh ginger, peeled and sliced into thin matchsticks

4 tablespoons teriyaki sauce

2 tablespoons sesame seeds, toasted

1 tablespoon poppy seeds

DIRECTIONS:

1. *For brine:* in a large bowl, add water, sugar and salt, and beat until sugar dissolves.
2. Add tuna fillets and refrigerate, covered, for 45 minutes.
3. Attach the sous vide immersion circulator using an adjustable clamp to a Cambro container or pot filled with water and preheat to 115 °F.
4. Remove tuna fillets from brine and, with paper towels, pat dry.
5. Into a large cooking pouch, place tuna fillets and olive oil. Seal pouch tightly after squeezing out the excess air. Place pouch in sous vide bath and set the cooking time for 30 minutes.
6. Remove pouch from sous vide bath and immediately plunge into a large bowl of ice water. Keep aside to cool completely.

7. Remove tuna fillets from pouch. With plastic wrap, cover tuna fillets and refrigerate for a further 6 hours.

8. ***Meanwhile, for dipping sauce:*** in a bowl, mix together ginger and teriyaki sauce. Keep aside until serving.

9. In a shallow bowl, mix together sesame seeds and poppy seeds.

10. Coat tuna fillets with evenly seeds mixture and cut into thin slices.

11. Serve tuna slices alongside ginger sauce.

COD IN TOM YUM BROTH

Preparation Time: 15 mins
Cooking Time: 30 mins
Cooking Temperature: 130 °F

INGREDIENTS:

2 cod fillets, cut lengthwise into 2 slices

2 tablespoons olive oil

salt and freshly ground black pepper, to taste

2 kaffir lime leaves, torn

2 thick galangal slices

1 lemongrass stalk (white part only), cut into 3-inch segments and bruised

2 cups chicken broth

2 small red chilies, bruised

1 teaspoon palm sugar or light brown sugar

1 teaspoon fresh lime juice

1 teaspoon fish sauce

1 tablespoon fresh cilantro, roughly chopped

DIRECTIONS:

1. Attach the sous vide immersion circulator using an adjustable clamp to a Cambro container or pot filled with water and preheat to 130 °F.
2. In 2 cooking pouches, divide cod, oil, salt and black pepper. Seal pouches tightly after squeezing out the excess air. Place pouches in sous vide bath and set the cooking time for 30 minutes.
3. Meanwhile, in a pan, add kaffir lime leaves, galangal slices, lemongrass and broth and bring to a boil. Simmer for 10 minutes.
4. Stir in remaining ingredients (except cilantro), and remove from heat.
5. Remove pouches from sous vide bath and carefully open them. Transfer fish pieces into serving bowls evenly and top with hot broth.
6. Garnish with cilantro and serve.

LEMON COD

Preparation Time: 15 mins
Cooking Time: 30 mins
Cooking Temperature: 130 °F

INGREDIENTS:

2 x 6-ounce cod fillets

kosher salt and freshly ground black pepper, to taste

zest and juice of 1 lemon

1 tablespoon extra-virgin olive oil

DIRECTIONS:

1. Attach the sous vide immersion circulator using an adjustable clamp to a Cambro container or pot filled with water and preheat to 130 °F.

2. Season cod fillets evenly with salt and pepper.

3. Into a cooking pouch, add cod fillets, lemon zest, lemon juice and oil. Seal pouch tightly after squeezing out the excess air. Place pouch in sous vide bath and set the cooking time for 30 minutes.

4. Remove pouch from sous vide bath and carefully open it. Remove cod fillets from pouch. With paper towels, pat cod fillets completely dry.

5. Serve immediately.

SCALLOPS WITH LEMON MEYER GLAZE

Preparation Time: 15 mins
Cooking Time: 40 mins
Cooking Temperature: 122 °F

INGREDIENTS:

2 pounds sea scallops, muscles removed

4 slices Meyer lemon

Salt and freshly ground black pepper, to taste

½ cup fresh orange juice

juice and zest of 2 Meyer lemons

2 tablespoons butter

2 tablespoon scallions, white and green parts separated, finely chopped (greens reserved for garnish)

pinch of red chili flakes

4 tablespoons dry sherry

2 teaspoons honey

DIRECTIONS:

1. Attach the sous vide immersion circulator using an adjustable clamp to a Cambro container or pot filled with water and preheat to 122 °F.

2. Into 2 cooking pouches, divide scallops, salt and black pepper. In each pouch, place 2 lemon slices. Seal pouches tightly after squeezing out the excess air. Place pouches in sous vide bath and set the cooking time for 30 minutes.

3. In a bowl, mix together orange juice and enough lemon juice to get ⅔ cup liquid. Keep aside.

4. Remove pouches from sous vide bath and carefully open them. Remove scallops from the pouches.

5. *For the sauce:* in a skillet, melt butter over medium-high heat and sauté white part of scallion and chili flakes until soft. With a slotted spoon, transfer scallion into a bowl and keep aside.

6. To the same skillet, add scallops and gently sear for 90 seconds per side. With a slotted spoon, transfer scallops onto a platter.

7. To the same skillet, add sherry and scrape browned pieces from bottom.

8. Add cooked scallion whites, juice mixture, and some of lemon zest and bring to a boil. Cook until desired thickness sauce is achieved.

9. Add honey 1 teaspoon at a time, and stir to combine.

10. Place sauce over scallops evenly. Garnish with scallion greens and some lemon zest, and serve immediately.

COCONUT SHRIMP

Preparation Time: 10 mins
Cooking Time: 35 mins
Cooking Temperature: 135 °F

INGREDIENTS:

1 package shrimp *

¼ cup bone broth

¼ cup coconut milk

butter, as required

1 x 1-inch piece fresh ginger, finely chopped

3 kaffir lime leaves, sliced

1 tablespoon flavored garlic lovers' seasoning

chopped fresh cilantro, for garnishing

DIRECTIONS:

1. Attach the sous vide immersion circulator using an adjustable clamp to a Cambro container or pot filled with water and preheat to 135 °F.
2. Into a cooking pouch, add all ingredients except cilantro. Seal pouch tightly after squeezing out the excess air. Place pouch in sous vide bath and set the cooking time for 35 minutes.
3. Remove pouch from sous vide bath and carefully open it. Remove shrimp mixture from pouch and transfer into a serving bowl.
4. Garnish with cilantro and serve immediately.

SHRIMP COCKTAIL

Preparation Time: 15 mins
Cooking Time: 35 mins
Cooking Temperature: 132 °F

INGREDIENTS:

For Shrimp:

 1 pound raw shrimp, peeled and deveined

 salt and freshly ground black pepper, to taste

 1 tablespoon butter

For Cocktail Sauce:

 2 small tomatoes

 ¼ cup fresh cilantro, plus more for garnishing

 1 chipotle pepper in adobo sauce

 3 cloves garlic

 ¼ cup tomato paste

 1 tablespoon honey

 1 tablespoon lime juice

 salt and freshly ground black pepper, to taste

DIRECTIONS:

1. Attach the sous vide immersion circulator using an adjustable clamp to a Cambro container or pot filled with water and preheat to 132 °F.
2. Season shrimp evenly with salt and black pepper.

3. Into a cooking pouch, add shrimp and butter. Seal pouch tightly after squeezing out the excess air. Place pouch in sous vide bath and set the cooking time for 15-35 minutes.

4. Remove pouch from sous vide bath and carefully open it. Remove shrimp from pouch. With paper towels, pat shrimp completely dry. Refrigerate until chilled.

5. *For cocktail sauce:* in a food processor, add all ingredients and pulse until well-combined.

6. Remove shrimp cocktail from refrigerator.

7. Into a large serving bowl, place cocktail sauce and shrimp.

8. Garnish with cilantro and serve.

BROWN BUTTER SCALLOPS

Preparation Time: 15 mins
Cooking Time: 40 mins
Cooking Temperature: 140 °F

INGREDIENTS:

1 x 4¼-ounce package scallops

2 teaspoons brown butter, divided

salt and freshly ground black pepper, to taste

DIRECTIONS:

1. Attach the sous vide immersion circulator using an adjustable clamp to a Cambro container or pot filled with water and preheat to 140 °F.

2. With paper towels, pat scallops.

3. Into a cooking pouch, add scallops, 1 teaspoon brown butter, salt and black pepper. Seal pouch tightly after squeezing out the excess air.

Place pouch in sous vide bath and set the cooking time for 35-40 minutes.

4. Remove pouch from sous vide bath and carefully open it. Remove scallops from pouch. With paper towels, pat scallops completely dry.

5. In a pan, melt remaining brown butter over high heat, and sear scallops for 30 seconds per side.

6. Serve immediately.

BACON WRAPPED SCALLOPS

Preparation Time: 15 mins
Cooking Time: 40 mins
Cooking Temperature: 140 °F

INGREDIENTS:

8 large diver scallops

8 bacon slices

1-2 tablespoons shallots, chopped

fresh thyme leaves from 3-4 sprigs

DIRECTIONS:

1. Attach the sous vide immersion circulator using an adjustable clamp to a Cambro container or pot filled with water and preheat to 140 °F.

2. Wrap each scallop with 1 bacon slice.

3. Into a cooking pouch, add wrapped scallops in a single layer, then add shallots and thyme. Seal pouch tightly after squeezing out the excess air. Place pouch in sous vide bath and set the cooking time for 20-40 minutes.

4. Remove pouch from sous vide bath and carefully open it. Remove scallops from the pouch. With paper towels, pat scallops completely dry.

5. Heat a cast iron grill pan over high heat, and sear scallops until golden brown.

6. Serve immediately.

GREEK STYLE OCTOPUS

Preparation Time: 20 mins
Cooking Time: 8 hours
Cooking Temperature: 165 °F

INGREDIENTS:

8 pounds frozen octopus, defrosted and cleaned

1½ cups extra-virgin olive oil, divided

1 cup fresh oregano, chopped

1 cup onion, chopped

1 bulb garlic, minced

¼ cup red wine vinegar

zest and juice of 1 lemon

salt, to taste

DIRECTIONS:

1. Attach the sous vide immersion circulator using an adjustable clamp to a Cambro container or pot filled with water and preheat to 165 °F.

2. Cut octopus's legs from body and chop each leg into 8 pieces.

3. Cut body in half longitudinally.

4. Into a cooking pouch, add octopus, ½ cup olive oil, and a handful of fresh oregano. Seal pouch tightly after squeezing out the excess air. Place pouch in sous vide bath and set the cooking time for 4½-8 hours.

5. Remove pouch from sous vide bath and carefully open it. Remove octopus from the pouch. With paper towels, pat octopus completely dry.

6. In a skillet, heat remaining olive oil and sauté onion for 2-3 minutes.

7. Add garlic and sauté for 1 minute more.

8. Stir in remaining oregano and remove from heat. Immediately, stir in vinegar, lemon juice and salt.

9. Into a clean, sealable plastic bag, add octopus and the vinegar mixture. Seal the bag and refrigerate to marinate for 24 hours.

10. Preheat the grill.

11. Remove octopus from bag, reserving marinade. Grill octopus over hot coals until cooked to taste.

12. Serve octopus with the topping of reserved marinade.

EASY LOBSTER TAILS

Preparation Time: 20 mins
Cooking Time: 40 mins
Cooking Temperature: 140 °F

INGREDIENTS:

2 x 10-ounce lobster tails

2 teaspoons seafood seasoning (of your choice), divided

4 tablespoons butter, divided

quartered lemons, for serving

DIRECTIONS:

1. Attach the sous vide immersion circulator using an adjustable clamp to a Cambro container or pot filled with water and preheat to 140 °F.

2. Remove meat from lobster tails.

3. In 2 cooking pouches, divide lobster tail meat, seasoning sand 2 tablespoons of butter. Seal pouches tightly after squeezing out the excess air. Place pouches in sous vide bath and set the cooking time for 40 minutes.

4. Remove pouches from sous vide bath and carefully open them. Remove lobster meat from the pouches.

5. Transfer lobster meat onto a serving platter. Top with remaining butter and serve alongside lemon quarters.

POACHED LOBSTER PASTA

Preparation Time: 20 mins
Cooking Time: 55 mins
Cooking Temperature: 140 °F

INGREDIENTS:

For Lobster:

4-5 frozen lobster tails, thawed and removed from shells, reserving the shells

1 teaspoon salt

½ cup unsalted butter

1 tablespoon chili paste

1 clove garlic, crushed

1-2 fresh parsley sprigs

1-2 fresh thyme sprigs

For Sauce:

3 tablespoons olive oil

reserved lobster shells

¼ cup tomato paste

2 plum tomatoes, chopped

2 cloves garlic, sliced

2 fresh parsley sprigs

2 fresh thyme sprigs

½ cup dry white wine

2 tablespoons white wine vinegar

4-5 cups whipping cream

1 pound linguine (or pasta of your choice)

salt and freshly ground white pepper, to taste

DIRECTIONS:

1. Attach the sous vide immersion circulator using an adjustable clamp to a Cambro container or pot filled with water and preheat to 140 °F.

2. Remove lobster meat from tails and season with a little salt.

3. Into a cooking pouch, add lobster, butter, chili paste, garlic and herbs. Seal pouch tightly after squeezing out the excess air. Place pouch in sous vide bath and set the cooking time for 30 minutes.

4. Remove pouch from sous vide bath and carefully open it. Remove lobster meat from the pouch and cut into small chunks.

5. Meanwhile, for the sauce: in a heavy large pan, heat oil over high heat and cook reserved lobster shells for 4-5 minutes.

6. Reduce heat to low and stir in the tomato paste. Cook for a few minutes.

7. Add tomatoes, garlic, herbs, wine and vinegar, and stir to combine.

8. Add cream and bring to a boil, then reduce heat to medium-low and simmer for 20 minutes, stirring occasionally.

9. Meanwhile, prepare pasta according to package's directions, then drain.

10. With a metal strainer, strain sauce into large bowl, pressing on solids to extract as much liquid as possible.

11. Transfer liquid into another pan over low heat. Add cooked pasta, lobster meat, salt and white pepper and toss to coat well.

12. Serve immediately.

TUNA

Preparation Time: 15 mins
Cooking Time: 45 mins
Cooking Temperature: 120 °F

INGREDIENTS:

2 x 10- or 12-ounce (1½-2 inch thick) tuna steaks

kosher salt and freshly ground black pepper, to taste

2 tablespoons extra-virgin olive oil

chopped fresh herbs (thyme, dill or parsley) as desired

sliced shallots, as desired

citrus zest, as desired

½ cup black sesame seeds

2 teaspoons vegetable oil

DIRECTIONS:

1. Season tuna generously with salt and black pepper.

2. In 2 cooking pouches, place tuna steaks in a single layer. Divide olive oil into each pouch and turn to coat. Add herbs, shallots and citrus zest. Seal pouches and refrigerate for at least 30 minutes or up to overnight.

3. Attach the sous vide immersion circulator using an adjustable clamp to a Cambro container or pot filled with water and preheat to 120 °F.

4. Remove pouches from refrigerator and seal after squeezing out the excess air. Place pouches in sous vide bath and set the cooking time for 45 minutes.

5. Remove pouches from sous vide bath and carefully open them. Remove steaks from pouches. With paper towels, pat steaks completely dry.

6. In a cast iron skillet, heat vegetable oil over high heat and cook steaks for 30-45 seconds, without moving.
7. Carefully flip and cook the other side for a further 30-45 seconds.
8. Serve immediately.

SALMON WITH LEMON MISO SAUCE

Preparation Time: 10 mins
Cooking Time: 1 hour
Cooking Temperature: 118 °F

INGREDIENTS:

2 x 4-6-ounce fresh salmon fillets

2 tablespoons lemon juice

2 tablespoons white miso paste

salt and freshly ground black pepper, to taste

DIRECTIONS:

1. Attach the sous vide immersion circulator using an adjustable clamp to a Cambro container or pot filled with water and preheat to 118 °F.
2. Into a large cooking pouch, place salmon fillets. Seal pouch tightly after squeezing out the excess air. Place pouch in sous vide bath and set the cooking time for 1 hour.
3. *For the sauce:* in a bowl, mix together remaining ingredients.
4. Remove pouch from sous vide bath and carefully open it.
5. Transfer salmon fillets onto a serving plate. Top with sauce and serve.

CRANBERRY BBQ SALMON

Preparation Time: 10 mins
Cooking Time: 35 mins
Cooking Temperature: 140 °F

INGREDIENTS:

2 tablespoons BBQ sauce

2 tablespoons cranberry sauce

1 tablespoon cranberry juice

1 tablespoon extra-virgin olive oil

1 teaspoon fresh lime juice

⅛ teaspoon salt

2 x 5-ounce boneless salmon fillets

fresh cilantro, for garnishing

DIRECTIONS:

1. Into a large bowl, add all ingredients except salmon fillets and cilantro, and mix until well-combined.

2. Set aside 1½ tablespoons of marinade in a small bowl.

3. Add salmon fillets to large bowl of marinade and coat generously.

4. Refrigerate, covered for 1-2 hours.

5. Attach the sous vide immersion circulator using an adjustable clamp to a Cambro container or pot filled with water and preheat to 140 °F.

6. Remove the salmon fillets from marinade and place into a cooking pouch. Seal pouch tightly after squeezing out the excess air. Place pouch in sous vide bath and set the cooking time for 25-30 minutes.

7. Preheat broiler to high.

8. Remove pouch from sous vide bath and carefully open it. Remove fillets from pouch. With paper towels, pat fillets completely dry.

9. Coat fillets evenly with reserved marinade.

10. Arrange salmon fillets onto a broiler-safe pan and broil for 1-2 minutes.

11. Garnish with cilantro and serve immediately.

SALMON TERIYAKI

Preparation Time: 15 mins
Cooking Time: 30 mins
Cooking Temperature: 126 °F

INGREDIENTS:

¼ cup low-sodium soy sauce

3 tablespoons sugar

2 tablespoons mirin

1 clove garlic, minced

¼ teaspoon fresh ginger, grated finely

¼ teaspoon cornstarch

4 x 6-ounce salmon fillets

2 teaspoons vegetable oil

½ teaspoon sesame seeds, toasted

1 scallion, thinly sliced

steamed rice, for serving

DIRECTIONS:

1. Into a small pan, add soy sauce, sugar, mirin, garlic, ginger and cornstarch over medium-high heat and bring to a boil, stirring continuously.

2. Cook for 1 minute.

3. Remove from heat and keep in room temperature to cool completely. Set aside ¼ cup of sauce into a bowl.

4. In 2 cooking pouches, divide salmon fillets and remaining sauce evenly. Seal pouches tightly after squeezing out the excess air and refrigerate for 1-4 hours.

5. Attach the sous vide immersion circulator using an adjustable clamp to a Cambro container or pot filled with water and preheat to 126 °F.

6. Remove pouches from refrigerator and place in sous vide bath. Set the cooking time for 30 minutes.

7. Remove pouches from sous vide bath and carefully open them. Remove fillets from pouches. With paper towels, pat fillets completely dry.

8. Into a small pan, add reserved marinade over medium-high heat and cook for 1-2 minutes.

9. *Meanwhile,* in a large nonstick frying pan, heat oil over medium-high heat. Place salmon fillets skin side up and sear for 20 seconds.

10. Flip and sear for a further 20 seconds.

11. Transfer fillets onto a platter and top with warm sauce.

12. Garnish with sesame seeds and scallion and serve immediately alongside steamed rice.

HALIBUT WITH SCALLIONS

Preparation Time: 15 mins
Cooking Time: 40 mins
Cooking Temperature: 128 °F

INGREDIENTS:

4 x 6-ounce halibut fillets

salt, to taste

⅔ cup scallions (green and pale parts), cut into ½-inch lengths

⅔ cup grapeseed oil

zest of 1 lemon, grated

½ teaspoon coriander seeds, crushed

1 tablespoon butter, melted

2 teaspoons Dijon mustard

DIRECTIONS:

1. Season halibut fillets evenly with salt and refrigerate for 1-24 hours.
2. Into a pan, add scallions, grapeseed oil, lemon zest and coriander, and bring to a gentle boil.
3. Reduce heat to low and simmer for 5 minutes, swirling the pan occasionally.
4. Remove from heat and keep aside to cool.
5. Strain mixture, and reserve oil and solids in separate bowls.
6. Attach the sous vide immersion circulator using an adjustable clamp to a Cambro container or pot filled with water and preheat to 128 °F.

7. In 2 cooking pouches, divide halibut fillets and reserved oil. Seal pouches tightly after squeezing out the excess air. Place pouches in sous vide bath and set the cooking time for 25-30 minutes.

8. In the same skillet, add reserved solids over medium-high heat and until browned, stirring occasionally.

9. Into a bowl, add butter and mustard and mix until smooth.

10. Preheat broiler to high. Arrange oven rack 2 inches from the heating element.

11. Remove pouches from sous vide bath and carefully open them. Remove fillets from pouches. With paper towels, pat fillets completely dry.

12. Arrange fillets onto a broiler-safe pan and top with a thin layer of butter mixture.

13. Broil until golden brown.

14. Divide fish fillets and solids mixture onto serving plates evenly and serve.

DILL MACKEREL

Preparation Time: 10 mins
Cooking Time: 25 mins
Cooking Temperature: 122 °F

INGREDIENTS:

2 mackerel fillets, pin boned

sea salt, to taste

fresh lemon rind, as required

oil, as required

DIRECTIONS:

1. Attach the sous vide immersion circulator using an adjustable clamp to a Cambro container or pot filled with water and preheat to 122 °F.

2. Season mackerel fillets evenly with a little salt.

3. Into a cooking pouch, add mackerel fillets and lemon zest. Seal pouch tightly after squeezing out the excess air. Place pouch in sous vide bath and set the cooking time for 20 minutes.

4. Remove pouches from sous vide bath and carefully open it. Remove fillets from pouch. With paper towels, pat fillets completely dry.

5. In a skillet, heat some oil over high heat and cook fillets for 1-2 minutes.

6. Serve immediately.

RED SNAPPER

Preparation Time: 15 mins
Cooking Time: 30 mins
Cooking Temperature: 132 °F

INGREDIENTS:

30-ounce skinless red snapper fillet, cut into 6 pieces and chilled

6 small, fresh bay leaves

A few strings of freshly cut chilies

1 teaspoon fennel seeds

sea salt, to taste

1½ tablespoons cold butter, cubed

DIRECTIONS:

1. Attach the sous vide immersion circulator using an adjustable clamp to a Cambro container or pot filled with water and preheat to 132 °F.

2. Into a large cooking pouch, place snapper pieces, bay leaves, chilies and fennel seeds. Seal pouch tightly after squeezing out the excess air. Place pouch in sous vide bath and set the cooking time for 25 minutes.

3. Remove pouch from sous vide bath and carefully open it. Remove fillets from pouch, reserving cooking liquid.

4. Transfer fillets onto warm serving plates and sprinkle with salt.

5. Into a small pan, add butter and reserved cooking liquid, and cook until desired thickness is achieved.

6. Pour sauce over snapper fillets and serve.

REDFISH WITH CREOLE MAYO

Preparation Time: 15 mins
Cooking Time: 25 mins
Cooking Temperature: 122 °F

INGREDIENTS:

For fish:

red fish fillets *

Creole seasoning, as required

olive oil, as required

For Mayo:

1 egg yolk

½ cup olive oil

½ teaspoon Creole mustard

1 small clove garlic, minced

pinch of salt

¼ teaspoon cayenne pepper

chopped fresh parsley, as required

DIRECTIONS:

1. Attach the sous vide immersion circulator using an adjustable clamp to a Cambro container or pot filled with water and preheat to 122 °F.

2. Season fish fillets with Creole seasoning evenly.

3. Into a large cooking pouch, place fish fillets. Seal pouch tightly after squeezing out the excess air. Place pouch in sous vide bath and set the cooking time for 20 minutes.

4. ***Meanwhile, for mayo:*** to a bowl, add egg yolk and beat until smooth.

5. Slowly add oil, beating continuously until a heavy cream like mixture is formed.

6. Add all remaining ingredients except parsley, and beat until well-combined. Keep aside until serving.

7. Preheat broiler to high.

8. Remove pouches from sous vide bath and carefully open them. Remove fillets from pouches. With paper towels, pat fillets completely dry.

9. Arrange fillets onto a broiler-safe pan and drizzle with some oil. Broil until golden brown.

10. Add parsley into mayo and stir to combine.

11. Serve fish with the topping of mayo.

KOHLRABI STUFFED WITH PRAWN, APPLE & LEMON

Preparation Time: 25 mins
Cooking Time: 40 mins
Cooking Temperature: 100 °F

INGREDIENTS:

For Pickled Kohlrabi:

1 kohlrabi

⅔ cup water

3 tablespoons plus 1 teaspoon cider vinegar

5 teaspoons sugar

1 teaspoon salt

For Kohlrabi Stuffing:

1 Granny Smith apple, peeled, cored and quartered

1-2 drops lemon juice

1 Granny Smith apple, cored and cubed

1 Granny Smith apple, cored and sliced into thin batons

5 cooked king prawns, cut into thirds

5 cooked whole king prawns

For Candied Lemon:

1 lemon

½ cup sugar

3 tablespoons plus 1 teaspoon water

1 tablespoon plus 2 teaspoons white wine vinegar

For Serving:

pinch of salt and Nepalese pepper

fresh cilantro leaves, for garnishing

DIRECTIONS:

1. *For pickled kohlrabi:* with a meat slicer, cut kohlrabi into fine slices and immediately place into a bowl of iced water.
2. Remove one slice from iced water. With a round cutter, punch out a 2-inch circle, and immediately return in to the iced water. Discard the remaining part of slice.
3. Repeat with the remaining slices.
4. Into a pan, add water, cider vinegar, sugar and salt, and bring to a boil.
5. Remove from heat and keep aside to cool slightly.

6. Drain water from kohlrabi slices.

7. Into a cooking pouch, add kohlrabi slices and warm pickling liquid. Seal pouch tightly after squeezing out the excess air. Refrigerate for at least 1 hour.

8. Attach the sous vide immersion circulator using an adjustable clamp to a Cambro container or pot filled with water and preheat to 100 °F.

9. Into a cooking pouch, add quartered apple. Seal pouch tightly after squeezing out the excess air. Place pouch in sous vide bath and set the cooking time for 20 minutes.

10. Remove pouch from sous vide bath and carefully open it. Remove apple from pouch.

11. Into a blender, add cooked apple and pulse until pureed.

12. Through a fine sieve, strain apple puree and place into a piping bag. Refrigerate the piping bag until used.

13. Into a bowl of iced water, add 1-2 drops of lemon juice and cubed apple.

14. *For candied lemon:* with a vegetable peeler, shave off lemon peel.

15. Place a small pan of water on the stove and bring to the boil.

16. *Meanwhile,* trim white pith from peel, and slice peel into a fine julienne.

17. Place lemon peel into boiling water for a few seconds, then drain water.

18. Repeat this process twice, replacing with fresh water each time.

19. After draining for a third time, finely chop lemon peel.

20. In another small pan, mix together sugar, water and vinegar and bring to a boil. Simmer until mixture becomes thick and syrupy, stirring continuously.

21. Stir in lemon peel and keep aside until candied.

22. Remove kohlrabi from pouch, discarding pickling liquid.

23. Arrange 1 slice on each plate, flat.

24. Carefully place a few pieces of cut prawn, apple cubes and a little candied lemon zest in the center of each slice and top with a few dots of apple puree.

25. Lift up one edge of kohlrabi slice and gently fold it over filling to create a parcel (similarly to a taco).

26. Sprinkle with a pinch of salt and pepper, and top with cilantro leaves.

27. Place 2 whole prawns beside each kohlrabi parcel, top evenly with apple batons, and serve.

PRAWNS DIABLO

Preparation Time: 15 mins
Cooking Time: 20 mins
Cooking Temperature: 135 °F

INGREDIENTS:

1½ pound fresh tiger prawns

2 tablespoons butter

1 tablespoon garlic, minced

1 tablespoon fresh cilantro, chopped

4 lime wedges

1 teaspoon sesame oil

1 teaspoon ground coriander

1 teaspoon ground cumin

1 teaspoon cayenne pepper

1 teaspoon chili flakes

1 teaspoon kosher salt

DIRECTIONS:

1. Attach the sous vide immersion circulator using an adjustable clamp to a Cambro container or pot filled with water and preheat to 135 °F.

2. Into a cooking pouch, add all ingredients. Seal pouch tightly after squeezing out the excess air. Place pouch in sous vide bath and set the cooking time for 20 minutes.

3. Remove pouch from sous vide bath and carefully open it. Remove prawns from pouch.

4. Serve alongside your favorite salad.

AHI TUNA

Preparation Time: 15 mins
Cooking Time: 30 mins
Cooking Temperature: 120 °F

INGREDIENTS:

⅓ cup honey

¼ cup ponzu sauce

1 tablespoon chili-garlic sauce

1 pound ahi tuna

DIRECTIONS:

1. Into a small bowl, add all ingredients except tuna, and beat until well-combined.

2. Into a cooking pouch, add tuna and honey mixture. Seal pouch tightly after squeezing out the excess air and refrigerate for 1 hour.

3. Attach the sous vide immersion circulator using an adjustable clamp to a Cambro container or pot filled with water and preheat to 120 °F.

4. Place pouch in sous vide bath and set the cooking time for 30 minutes.

5. Remove pouch from sous vide bath and carefully open it. Remove tuna from pouch.

6. Cut tuna into desired sized slices, and serve immediately.

BUTTER & HERB HALIBUT

Preparation Time: 15 mins
Cooking Time: 50 mins
Cooking Temperature: 120 °F

INGREDIENTS:

4 x 6-ounce (1-inch thick) halibut fillets

kosher salt and freshly ground black pepper, to taste

4 tablespoons unsalted butter, divided

shallots, as required (optional), thinly sliced

citrus zest, as required (optional), grated

fresh herbs (thyme, parsley or dill), as required (optional)

garlic cloves, as required, minced

DIRECTIONS:

1. Season each halibut slice generously with salt and black pepper.

2. Between 2 cooking pouches, divide halibut fillets and 2 tablespoons of butter (i.e. 1 tablespoon per pouch). Add shallots, citrus zest and your favorite herbs. Seal pouch tightly after squeezing out the excess air and refrigerate for at least 30 minutes and up to overnight.

3. Attach the sous vide immersion circulator using an adjustable clamp to a Cambro container or pot filled with water and preheat to 130 °F.

4. Place pouches in sous vide bath and set the cooking time for 30-45 minutes.

5. Remove pouches from sous vide bath and carefully open them. Remove fillets from pouches, discarding shallots, zest and herbs. Remove halibut skin. With paper towels, pat fillets completely.

6. In a large, heavy skillet, melt remaining butter over medium-high heat.

7. Place halibut fillets presentation-side-down and cook for 30-45 seconds, without stirring.

8. Add a little of the shallots, herbs and garlic, and cook for 1½ minutes, tilting pan and basting halibut with hot butter.

9. Flip and cook the other side for a further 15-30 seconds.

10. Transfer halibut fillets onto a paper-towel-lined plate to remove excess grease.

11. Serve immediately.

Saffron Infused Halibut

Preparation Time: 25 mins
Cooking Time: 25 mins
Cooking Temperature: 140 °F

INGREDIENTS:

For Halibut:

4 x 5-ounce boneless fresh halibut fillets, cut into thick cubes

kosher salt, to taste

⅓ cup fish broth

3 tablespoons butter

1 tablespoon fresh orange zest, finely chopped

15 Spanish saffron threads

For Tomato Compote:

2 tablespoons extra-virgin olive oil

2 tablespoons garlic, finely chopped

2 tablespoons water

2 tablespoons shallots, finely chopped

½ cup cherry tomatoes, halved lengthwise

3 tablespoons fresh basil, chopped

1 tablespoon fresh orange zest, finely chopped

½ teaspoon freshly ground black pepper

For Zucchini:

2 zucchinis

1 tablespoon extra-virgin olive oil

1 tablespoon fresh parsley, chopped

1 tablespoon fresh mint, chopped

1 teaspoon fresh lemon zest, grated

pinch of salt

For Garnish:

2 tablespoons fresh chives, minced

DIRECTIONS:

1. Attach the sous vide immersion circulator using an adjustable clamp to a Cambro container or pot filled with water and preheat to 140 °F.
2. *For the halibut:* season halibut cubes with a little kosher salt and keep aside.
3. Into a pan over a low heat, add remaining ingredients and cook for 3 minutes, beating continuously.
4. Remove from heat.
5. Between 2 cooking pouches, divide halibut cubes and butter mixture evenly. Seal pouches tightly after squeezing out the excess air and keep aside.
6. *For the tomato compote:* in a pan, heat oil over medium heat and sauté garlic until golden.
7. Add water and shallots and cook for 3-4 minutes.
8. Stir in remaining ingredients and remove from heat. Keep aside to cool.
9. Into a cooking pouch, add tomato mixture. Seal pouch tightly after squeezing out the excess air and keep aside.
10. *For zucchini in a bowl:* add all ingredients and toss to coat well.
11. Into a cooking pouch, add zucchini mixture. Seal pouch tightly after squeezing out the excess air.

12. Place all pouches in sous vide bath and set the cooking time for 17 minutes, plus a separate timer for 12 minutes.

13. *After 12 minutes,* remove pouches of tomato compote and zucchini.

14. Carefully, open pouches. Remove zucchini from pouch, reserving cooking liquid into bowl. Transfer tomato compote into another bowl.

15. With vegetable peeler, shape zucchini into ribbons.

16. Transfer zucchini ribbons into the bowl of reserved cooking liquid and toss to coat.

17. *After the full 17 minutes,* remove pouches of halibut from sous vide bath and carefully open them. Remove halibut cubes from pouches.

18. Divide zucchini ribbons onto serving plates evenly. Place fish cubes over ribbons, followed by tomato compote evenly.

19. Garnish with chives and serve.

SWORDFISH WITH MANGO SALSA

Preparation Time: 20 mins
Cooking Time: 35 mins
Cooking Temperature: 127 °F

INGREDIENTS:

For Salsa:

5½ ounces fresh raspberries, washed

5½ ounces fresh mango, peeled, pitted and chopped

1½ ounces red onion, minced

⅓ cup fresh cilantro, chopped

1 small jalapeño pepper, minced

2 tablespoons fresh lime juice

For Swordfish:

3 tablespoons sugar

3 tablespoons fine sea salt

4-4½ cups cool water

4 x 4-ounce swordfish fillets

½ cup butter

3 tablespoons balsamic vinegar

1¾ tablespoons honey

1½ tablespoons Dijon mustard

salt and freshly ground white pepper, to taste

DIRECTIONS:

1. ***For the salsa:*** to a bowl, add all ingredients and mix. Refrigerate overnight, covered.

2. ***For the swordfish:*** in a large bowl, dissolve sugar and salt in cool water. Place swordfish fillets and refrigerate for 3 hours.

3. Attach the sous vide immersion circulator using an adjustable clamp to a Cambro container or pot filled with water and preheat to 127 °F.

4. Into a pan, add butter and cook until golden brown, swirling pan continuously.

5. Remove from heat and add vinegar, honey, Dijon mustard, salt and white pepper, beating until well-combined.

6. Remove fish fillet from bowl of cold water and lightly season with salt and white pepper.

7. Between 4 cooking pouches, divide fish fillets. Add 2-3 tablespoons of brown butter to each pouch. Seal pouches tightly after squeezing out the excess air.

8. Place pouches in sous vide bath and set the cooking time for 30 minutes.

9. Remove pouches from sous vide bath and carefully open them. Remove fish fillets from pouches. With paper towels, pat fillets completely dry.

10. With a blow torch, toast each fillet until a slight crust is formed.

11. Divide fillets onto serving plates and drizzle evenly with brown butter.

12. Place salsa evenly alongside each fillet and serve.

FISH TACOS

Preparation Time: 20 mins
Cooking Time: 20 mins
Cooking Temperature: 132 °F

INGREDIENTS:

For Fish:

1 teaspoons fresh cilantro, chopped

½ teaspoon chili powder

pinch of salt and freshly ground black pepper

1 pound thick, flaky fish (cod/halibut)

For Marinated Onion:

½ large red onion, thinly sliced

1 tablespoon white wine vinegar

1 teaspoons fresh cilantro, chopped

pinch of salt and freshly ground black pepper

For Tacos:

⅓ cup sour cream

1 teaspoon hot sauce

4 corn or flour tortillas

lettuce, as required, shredded

1 avocado, peeled, pitted and sliced

10-12 cherry tomatoes, halved

4 lime wedges

DIRECTIONS:

1. Attach the sous vide immersion circulator using an adjustable clamp to a Cambro container or pot filled with water and preheat to 132 °F.

2. ***For the fish:*** in a small bowl, mix together cilantro, chili powder, salt and black pepper. Season fish with cilantro mixture evenly.

3. Into a cooking pouch, add fish. Seal pouch tightly after squeezing out the excess air. Place pouch in sous vide bath and set the cooking time for 20 minutes.

4. ***Meanwhile for the marinated onion:*** in a small bowl, mix together all ingredients and keep aside.

5. In another bowl, mix together sour cream and hot sauce and keep aside.

6. Remove pouch from sous vide bath and carefully open it. Remove fish from pouch.

7. Arrange tacos onto serving plates.

8. Place a heaped spoonful of cooked fish onto the center of each tortilla. Top with the shredded lettuce, followed by marinated onion, avocado and tomato evenly.

9. Drizzle with sour cream and serve alongside lime wedges.

BLACK COD

Preparation Time: 10 mins
Cooking Time: 35 mins
Cooking Temperature: 130 °F

INGREDIENTS:

2 medium bone-in black cod fillets

1 x 1-inch piece fresh ginger, grated

1 cup soy sauce

½ cup mirin

2 dashes fish sauce

DIRECTIONS:

1. Attach the sous vide immersion circulator using an adjustable clamp to a Cambro container or pot filled with water and preheat to 130 °F.

2. Into a cooking pouch, add all ingredients. Seal pouch tightly after squeezing out the excess air. Place pouch in sous vide bath and set the cooking time for 30 minutes.

3. Preheat broiler to high.

4. Remove pouch from sous vide bath and carefully open it. Remove fillets from pouch. With paper towels, pat fillets completely dry.

5. Broil until golden brown.

Miso Tilapia

Preparation Time: 15 mins
Cooking Time: 25 mins
Cooking Temperature: 132 °F

Ingredients:

1 teaspoon fresh ginger, grated finely

3-4 tablespoons low-sodium white miso

½ tablespoon cooking wine

1 teaspoon vegetable oil

1 teaspoon sugar

2 tilapia fillets, rinsed and pat-dried

½ tablespoon butter

white sesame seeds, for garnishing

Directions:

1. Attach the sous vide immersion circulator using an adjustable clamp to a Cambro container or pot filled with water and preheat to 132 °F.

2. In a small bowl mix together ginger, miso, wine, oil and sugar.

3. Into a large cooking pouch, place tilapia fillets. Coat each fillet with miso mixture evenly. Seal pouch tightly after squeezing out the excess air. Place pouch in sous vide bath and set the cooking time for 20 minutes.

4. Remove pouch from sous vide bath and carefully open it. Remove tilapia fillets from pouch.

5. In a cast iron skillet, melt butter over high heat, and sear fillets for 30 seconds per side.

6. Sprinkle with sesame seeds and serve.

Coconut and Thai Seasoned Hake

Preparation Time: 15 mins
Cooking Time: 40 mins
Cooking Temperature: 122 °F

INGREDIENTS:

4 x 7-ounce skinless hake fillets

pinch of sugar

sea salt, to taste

6¾ ounces coconut milk, divided as 5 ounces and 1¾ ounces

1 tablespoon palm sugar

3 teaspoons red Thai spice paste

1 bunch fresh cilantro, finely chopped

fresh zest of 2 limes

2 lime leaves, finely chopped

5⅓ ounces rice noodles, soaked

DIRECTIONS:

1. Season hake fillets pinch of sugar and salt, and refrigerate for 3 hours.

2. Attach the sous vide immersion circulator using an adjustable clamp to a Cambro container or pot filled with water and preheat to 122 °F.

3. Into a small blender, add 5 ounces of coconut milk, the palm sugar, the Thai spice, half of the cilantro, half of the lime zest, and 1 lime leaf, and pulse until a paste is formed.

4. Divide hake fillets and coconut milk mixture into 4 cooking pouches evenly. Seal pouches tightly after squeezing out the excess air. Place pouches in sous vide bath and set the cooking time for 40 minutes.

5. Meanwhile, in a small pan, mix together remaining coconut milk, lime zest and lime leaf.

6. Add noodles and toss until completely heated.

7. Stir in salt and remove from heat.

8. Remove pouch from sous vide bath and carefully open it. Remove hake fillets from pouch.

9. Divide noodles into serving bowls and top with hake pieces.

10. Garnish with cilantro and serve.

CLAMS IN WHITE WINE SAUCE

Preparation Time: 15 mins
Cooking Time: 40 mins
Cooking Temperature: 132 °F

INGREDIENTS:

1 cup fish broth

3 tablespoons white wine

24 clams, cleaned

3 cloves garlic, sliced

2 tablespoons extra-virgin olive oil

1 cup marinated artichoke hearts, halved

1 tablespoon cornstarch

salt and freshly ground black pepper, to taste

chopped fresh parsley, for garnishing

DIRECTIONS:

1. Attach the sous vide immersion circulator using an adjustable clamp to a Cambro container or pot filled with water and preheat to 132 °F.

2. Into a pan, add broth and white wine over high heat and bring to a boil. Add clams and blanche for 1 minute.

3. Immediately strain clams through a strainer, reserving cooking liquid.

4. Set clams and cooking liquid aside to cool for 15 minutes.

5. Into a large cooking pouch, place clams, cooking liquid, garlic and oil. Seal pouch tightly after squeezing out the excess air. Place pouch in sous vide bath and set the cooking time for 10 minutes.

6. Remove pouch from sous vide bath and carefully open it. Remove clams from pouch, reserving cooking liquid.

7. Heat a skillet over medium heat and add reserved cooking liquid.

8. Add cornstarch and stir to combine.

9. Add artichoke hearts and toss until warmed.

10. Stir in clams and immediately remove from heat.

11. Serve hot, with a garnishing of parsley.

SHERRY PAPRIKA SHRIMP

Preparation Time: 15 mins
Cooking Time: 1 hour 10 mins
Cooking Temperature: 135 °F

INGREDIENTS:

1½ pounds large shrimp, peeled and deveined

½ teaspoon baking soda

kosher salt, to taste

6 tablespoons extra-virgin olive oil

6 medium cloves garlic, thinly sliced

2 bay leaves

1 tablespoon sweet smoked Spanish paprika

3 tablespoons sherry

1½ teaspoons sherry vinegar

2 tablespoons butter, softened

crusty bread, to serve

DIRECTIONS:

1. Attach the sous vide immersion circulator using an adjustable clamp to a Cambro container or pot filled with water and preheat to 135 °F.
2. Into a large bowl, add shrimp, baking soda and ½ teaspoon of salt, and mix well. Keep aside.
3. Place a large skillet on a medium-low heat and add olive oil and garlic. Sauté for 3 minutes.
4. Add bay leaves and paprika, and sauté for 30 seconds.
5. Stir in sherry and vinegar, and increase heat to high for 2 minutes.

6. Remove from heat and stir in butter and salt. Keep aside for 5 minutes to cool.

7. Into a cooking pouch, add shrimp and sherry mixture. Seal pouch tightly after squeezing out the excess air. Place pouch in sous vide bath and set the cooking time for 15-60 minutes.

8. Remove pouch from sous vide bath and carefully open it. Transfer shrimp and cooking liquid into a warm bowl and serve and serve immediately with bread.

6

SOUPS & STEWS

BUTTERNUT SQUASH & APPLE SOUP

Preparation Time: 20 mins
Cooking Time: 2 hours
Cooking Temperature: 185 °F

INGREDIENTS:

1 large Granny Smith apple, cored and sliced

1 medium butternut squash, peeled and sliced

½ of onion, sliced

¾ cup light cream

1 teaspoon sea salt

DIRECTIONS:

1. Attach the sous vide immersion circulator to a Cambro container or pot with water using an adjustable clamp and preheat water to 185 °F.

2. Into a large cooking pouch, place apple, squash and onion. Seal pouch tightly after squeezing out the excess air. Place pouch in sous vide bath and set the cooking time for 2 hours.

3. Remove pouch from sous vide bath and keep aside to cool slightly. Transfer squash mixture into blender.

4. Add cream and salt, and pulse until smooth.

5. Serve immediately.

Easy Chicken Broth

Preparation Time: 15 mins
Cooking Time: 9 hours 30 mins
Cooking Temperature: 194 °F

Ingredients:

10-12 pounds chicken (necks, legs, wings and bones)

170-200 fluid ounces cold water, divided

1 pound yellow onion, cut into halves

8 ounces celery, roughly chopped

8 ounces carrots, roughly chopped

10 fresh thyme sprigs

small handful parsley stems

3 bay leaves

½ teaspoon black peppercorn

Directions:

1. Preheat the oven to 400 °F.
2. Arrange chicken pieces onto a roasting pan and roast for 1½ hours.
3. Attach the sous vide immersion circulator using an adjustable clamp to a Cambro container or pot filled with water and preheat to 194 °F.
4. Remove chicken pieces from oven and transfer into a bowl.
5. To the same roasting pan, add 1 cup of water and scrape to loosen browned pieces.
6. Into a large cooking pouch, place roasted chicken, water from roasting pan, and remaining ingredients. Seal pouch tightly after squeezing out

the excess air. Place pouch in sous vide bath and set the cooking time for 6-8 hours.

7. Remove pouch from sous vide bath and carefully open it. Through a strainer, strain broth into a bowl. Refrigerate overnight.

8. Remove fat from top surface. Transfer into a container and preserve in refrigerator.

OXTAIL STEW

Preparation Time: 20 mins
Cooking Time: 20 hours 40 mins
Cooking Temperature: 180 °F

INGREDIENTS:

For Stew:

4 pounds oxtail pieces

8 medium whole onions, unpeeled

1 whole garlic bulb, unpeeled

1 cup white wine

3½ ounces Demerara sugar

⅛ teaspoon ground cloves

Pinch of cayenne pepper

Salt and freshly ground black pepper, to taste

For Sauce:

1½ tablespoons butter

4 medium carrots, peeled and cut into half-moons

2 celery sticks, finely chopped

1 medium leek, thinly sliced

10 closed-cup mushrooms, thinly sliced

2 teaspoons English mustard

2 cups reserved cooking liquid

4 tablespoons onion puree from oxtail

pinch of cayenne pepper

salt and freshly ground black pepper, to taste

DIRECTIONS:

1. Preheat the oven to 390 °F and line a baking tray with a piece of foil.

2. Arrange onion and garlic bulb onto prepared baking tray and roast for 50 minutes. After 15 minutes, remove garlic from roasting tray and keep aside.

3. Remove onions from oven and keep aside with garlic to cool slightly, then squeeze the roasted onion pulp and garlic pulp from the skins.

4. Transfer squeezed pulp into a small pan with wine, sugar and seasonings and bring to a boil. Simmer for 10-15 minutes.

5. With an immersion blender, blend the onion mixture into a thick puree.

6. Keep aside to cool completely, reserving 4 tablespoons in another bowl.

7. Attach the sous vide immersion circulator using an adjustable clamp to a Cambro container or pot filled with water and preheat to 180 °F.

8. Into a cooking pouch, add oxtail pieces with remaining onion puree and freeze for 15 minutes.

9. Remove pouch from freezer and seal pouch tightly after squeezing out the excess air. Place pouch in sous vide bath and set the cooking time for 20 hours.

10. Remove pouch from sous vide bath and carefully open it. Remove oxtail pieces from pouch, reserving cooking liquid.

11. Through a sieve, strain cooking liquid into a bowl and refrigerate to cool.

12. After cooling, remove solidified fat from top.

13. Flake meat from bones of warm oxtail pieces and, using 2 forks, shred meat.

14. *For the sauce:* in a large pan, melt butter and sauté carrots, celery and leeks until they begin to soften.

15. Add flaked oxtail meat, cooking liquid, reserved onion puree and mustard, and bring to a boil.

16. Reduce heat and simmer, covered, for 15-20 minutes.

17. Add mushrooms in the last 5 minutes along with cayenne pepper, salt and black pepper to taste.

18. Serve immediately.

BEEF BONE BROTH

Preparation Time: 10 mins
Cooking Time: 12 hours 15 mins
Cooking Temperature: 176 °F

INGREDIENTS:

1½ pounds beef bones

3 cups water

1 carrot, peeled and chopped

1 celery stick, chopped

1 white onion, chopped

DIRECTIONS:

1. Attach the sous vide immersion circulator using an adjustable clamp to a Cambro container or pot filled with water and preheat to 176 °F.

2. Into a cooking pouch, add all ingredients. Seal pouch tightly after squeezing out the excess air. Place pouch in sous vide bath and set the cooking time for 12 hours.

3. Remove pouch from sous vide bath and carefully open it. Transfer bone mixture into a pan and bring to a boil. Boil for 10 minutes.

4. Through a strainer, strain broth and serve or preserve in refrigerator.

LENTIL SOUP

Preparation Time: 15 mins
Cooking Time: 2 hours
Cooking Temperature: 180 °F

INGREDIENTS:

3 tablespoons extra-virgin olive oil

1 yellow onion, finely chopped

4 carrots, peeled and finely chopped

3 celery stalks celery, finely chopped

2 garlic cloves, minced

kosher salt and freshly ground black pepper, to taste

2 cups brown lentils

8 cups chicken broth

3 fresh thyme sprigs

1 bay leaf

1 tablespoon ground cumin

fresh lemon juice, as required

DIRECTIONS:

1. Attach the sous vide immersion circulator using an adjustable clamp to a Cambro container or pot filled with water and preheat to 180 °F.

2. In a large non-stick skillet, heat oil over medium heat and cook onion, carrots, celery, garlic, salt and black pepper for 5 minutes, stirring occasionally.

3. Into a large cooking pouch, place onion mixture, lentils, broth, thyme, bay leaf and cumin. Seal pouch tightly after squeezing out the excess air. Place pouch in sous vide bath and set the cooking time for 2 hours.

4. Remove pouch from sous vide bath and carefully open it. Transfer soup into serving bowls and season with salt and black pepper.

5. Drizzle with lemon juice and serve hot.

Avgolemono Soup

Preparation Time: 15 mins
Cooking Time: 6 hours 35 minutes
Cooking Temperature: 150 °F

INGREDIENTS:

---

1 x 4-pound whole chicken, trussed

6 cups water

2 cups white onion, chopped

2 cups celery, chopped

2 cups carrots, peeled and chopped

kosher salt and freshly ground black pepper, to taste

1 tablespoon extra-virgin olive oil

½ cup white onion, finely chopped

2 cloves garlic, minced

½ cup uncooked long-grain white rice

1 egg, beaten

¼ cup fresh lemon juice

1 tablespoon cornstarch

2 tablespoons scallion, chopped

2 tablespoons fresh parsley, chopped

lemon wedges, for garnishing

DIRECTIONS:

---

1. Attach the sous vide immersion circulator using an adjustable clamp to a Cambro container or pot filled with water and preheat to 150 °F.

2. Into a large cooking pouch, place chicken, 2 cups of onion, celery, carrot, salt and black pepper. Seal pouch tightly after squeezing out the excess air. Place pouch in sous vide bath and set the cooking time for 6 hours.

3. Remove pouch from sous vide bath and carefully open it. Carefully, transfer chicken onto a plate and keep aside for at least 20 minutes.

4. Through a fine-mesh strainer, strain cooking liquid into a large bowl. Discard vegetable solids.

5. Remove chicken meat from bones and shred. Discard bones.

6. In a Dutch oven, heat oil over medium heat and sauté finely chopped onion for 5 minutes.

7. Add garlic and rice and sauté for 2 minutes.

8. Add strained cooking liquid and bring to a boil. Simmer for 20 minutes.

9. Into a small bowl, add egg, lemon juice and cornstarch and beat until well-combined.

10. Add egg mixture into soup, beating continuously.

11. Add shredded chicken and simmer for 5 minutes.

12. Stir in salt and black pepper and remove from heat.

13. Divide soup into serving bowls and serve with a garnish of scallions, parsley and lemon wedges.

PORK & WHITE BEANS STEW

Preparation Time: 15 mins
Cooking Time: 10 hours
Cooking Temperature: 140 °F

INGREDIENTS:

2 tablespoons vegetable oil

1 tablespoon unsalted butter

1 x 2-pound pork loin, trimmed and cut into 1-inch pieces

salt and freshly ground black pepper, to taste

2 large carrots, peeled and cut into ½-inch pieces

2 cups frozen pearl onions

2 cloves garlic, minced

2 tablespoons all-purpose flour

1 cup dry white wine

1 x 15-ounce can white beans, rinsed and drained

2 cups chicken broth

4 large fresh rosemary sprigs

2 bay leaves

chopped fresh rosemary, for garnishing

DIRECTIONS:

1. Attach the sous vide immersion circulator using an adjustable clamp to a Cambro container or pot filled with water and preheat to 140 °F.

2. Season pork evenly with salt and black pepper.

3. In a large nonstick skillet, heat oil and butter over medium-high heat, and sear pork for 5-7 minutes.

4. Add carrots and onions and cook for 5 minutes. Add garlic and cook for 1 minute.

5. Stir in flour and cook for 2 minutes, stirring continuously.

6. Add wine and bring to a boil, scraping up the browned bits from bottom of skillet.

7. Stir in beans, broth, rosemary and bay leaves and remove from heat.

8. Between 2 cooking pouches, divide pork mixture, placing 2 rosemary sprigs and 1 bay leaf in each pouch. Seal pouches tightly after squeezing out the excess air. Place pouches in sous vide bath and set the cooking time for at least 7 and no more than 10 hours.

9. Remove pouches from sous vide bath and carefully open them.

10. Divide stew into serving bowls and serve with the garnishing of chopped rosemary.

OYSTER STEW

Preparation Time: 15 mins
Cooking Time: 1 hour 5 mins
Cooking Temperature: 120 °F

INGREDIENTS:

4 tablespoons unsalted butter

1 small clove garlic, minced

1 cup thinly sliced leeks

2 cups oysters with liquid, shucked

2 cups heavy cream

2 cups whole milk

1 bay leaf

kosher salt and freshly ground black pepper, to taste

DIRECTIONS:

1. Attach the sous vide immersion circulator using an adjustable clamp to a Cambro container or pot filled with water and preheat to 120 °F.

2. In a large skillet, melt butter over medium heat and cook garlic and leeks for 5 minutes, stirring occasionally.

3. Into a large cooking pouch, place leek mixture, oysters, cream, milk and bay leaf. Seal pouch tightly after squeezing out the excess air. Place pouch in sous vide bath and set the cooking time for 1 hour.

4. Remove pouch from sous vide bath and carefully open it.

5. Divide stew into serving bowls and season with salt and black pepper. Serve hot.

THAI COCONUT CHICKEN CURRY SOUP

Preparation Time: 15 mins
Cooking Time: 1 hour 10 mins
Cooking Temperature: 149 °F

INGREDIENTS:

1 tablespoon coconut oil

1 red bell pepper, seeded and cut into ½-inch pieces

½ of yellow onion, sliced into half moons

3 cloves garlic, thinly sliced

1 x 1-inch piece fresh ginger, minced

2 tablespoons red curry paste

¼ cup water

1 pound skinless, boneless chicken breasts, cut into 1-inch pieces

1 x 13½-ounce can full-fat coconut milk

1 cup chicken broth

2 tablespoons fish sauce

2 tablespoons granulated sugar

1 tablespoon fresh lime juice

1 ounce dried rice vermicelli noodles

1 cup frozen shelled edamame

fresh cilantro and lime wedges, for serving

DIRECTIONS:

1. Attach the sous vide immersion circulator using an adjustable clamp to a Cambro container or pot filled with water and preheat to 149 °F.

2. In a large skillet, melt coconut oil over medium heat and sauté bell pepper, onion, garlic, ginger and curry paste for 3 minutes.

3. Add water and with an edged wooden spoon, scrape browned bits from the bottom of skillet.

4. Cook for 5 minutes, then remove from heat.

5. Into a cooking pouch, place onion mixture, chicken, coconut milk, broth, fish sauce, sugar and lime juice. Seal pouch tightly after squeezing out the excess air. Place pouch in sous vide bath and set the cooking time for 1 hour.

6. Meanwhile, boil a large pan of water and cook noodles according to directions on the packet. For the last 4 minutes of cooking, place frozen edamame in pan.

7. Drain rice and edamame mixture well and run under cold water for 1 minute.

8. Remove pouch from sous vide bath and carefully open it.

9. Divide noodle mixture into serving bowls and top evenly with hot soup.

10. Garnish with cilantro and lime wedges and serve immediately.

CREAMY TOMATO SOUP

Preparation Time: 15 mins
Cooking Time: 1 hour 20 mins
Cooking Temperature: 172 °F

INGREDIENTS:

½ cup plus 2 tablespoons butter, divided

⅓ cup flour

4 cups milk

1 cup heavy cream

1 green bell pepper, seeded and chopped

½ large onion, chopped

1 clove garlic, chopped

3 large cans diced tomatoes with liquid

1-2 fresh tomatoes, chopped

2 tablespoons dried basil, crushed

pinch of cayenne pepper

1 teaspoon salt

1 teaspoon freshly ground black pepper

DIRECTIONS:

1. Attach the sous vide immersion circulator using an adjustable clamp to a Cambro container or pot filled with water and preheat to 172 °F.

2. ***For the roux:*** in a large pan, melt ½ cup of butter over medium heat.

3. Slowly add flour, stirring continuously, and cook for 1-2 minutes.

4. Stir in milk and cook for 1-2 minutes or until mixture just starts to thicken, stirring continuously.

5. Stir in cream and cook for 1-2 minutes or until mixture becomes thick, stirring continuously.

6. Remove from heat and keep aside.

7. In another pan, melt coconut oil and sauté bell pepper, onion and garlic until onion becomes translucent.

8. Add tomatoes with liquid and basil and bring to a gentle boil. Simmer for 30 minutes.

9. With immersion blender, blend soup mixture slightly.

10. Add white sauce and stir to combine.

11. Add white sauce, cayenne pepper, salt and black pepper and cook until well-combined. Remove from heat.

12. Into a cooking pouch, add tomato mixture. Seal pouch tightly after squeezing out the excess air. Place pouch in sous vide bath and set the cooking time for 30-40 minutes.

13. Remove pouch from sous vide bath and carefully open it.

14. Divide soup into serving bowls and serve.

LAMB STEW

Preparation Time: 15 mins
Cooking Time: 24 hours 10 mins
Cooking Temperature: 149 °F

INGREDIENTS:

1 whole lamb breast *

dried Italian seasoning, to taste

chopped seasonal vegetables of your choice *

2-3 lamb stock cubes

gravy granules *

salt and freshly ground black pepper, to taste

DIRECTIONS:

1. Attach the sous vide immersion circulator using an adjustable clamp to a Cambro container or pot filled with water and preheat to 149 °F.

2. Season lamb breast lightly with Italian seasoning.

3. Into a cooking pouch, place lamb breast. Seal pouch tightly after squeezing out the excess air. Place pouch in sous vide bath and set the cooking time for 24 hours.

4. Meanwhile, in a large pan, cook vegetables according to your taste.

5. Remove pouch from sous vide bath and carefully open it. Remove lamb neck from pouch, reserving pouch juices in a jug. Add 2 stock cubes and some boiling water and stir to combine well. (If mixture is thin, then add another stock cube or some gravy granules).

6. Cut lamb breast into desired sized pieces and transfer into the pan with vegetables.

7. Add gravy and mix until well-combined, and cook until heated through.

8. This stew is great served with a delicious crusty bread roll or creamy mashed potatoes.

BEEF STEW

Preparation Time: 20 mins
Cooking Time: 49 hours
Cooking Temperature: 140 °F / 185 °F

INGREDIENTS:

good quality beef stew meat *

butternut squash, peeled and chopped *

turnips, peeled and chopped *

potatoes, chopped *

bacon *

celery, chopped *

carrots, peeled and chopped *

onions, chopped *

seasoning of your choice *

red wine *

beef broth *

xanthan gum *

DIRECTIONS:

1. Attach the sous vide immersion circulator using an adjustable clamp to a Cambro container or pot filled with water and preheat to 140 °F.

2. Into a cooking pouch, add stew meat. Seal pouch tightly after squeezing out the excess air. Place pouch in sous vide bath and set the cooking time for 48 hours.

3. Remove pouch from sous vide bath and carefully open it. Remove stew meat from pouch.

4. ***For the vegetables:*** preheat the water now to 185 °F.

5. In 3 different cooking pouches, place squash, turnips and potatoes separately. Seal pouches tightly after squeezing out the excess air. Place pouches in sous vide bath and set the cooking time for 45 minutes.

6. Heat a large non-stick pan over medium-high heat and cook bacon until crisp.

7. Transfer bacon onto a plate, reserving grease in the pan.

8. To the same pan, add stew meat and sear for 1-2 minutes (or until browned).

9. Transfer meat into the plate with bacon.

10. To the same pan, add celery, carrots, onions and seasoning, and sauté for 4-5 minutes.

11. Add wine and scrape browned pieces from the bottom.

12. Remove pouches of vegetables from sous vide bath and carefully open them. Remove vegetables from pouches, reserving cooking liquids.

13. Add some beef broth and cooking liquid into pan and cook until desired doneness is achieved.

14. For a thicker and creamier texture, add xanthan gum and cook until desired thickness, stirring continuously.

15. Add meat, bacon and cooked vegetables, and cook until heated through.

MINESTRONE SOUP

Preparation Time: 15 mins
Cooking Time: 1 hour
Cooking Temperature: 185 °F

INGREDIENTS:

5½ cups water

¾ ounce Parmesan rind

1½ cups onion, chopped

1 cup carrot, peeled and chopped

⅓ cup celery, chopped

2 cloves garlic, pressed

2 teaspoons tomato paste

salt, to taste

1 cup canned cannellini beans, rinsed and drained

⅓ cup cooked orzo pasta

leaves from 1 sprig fresh rosemary, minced

4 fresh basil leaves, chopped

olive oil, as required

Parmesan shaving, as required

DIRECTIONS:

1. Attach the sous vide immersion circulator using an adjustable clamp to a Cambro container or pot filled with water and preheat to 185 °F.

2. Into a large cooking pouch, place water, Parmesan rind, onion, carrot, celery, garlic, tomato paste and salt.

3. Seal pouch tightly after squeezing out the excess air. Place pouch in sous vide bath and set the cooking time for 1 hour.

4. Remove pouch from sous vide bath and carefully open it. Remove Parmesan rind and discard.

5. Divide beans, pasta and herbs into hot serving bowls and top evenly with hot soup.

6. Drizzle each bowl with olive oil generously. Garnish with Parmesan shavings and serve immediately.

7

VEGETABLES & SIDES

BROCCOLI WITH ROASTED RED PEPPERS

Preparation Time: 15 mins
Cooking Time: 50 minutes
Cooking Temperature: 183°F

INGREDIENTS:

2 canned roasted red peppers, rinse, seeded and cut into strips lengthwise

2 cups broccoli florets

1 garlic clove, minced

½ teaspoon salt

¼ teaspoon freshly ground black pepper

1 tablespoon butter

¼ cup Parmesan cheese, grated freshly

DIRECTIONS:

1. Attach the sous vide immersion circulator to a Cambro container or pot with water using an adjustable clamp and preheat water to 183°F.

2. Place red pepper strips in a cooking pouch.

3. In a bowl, mix together broccoli, garlic, salt, and black pepper. In another cooking pouch, place broccoli mixture and butter.

4. Seal pouches tightly after squeezing out the excess air. Place the pouch of broccoli in sous vide bath and set the cooking time for about 30 minutes. After 10-15 minutes, add pouch of red peppers to the sous vide bath.

5. Remove pouches from the sous vide bath and carefully open them. Remove vegetables from pouch and discard cooking liquid.

6. Transfer vegetables into warm serving bowls evenly. Garnish with Parmesan cheese and serve immediately.

Marinated Eggplant

Preparation Time: 15 mins, plus 2 hours for marinating
Cooking Time: 1 hour 40 mins
Cooking Temperature: 185°F

Ingredients:

2 pound eggplant, cut into ½-inch slices

sea salt, to taste

1 tablespoon garlic, chopped

2 teaspoons fresh lemon zest, grated

handful of fresh oregano, chopped

dash of olive oil

1 tablespoon smoked paprika

freshly cracked black pepper, to taste

Directions:

1. Season eggplant slices with salt generously.

2. Arrange eggplant slices onto a large flat tray, smaller round down. Sprinkle with more salt and set aside for about 2 hours.

3. Attach the sous vide immersion circulator to a Cambro container or pot with water using an adjustable clamp and preheat water to 185°F.

4. Rinse the eggplant slices completely and pat dry with paper towels.

5. In a large bowl, add remaining ingredients and mix until well combined. Add eggplant slices and coat generously with mixture.

6. In 2-3 cooking pouches, place eggplant slices in a single layer. Seal pouches tightly after squeezing out the excess air. Place the pouches in the sous vide bath and set the cooking time for about 1½ hours.

7. Remove pouches from the sous vide bath and immediately immerse in a bowl of ice water. After cooling, remove eggplant slices from pouch. With paper towels, pat dry eggplant slices completely.

8. Coat the eggplant slices with a coating of your choice, such as breadcrumbs, sesame seeds, or Parmesan cheese.

9. Fry the coated slices in some butter and olive oil over low heat until golden brown. Serve alongside tomato salsa, goat cheese, and basil.

PARSNIPS

Preparation Time: 15 mins
Cooking Time: 1 hour 40 mins
Cooking Temperature: 185°F

INGREDIENTS:

vegetable broth, enough to cover parsnips in cooking bag

2-3 parsnips, peeled and cut into thick rounds

2-3 teaspoons fresh thyme leaves

butter, as required

DIRECTIONS:

1. Attach the sous vide immersion circulator to a Cambro container or pot with water using an adjustable clamp and preheat water to 185°F.

2. In a cooking pouch, place parsnip rounds, thyme, and enough broth to cover. Seal pouch tightly after squeezing out the excess air. Place pouch in sous vide bath and set the cooking time for about 45 minutes and no more than 90 minutes.

3. Remove pouch from the sous vide bath and carefully open it. Remove parsnips from pouch, reserving broth in a bowl. With paper towels, pat dry parsnip rounds completely.

4. In a non-stick frying pan, melt butter over high heat and cook parsnip rounds until browned on both sides.

5. Add reserved broth with some water over high heat and cook until sauce becomes thick, basting parsnips occasionally with sauce.

6. Serve parsnips with pan sauce.

PICKLED RADISHES

Preparation Time: 15 mins
Cooking Time: 45 mins
Cooking Temperature: 190°F

INGREDIENTS:

2/3 cup water

2/3 cup white wine vinegar

2 garlic cloves, sliced in half lengthwise

3 tablespoons sugar

1 bay leaf

1 tablespoon salt

½ teaspoon yellow mustard seeds

¼ teaspoon coriander seeds

½ teaspoon whole peppercorns

12 ounces (3/4 pound) of radishes, trimmed and quartered

DIRECTIONS:

1. Attach the sous vide immersion circulator to a Cambro container or pot with water using an adjustable clamp and preheat water to 190°F.

2. In a pot, add all ingredients except radishes and bring to a boil, stirring continuously until sugar melts.

3. Place radishes in a single layer in a cooking pouch. Pour sugar mixture over radishes. Seal pouch tightly after squeezing out the excess air. Place pouch in sous vide bath and set the cooking time for about 45 minutes.

4. Remove pouch from the sous vide bath and immediately immerse in a bowl of ice water. After cooling, remove radishes from pouch and serve immediately.

5. Radishes can be stored in the refrigerator in an airtight container.

STEAK FRIES

Preparation Time: 15 mins
Cooking Time: 1 hour 30 mins
Cooking Temperature: 190°F

INGREDIENTS:

¼ cup butter, melted

½ teaspoon paprika

¼ teaspoon cayenne pepper

¼ teaspoon onion powder

¼ teaspoon garlic powder

¼ teaspoon salt

5 russet potatoes, cut in half lengthwise

DIRECTIONS:

1. Attach the sous vide immersion circulator to a Cambro container or pot with water using an adjustable clamp and preheat water to 190°F.

2. In a bowl, add all ingredients except potatoes and mix well.

3. Place potatoes in a single layer in a cooking pouch. Pour butter mixture over potatoes evenly. Seal pouch tightly after squeezing out the excess air. Place pouch in sous vide bath and set the cooking time for about 1½ hours.

4. Preheat the broiler of oven to high.

5. Remove pouch from the sous vide bath carefully open it. Remove potatoes from pouch. With paper towels, pat potatoes completely dry.

6. Arrange potatoes in a single layer on a baking sheet and broil for about 2-3 minutes per side. Serve immediately.

TAIWANESE CORN

Preparation Time: 15 mins
Cooking Time: 22 mins
Cooking Temperature: 185°F

INGREDIENTS:

3 ears of summer corn

3 garlic cloves

1 stalk scallion, chopped roughly

2 tablespoons butter

3 tablespoons dark soy sauce

2 tablespoons chili sauce

1 tablespoon sugar

salt, to taste

DIRECTIONS:

1. Attach the sous vide immersion circulator to a Cambro container or pot with water using an adjustable clamp and preheat water to 185°F.

2. In a food processor, add all ingredients except corn and salt and pulse until smooth.

3. Place corn and butter mixture in a cooking pouch. Seal pouch tightly after squeezing out the excess air. Place pouch in sous vide bath and set the cooking time for about 20 minutes.

4. Preheat the broiler of oven to high.

5. Remove pouch from the sous vide bath carefully open it. Remove corn ears from pouch.

6. Arrange corn ears onto a baking sheet and broil for about 2 minutes. Serve immediately.

CORN ON THE COB

Preparation Time: 15 mins
Cooking Time: 30 mins
Cooking Temperature: 183°F

INGREDIENTS:

4 ears corn, in the husk, both ends trimmed

2 tablespoons butter, plus extra for serving

kosher salt, to taste

fresh cilantro, chopped, as required

garlic cloves, minced, as required

DIRECTIONS:

1. Attach the sous vide immersion circulator to a Cambro container or pot with water using an adjustable clamp and preheat water to 183°F.

2. In 2 cooking pouches, divide all ingredients evenly. Seal pouch tightly after squeezing out the excess air. Place pouches in sous vide bath and set the cooking time for about 30 minutes.

3. Remove pouches from the sous vide bath and carefully open them. Remove corn ears from pouches.

4. Carefully, remove corn from husks. Discard husks.

5. Serve corn with extra butter.

CARROTS WITH BUTTER

Preparation Time: 10 mins
Cooking Time: 25 mins
Cooking Temperature: 185°F

INGREDIENTS:

baby carrots

olive oil, as required

pinch of salt

butter, as required

DIRECTIONS:

1. Attach the sous vide immersion circulator to a Cambro container or pot with water using an adjustable clamp and preheat water to 185°F.

2. Place carrots in a single layer in a cooking pouch. Add a little olive oil and salt. Seal pouch tightly after squeezing out the excess air. Place pouch in sous vide bath and set the cooking time for about 25 minutes.

3. Remove pouch from the sous vide bath and carefully open it. Remove carrots from pouch. With paper towels, pat dry carrots completely

4. Serve immediately with a topping of butter.

GLAZED CARROTS

Preparation Time: 10 mins
Cooking Time: 1 hour
Cooking Temperature: 183°F

INGREDIENTS:

1 pound whole baby carrots

2 tablespoons unsalted butter

1 tablespoon granulated sugar

kosher salt, to taste

1 tablespoon fresh parsley, chopped

freshly ground black pepper, to taste

DIRECTIONS:

1. Attach the sous vide immersion circulator to a Cambro container or pot with water using an adjustable clamp and preheat water to 183°F.

2. Place carrots, butter, sugar, and salt in a cooking pouch. Seal pouch tightly after squeezing out the excess air. Place pouch in sous vide bath and set the cooking time for about 1 hour.

3. Remove pouch from the sous vide bath and carefully open it.

4. Transfer carrots and cooking liquid to a 12-inch, heavy-bottomed skillet over high heat and cook for about 2 minutes, stirring continuously.

5. Stir in parsley, salt, and black pepper and remove from heat. Serve immediately.

GARLIC & HERB POTATOES

Preparation Time: 15 mins
Cooking Time: 1 hour
Cooking Temperature: 183°F

INGREDIENTS:

1 stick butter, melted

2 garlic cloves, chopped

½ teaspoon basil

½ teaspoon oregano

pinch of dried rosemary

½ teaspoon paprika

½ teaspoon salt

5 pounds russet potatoes, peeled and cubed

DIRECTIONS:

1. Attach the sous vide immersion circulator to a Cambro container or pot with water using an adjustable clamp and preheat water to 183°F.

2. In a bowl, add all ingredients except potatoes and mix until well combined.

3. In 2 cooking pouch, divide potatoes and butter mixture. Seal pouch tightly after squeezing out the excess air. Place pouch in sous vide bath and set the cooking time for about 1 hour.

4. Preheat the broiler of oven to high.

5. Remove pouch from the sous vide bath and carefully open them. Transfer carrot mixture onto a broiler pan.

6. Broil for about 2-3 minutes.

BUTTER POACHED POTATOES

Preparation Time: 15 mins
Cooking Time: 1 hour
Cooking Temperature: 190°F

INGREDIENTS:

1 pound small Yukon gold potatoes, halved

2 tablespoons unsalted butter

1 tablespoon extra-virgin olive oil

1 tablespoon fresh thyme or rosemary, minced

2 teaspoons kosher salt

1 teaspoon freshly ground black pepper

DIRECTIONS:

1. Attach the sous vide immersion circulator to a Cambro container or pot with water using an adjustable clamp and preheat water to 190°F.

2. Place all ingredients in a cooking pouch. Seal pouch tightly after squeezing out the excess air. Place pouch in sous vide bath and set the cooking time for about 1 hour.

3. Remove pouch from the sous vide bath and carefully open it. Transfer potato mixture to a platter and serve immediately.

ARTICHOKES

Preparation Time: 10 mins
Cooking Time: 1 hour
Cooking Temperature: 183°F

INGREDIENTS:

artichokes, peeled, stems and lower leaves removed

DIRECTIONS:

1. Attach the sous vide immersion circulator to a Cambro container or pot with water using an adjustable clamp and preheat water to 183°F.

2. Place artichokes in a cooking pouch. Seal pouch tightly after squeezing out the excess air. Place pouch in sous vide bath and set the cooking time for about 1 hour.

3. Remove pouch from the sous vide bath and carefully open it. Remove artichokes from pouch and serve immediately.

MASHED POTATOES WITH GARLIC

Preparation Time: 15 mins
Cooking Time: 1 hour 30 mins
Cooking Temperature: 194°F

INGREDIENTS:

2 pound russet potatoes, peeled and cut into 1/8-inch pieces

1 cup whole milk

1 cup unsalted butter

3 fresh rosemary sprigs

5 garlic cloves, smashed

2 teaspoons kosher salt

DIRECTIONS:

1. Attach the sous vide immersion circulator to a Cambro container or pot with water using an adjustable clamp and preheat water to 194°F.

2. Place all ingredients in a cooking pouch. Seal pouch tightly after squeezing out the excess air. Place pouch in sous vide bath and set the cooking time for about 1½ hours.

3. Remove pouch from the sous vide bath and carefully open it. Remove potatoes from pouch, reserving cooking liquid in a bowl. Discard rosemary sprigs.

4. Transfer potatoes into a large bowl and mash well.

5. Gently beat reserved cooking liquid. Add reserved liquid into mashed potatoes and stir to combine.

6. Serve immediately.

GARLIC & PAPRIKA SWEET POTATOES

Preparation Time: 15 mins
Cooking Time: 1 hour
Cooking Temperature: 185°F

INGREDIENTS:

7 tablespoons salted butter, softened

4½ tablespoons maple syrup

10 roasted, smoked garlic cloves

2 teaspoons fresh thyme, chopped

2 teaspoons smoked paprika

sea salt, to taste

2.2 pounds (1 kg) sweet potatoes, peeled and chopped

DIRECTIONS:

1. Attach the sous vide immersion circulator to a Cambro container or pot with water using an adjustable clamp and preheat water to 185°F.

2. In a bowl, add all ingredients except sweet potatoes and mix until well combined.

3. Place sweet potatoes and butter mixture in a cooking pouch. Seal pouch tightly after squeezing out the excess air. Place pouch in sous vide bath and set the cooking time for about 45-60 minutes.

4. Remove pouch from the sous vide bath and carefully open it. Remove sweet potatoes from pouch.

5. Heat a sauté pan and cook sweet potatoes until golden brown.

WHISKEY SUGARED SWEET POTATOES

Preparation Time: 15 mins
Cooking Time: 1 hour 25 mins
Cooking Temperature: 150°F

INGREDIENTS:

½ cup brown sugar

½ teaspoon cinnamon

½ teaspoon ground allspice

¼ teaspoon cayenne pepper

pinch of granulated onions

pinch of granulated garlic

1 teaspoon salt

¼ cup American whiskey

4 sweet potatoes, peeled, and cut into ½-inch cubes

4 tablespoons butter

1 tablespoon cider vinegar

DIRECTIONS:

1. Attach the sous vide immersion circulator to a Cambro container or pot with water using an adjustable clamp and preheat water to 150°F.

2. In a bowl, mix together sugar, spices, and salt. Set aside.

3. In a small pan, bring whiskey to a boil. Cook until it reduces by half. Add sugar mixture and cook until a paste is formed.

4. Transfer sugar paste into a large bowl. Add sweet potato cubes and butter to the bowl and mix until well combined.

5. Place sweet potato mixture in a cooking pouch. Seal pouch tightly after squeezing out the excess air. Place pouch in sous vide bath and set the cooking time for about 1 hour.

6. Preheat oven to 400°F. Line a baking sheet with parchment paper.

7. Remove pouch from the sous vide bath and carefully open it. Remove sweet potato cubes from pouch, reserving cooking liquid in a pan.

8. Place sweet potato cubes onto prepared baking sheet. Roast for about 25 minutes, stirring once after 15 minutes.

9. Meanwhile, cook reserved cooking liquid until desired thickness.

10. Remove sweet potatoes from oven and transfer into a bowl. Add thickened sauce and vinegar and toss to coat well.

11. Serve immediately.

MARINATED MUSHROOMS

Preparation Time: 15 mins
Cooking Time: 1 hour
Cooking Temperature: 185°F

INGREDIENTS:

10 ounces white mushrooms, quartered

3 tablespoons olive oil

2 tablespoons dry sherry

1 teaspoon Worcestershire sauce

1 lemon peel strip

½ teaspoon dried thyme, crushed

1 bay leaf

pinch of garlic powder

salt and freshly ground black pepper, to taste

DIRECTIONS:

1. Attach the sous vide immersion circulator to a Cambro container or pot with water using an adjustable clamp and preheat water to 185°F.

2. Place all ingredients in a cooking pouch. Seal pouch tightly after squeezing out the excess air. Place pouch in sous vide bath and set the cooking time for about 1 hour.

3. Remove pouch from the sous vide bath and let mushrooms cool in pouch. Drain and serve.

BRUSSELS SPROUTS WITH GARLIC

Preparation Time: 15 mins
Cooking Time: 1 hour
Cooking Temperature: 180°F

INGREDIENTS:

1 tablespoon olive oil

2 garlic cloves, smashed and minced

pinch of salt

freshly ground black pepper, to taste

1 pound Brussels sprouts, trimmed

DIRECTIONS:

1. Attach the sous vide immersion circulator to a Cambro container or pot with water using an adjustable clamp and preheat water to 180°F.

2. In a bowl, add all ingredients except Brussels sprouts and mix until well combined.

3. Place Brussels sprouts and oil mixture in a cooking pouch. Seal pouch tightly after squeezing out the excess air. Place pouch in sous vide bath and set the cooking time for about 1 hour.

4. Preheat a grill to medium heat.

5. Remove pouch from the sous vide bath and carefully open it. Remove Brussels sprouts from pouch.

6. Thread Brussels sprouts onto pre-soaked bamboo skewers. Grill for about 2-3 minutes per side.

Szechuan Style Green Beans

Preparation Time: 15 mins
Cooking Time: 1 hour
Cooking Temperature: 186°F

Ingredients:

12 ounces (3/4 pound) fresh, long green beans

1 tablespoon dried onions, minced

1 tablespoon red chili flakes

1 tablespoon Sriracha chili sauce

1 teaspoon sesame oil, toasted

½ teaspoon garlic salt

1 tablespoon sesame seeds, toasted

chopped scallions, for garnishing

DIRECTIONS:

1. Attach the sous vide immersion circulator to a Cambro container or pot with water using an adjustable clamp and preheat water to 186°F.

2. Place beans, onions, chili flakes, Sriracha, sesame oil, and garlic salt in a cooking pouch. Seal pouch tightly after squeezing out the excess air. Place pouch in sous vide bath and set the cooking time for about 45-60 minutes.

3. Remove pouch from the sous vide bath and carefully open it. Transfer beans onto a serving platter. Garnish with sesame seeds and scallions and serve.

GREEN BEAN CASSEROLE

Preparation Time: 15 mins
Cooking Time: 2 hours
Cooking Temperature: 185°F

INGREDIENTS:

2 cups fresh green beans, trimmed and cut into small pieces

½ medium shallot, chopped

7 ounce (207 mL) can condensed cream of mushroom soup

¼ cup panko bread crumbs

1 egg, beaten well

salt and freshly ground black pepper, to taste

1 (2.8-ounce) can crispy fried onions

DIRECTIONS:

1. Attach the sous vide immersion circulator to a Cambro container or pot with water using an adjustable clamp and preheat water to 185°F.

2. Place all ingredients except crispy onions in a large cooking pouch. Massage the pouch to combine all ingredients. Seal pouch tightly after squeezing out the excess air. Place pouch in sous vide bath and set the cooking time for about 2 hours.

3. Remove pouch from the sous vide bath and carefully open it. Transfer bean mixture onto a serving platter. Top with crispy onions and serve.

GREEN BEANS ALMANDINE

Preparation Time: 15 mins
Cooking Time: 2 hours
Cooking Temperature: 180°F

INGREDIENTS:

3-4 cups fresh green beans, trimmed

1 tablespoon lemon zest

2 tablespoon olive oil

2 tablespoons lemon juice

1 teaspoon salt

½ cup almonds, toasted and chopped roughly

DIRECTIONS:

1. Attach the sous vide immersion circulator to a Cambro container or pot with water using an adjustable clamp and preheat water to 180°F.

2. In a bowl, add green beans, lemon zest, and oil and toss to coat well.

3. Place bean mixture in a cooking pouch. Seal pouch tightly after squeezing out the excess air. Place pouch in sous vide bath and set the cooking time for about 1½-2 hours.

4. Remove pouch from the sous vide bath and carefully open it. Transfer bean mixture onto a serving platter. Drizzle with lemon juice and sprinkle with salt. Garnish with almonds and serve.

Acorn Squash

Preparation Time: 10 mins
Cooking Time: 1 hour
Cooking Temperature: 194°F

Ingredients:

2 tablespoons butter

pinch of dried rosemary

pinch of salt

1 acorn squash, seeded and cut into wedges

Directions:

1. Attach the sous vide immersion circulator to a Cambro container or pot with water using an adjustable clamp and preheat water to 194°F.

2. In a pan, melt butter over medium heat until light brown specks appear, stirring occasionally. Stir in rosemary and salt and remove from heat.

3. Place acorn squash in a cooking pouch. Pour brown butter over squash wedges evenly. Seal pouch tightly after squeezing out the excess air. Place pouch in sous vide bath and set the cooking time for about 1 hour.

4. Remove pouch from the sous vide bath and carefully open it. Transfer squash wedges onto a serving platter and serve.

CARAMELIZED ONIONS

Preparation Time: 15 mins
Cooking Time: 24 hours
Cooking Temperature: 186°F

INGREDIENTS:

1 tablespoon cooking oil

2 tablespoons butter

2 pound yellow onions, thinly sliced

1 garlic clove, crushed

¼ teaspoon salt

DIRECTIONS:

1. Attach the sous vide immersion circulator to a Cambro container or pot with water using an adjustable clamp and preheat water to 186°F.

2. In a skillet, heat oil and butter over medium heat and cook onions and salt until translucent. Add garlic and cook for about 1 minute. Remove from heat and set aside to cool completely.

3. Place cooled onions in a cooking pouch. Seal pouch tightly after squeezing out the excess air. Place pouch in sous vide bath and set the cooking time for about 24 hours. Cover the sous vide bath with plastic wrap to minimize water evaporation. Add water intermittently to maintain the proper water level.

4. Remove pouch from the sous vide bath and carefully open it. Transfer onions to a container.

5.   Onions can be stored in a refrigerator for up to 3 days.

ROOT VEGETABLES WITH BROWN BUTTER

Preparation Time: 20 mins
Cooking Time: 3 hours 10 minutes
Cooking Temperature: 185°F

INGREDIENTS:

8 baby carrots, cut into 1-inch pieces

1 medium rutabaga, peeled and cut into 1-inch pieces

1 medium turnip, peeled and cut into 1-inch pieces

1 medium parsnip, peeled and cut into 1-inch pieces

½ medium red onion, cut into 1-inch pieces

4 garlic cloves, crushed

4 fresh rosemary sprigs

2 tablespoons extra-virgin olive oil

kosher salt and freshly ground black pepper, to taste

2 tablespoons butter

DIRECTIONS:

1.   Attach the sous vide immersion circulator to a Cambro container or pot with water using an adjustable clamp and preheat water to 185°F.

2.   In a large bowl, add vegetables and mix.

3.   In 2 cooking pouches, divide vegetable mixture, rosemary sprigs, olive oil, salt, and black pepper. Seal pouch tightly after squeezing out the

excess air. Place pouch in sous vide bath and set the cooking time for about 3 hours.

4. Remove pouches from the sous vide bath and carefully open them. Remove vegetables from pouches, reserving cooking liquid.

5. Heat a large sauté pan over high heat and cook vegetables with reserved cooking liquid for about 5 minutes.

6. Stir in butter and cook for an additional 5 minutes, stirring occasionally. Serve warm.

RATATOUILLE

Preparation Time: 20 mins
Cooking Time: 1 hour
Cooking Temperature: 176°F

INGREDIENTS:

1 pound Japanese eggplants, halved lengthwise

½ pound zucchini, halved lengthwise

½ pound yellow squash, halved lengthwise

1 red bell pepper, seeded and cut into quarters

5 tablespoons extra-virgin olive oil, divided

salt and freshly ground black pepper, to taste

1 Spanish onion, cut in ½-inch pieces

3 garlic cloves, minced

1 teaspoon red pepper flakes

½ pound plum tomatoes, peeled and roughly chopped

½ cup dry white wine

1 teaspoon thyme leaves

2 tablespoons fresh parsley, chopped

½ cup fresh basil leaves

DIRECTIONS:

1. Attach the sous vide immersion circulator to a Cambro container or pot with water using an adjustable clamp and preheat water to 176°F.

2. In a large bowl, add eggplant, zucchini, squash, bell pepper, 3 tablespoons of oil, salt, and black pepper and toss to coat well.

3. Heat a large skillet over medium-high heat and sear vegetable mixture in batches for about 4 minutes per side. Transfer vegetable mixture back into the bowl.

4. In the same skillet, add 1 tablespoon of olive oil over medium-high heat and sauté onion for about 8 minutes. Add garlic and red pepper flakes and sauté for about 1 more minute.

5. Stir in tomatoes and cook for about 1 minute. Add white wine, bring to a boil, and cook for about 1 minute. Remove from heat and stir in thyme.

6. Cut all cooked vegetables into ½-inch pieces. Add vegetable mixture into tomato mixture and stir to combine.

7. Place vegetable mixture in a cooking pouch. Seal pouch tightly after squeezing out the excess air. Place pouch in sous vide bath and set the cooking time for about 40 minutes.

8. Remove pouch from the sous vide bath and carefully open it. Transfer vegetable mixture into a large serving bowl. Stir in parsley and drizzle with remaining oil.

9. Garnish with basil and serve.

DILL PICKLES

Preparation Time: 15 mins
Cooking Time: 30 mins
Cooking Temperature: 190°F

INGREDIENTS:

1 cup white wine vinegar

½ cup granulated sugar

3 tablespoons kosher salt

1 teaspoon black peppercorns

1/3 cup ice-cold water

4 pickling cucumbers, sliced into ¼-inch-thick coins

½ red onion, sliced into 1-inch pieces

4 fresh dill sprigs

2 garlic cloves, peeled

DIRECTIONS:

1. Attach the sous vide immersion circulator to a Cambro container or pot with water using an adjustable clamp and preheat water to 190°F.

2. For brine: in a medium pot, add vinegar, sugar, salt, and peppercorns over medium heat and bring to a boil, stirring until sugar and salt are dissolved. Remove from heat and add cold water. Set aside to cool completely.

3. Place cucumbers, dill, onion, garlic, and brine in a cooking pouch. Seal pouch tightly after squeezing out the excess air. Place pouch in sous vide bath and set the cooking time for about 30 minutes.

4. Remove pouch from the sous vide bath and immediately immerse in a large bowl of ice water to cool. Remove pickles from pouch and serve immediately.

PICKLED JALAPEÑO PEPPERS

Preparation Time: 15 mins
Cooking Time: 30 mins
Cooking Temperature: 180°F

INGREDIENTS:

1 cup white wine vinegar

3 tablespoons ultrafine sugar

2 teaspoons kosher salt

6 jalapeño peppers, sliced crosswise ¼-inch thick

½ white onion, thinly sliced

DIRECTIONS:

1. Attach the sous vide immersion circulator to a Cambro container or pot with water using an adjustable clamp and preheat water to 180°F.

2. In a large bowl, add vinegar, sugar, and salt and beat until sugar is dissolved.

3. Place jalapeño peppers, onion, and vinegar mixture in a cooking pouch. Seal pouch tightly after squeezing out the excess air. Place pouch in sous vide bath and set the cooking time for about 30 minutes.

4. Remove pouch from the sous vide bath and immediately immerse in a large bowl of ice water to cool. Remove peppers from pouch and serve immediately.

QUINOA

Preparation Time: 10 mins
Cooking Time: 1 hour
Cooking Temperature: 180°F

INGREDIENTS:

1 cup quinoa, rinsed

1 small, fresh basil sprig

2 garlic cloves, peeled

kosher salt, to taste

1½ cups water

DIRECTIONS:

1. Attach the sous vide immersion circulator to a Cambro container or pot with water using an adjustable clamp and preheat water to 180°F.

2. Mix together quinoa, basil, garlic, salt, and water in a cooking pouch. Seal pouch tightly after squeezing out the excess air. Place pouch in sous vide bath and set the cooking time for about 1 hour.

3. Remove pouch from the sous vide bath and carefully open it. Transfer quinoa mixture into a serving bowl, discarding basil and garlic. With a fork, fluff the quinoa and serve.

BASIC RISOTTO

Preparation Time: 15 mins
Cooking Time: 45 mins
Cooking Temperature: 183°F

INGREDIENTS:

1 cup Arborio rice

1/3 cup Romano cheese, grated

leaves from 1 fresh rosemary sprig, minced

2 tablespoons jarred roasted minced garlic

1 teaspoon extra-virgin olive oil

3 cups vegetable broth

salt and freshly ground black pepper, to taste

DIRECTIONS:

1. Attach the sous vide immersion circulator to a Cambro container or pot with water using an adjustable clamp and preheat water to 183°F.

2. Place all ingredients in a cooking pouch. Seal pouch tightly after squeezing out the excess air. Place pouch in sous vide bath and set the cooking time for about 45 minutes.

3. Remove pouch from the sous vide bath and carefully open it. Transfer rice mixture into a serving bowl. With a fork, fluff the rice and serve.

Spring Vegetables & Risotto

Preparation Time: 20 mins
Cooking Time: 40 mins
Cooking Temperature: 183°F

Ingredients:

For Risotto:

1 cup Arborio rice

2 4-ounce cans mushroom stems and pieces, chopped

leaves from 1 fresh rosemary sprig, minced

3 cups vegetable broth

½ teaspoon butter

salt and freshly ground black pepper, to taste

For Vegetables:

1 pound spring vegetables (asparagus, broccoli, peppers, summer squash), cut into bite sized pieces

salt and freshly ground black pepper, to taste

1-2 tablespoons butter

fresh herbs of choice

For Garnishing:

freshly grated Parmesan cheese, for serving

Directions:

1. Attach the sous vide immersion circulator to a Cambro container or pot with water using an adjustable clamp and preheat water to 183°F.

2. Place all risotto ingredients in a cooking pouch and all vegetable ingredients in a second pouch. Seal pouches tightly after squeezing out the excess air. Place pouches in sous vide bath and set the cooking time for about 40 minutes.

3. Remove pouches from the sous vide bath and carefully open them.

4. Transfer rice mixture into a serving bowl. With a fork, fluff the rice. Transfer vegetable mixture into another bowl.

5. Divide rice into serving plate and top with vegetables evenly. Sprinkle with cheese and serve.

LIGHTLY SEASONED BEETS

Preparation Time: 10 mins
Cooking Time: 1½ hours
Cooking Temperature: 185°F

INGREDIENTS:

12-16 small, fresh beets, trimmed, scrubbed and halved

2 tablespoons butter, softened

1/2 teaspoon salt

1/4 teaspoon freshly ground black pepper

DIRECTIONS:

1. Attach the sous vide immersion circulator to a Cambro container or pot with water using an adjustable clamp and preheat water to 185°F.

2. Place beets in a single layer in a cooking pouch. Add butter, salt, and pepper. Seal pouch tightly after squeezing out the excess air. Place pouch in sous vide bath and set the cooking time for about 1½ hours.

3. Remove pouch from the sous vide bath and carefully open it.

4.   Remove beets and serve immediately.

BISCUITS

Preparation Time: 15 mins
Cooking Time: 2 hours
Cooking Temperature: 195°F

INGREDIENTS:

1 cup all-purpose flour

½ teaspoon granulated sugar

1 teaspoon baking powder

¼ teaspoon baking soda

¼ teaspoon salt

½ cup chilled buttermilk

4 tablespoons unsalted butter, melted

DIRECTIONS:

1.   Attach the sous vide immersion circulator to a Cambro container or pot with water using an adjustable clamp and preheat water to 195°F. Grease 5 half-pint canning jars generously.

2.   In a medium bowl, mix together flour, sugar, baking powder, baking soda, and salt.

3.   In another bowl, add buttermilk and butter and stir until butter forms distinct clumps in the buttermilk. Add buttermilk mixture into flour mixture and stir until just combined.

4.   Divide dough between prepared jars evenly. With a damp towel, wipe off sides and tops of jars.

5. Cover each jar with the lid just tight. (Do not over-tighten jars; air will need to escape). Place jars in sous vide bath and set the cooking time for about 2 hours.

6. Remove the jars from the sous vide bath and carefully remove the lids. Place jars onto a wire rack to cool for about 5 minutes.

7. Carefully remove biscuits from jars and serve warm.

Brown Rice Pilaf

Preparation Time: 10 mins
Cooking Time: 3 hours
Cooking Temperature: 180°F

Ingredients:

1 tablespoon extra-virgin olive oil

1 medium leek (white and light green portion), halved and thinly sliced

1 garlic clove, minced

kosher salt, to taste

¼ cup currants

1 cup brown rice, rinsed

2 cups vegetable broth

¼ cup walnuts, toasted and chopped

Directions:

1. Attach the sous vide immersion circulator to a Cambro container or pot with water using an adjustable clamp and preheat water to 180°F.

2. In a small pan, heat the olive oil over medium heat and cook leek, garlic, and ½ teaspoon of salt until fragrant, stirring occasionally.

3. Remove from heat and stir in currants and rice.

4. Place rice mixture and broth in a cooking pouch. Seal pouch tightly after squeezing out the excess air. Place pouch in sous vide bath and set the cooking time for about 3 hours.

5. Remove pouch from the sous vide bath and carefully open it. Transfer rice mixture into a serving bowl and season with salt.

6. Sprinkle with walnuts and serve.

SPINACH CHEESE DIP

Preparation Time: 15 mins
Cooking Time: 1 hour
Cooking Temperature: 180°F

INGREDIENTS:

1 pound cream cheese, cubed

½ cup beer

2 ounces smoked Gouda cheese, grated

½ medium red bell pepper, seeded and chopped

½ cup fresh baby spinach leaves, chopped

1 garlic clove, peeled and pressed

1 tablespoon Dijon mustard

1 teaspoon Herbs de Provence

1 teaspoon salt

½ teaspoon ground white pepper

1 sourdough round loaf, for serving

DIRECTIONS:

1. Attach the sous vide immersion circulator to a Cambro container or pot with water using an adjustable clamp and preheat water to 180°F.

2. Place all ingredients except bread in a cooking pouch. Seal pouch tightly after squeezing out the excess air. Place pouch in sous vide bath and set the cooking time for about ½-1 hour.

3. Remove the pouch from the sous vide bath and carefully massage it to mix the dip mixture. Return pouch to sous vide bath until cheese melts completely.

4. Meanwhile, with a bread knife, remove the top from the loaf of bread. Carefully hollow out the middle of loaf to make a bread bowl. Cut the interior bread into bite-sized pieces.

5. Remove the pouch from the sous vide bath and carefully open it. Immediately, transfer dip into the bread bowl. Serve with bread pieces.

QUESO BLANCO DIP

Preparation Time: 15 mins
Cooking Time: 30 mins
Cooking Temperature: 175°F

INGREDIENTS:

1½ cups Asadero or Chihuahua cheese, shredded finely

¼ cup half-and-half cream

4 ounces (1/4 pound) green chilies, chopped

1 Serrano pepper, stemmed and chopped finely

2 tablespoons onion, grated

2 teaspoons ground cumin

½ teaspoon salt

DIRECTIONS:

1. Attach the sous vide immersion circulator to a Cambro container or pot with water using an adjustable clamp and preheat water to 175°F.

2. Place all ingredients except bread in a cooking pouch. Seal pouch tightly after squeezing out the excess air. Place pouch in sous vide bath and set the cooking time for about 30 minutes. Remove pouch from bath occasionally and massage mixture to mix.

3. Remove the pouch from the sous vide bath and carefully open it. Immediately, transfer dip into a bowl and serve.

CHEESY GRITS

Preparation Time: 15 mins
Cooking Time: 3 hours
Cooking Temperature: 180°F

INGREDIENTS:

1 cup old fashioned grits

3 cups vegetable broth

1 cup cream

2 tablespoons cold butter, cut into small pieces

4 ounces (1/4 pound) cheddar cheese, grated, plus extra for garnish

salt and freshly ground black pepper, to taste

paprika for garnish

DIRECTIONS:

1. Attach the sous vide immersion circulator to a Cambro container or pot with water using an adjustable clamp and preheat water to 180°F.

2. In a large bowl, add grits, broth, and cream and beat until well combined. Add butter and gently stir.

3. Place grits mixture in a cooking pouch. Seal pouch tightly after squeezing out the excess air. Place pouch in sous vide bath and set the cooking time for about 2-3 hours.

4. Remove pouch from the sous vide bath and carefully open it. Transfer grits into a bowl. Immediately, add cheese and beat until well combined. Stir in salt and black pepper.

5. Serve immediately with a sprinkling of extra cheese and paprika.

SOUTHERN BUTTERY GRITS

Preparation Time: 10 mins
Cooking Time: 3 hours
Cooking Temperature: 180°F

INGREDIENTS:

½ cup roughly ground grits

1 tablespoon unsalted butter

½ teaspoon kosher salt

2 cups water

DIRECTIONS:

1. Attach the sous vide immersion circulator to a Cambro container or pot with water using an adjustable clamp and preheat water to 180°F.

2. Place all ingredients in a cooking pouch. Seal pouch tightly after squeezing out the excess air. Place pouch in sous vide bath and set the cooking time for about 3 hours.

3. Remove pouch from the sous vide bath and carefully open it. Transfer grits into a bowl and serve immediately.

SQUASH CASSEROLE

Preparation Time: 15 mins
Cooking Time: 1 hour 17 mins
Cooking Temperature: 176°F

INGREDIENTS:

2 tablespoons unsalted butter

¾ cup onion, chopped

1½ pound summer squash, quartered lengthwise and cut into ¼-inch-thick pieces

kosher salt, to taste

2 large eggs

½ cup whole milk

freshly ground black pepper, to taste

½ cup plain potato chips, crumbled

DIRECTIONS:

1. Attach the sous vide immersion circulator to a Cambro container or pot with water using an adjustable clamp and preheat water to 176°F. Grease 4 half-pint canning jars generously.

2. In a large skillet, melt butter over medium-high heat and sauté onion for about 5-7 minutes. Add squash and a generous pinch of salt and sauté for an additional 10 minutes. Season with salt and black pepper and remove from heat.

3. Divide squash mixture into prepared jars evenly and set aside at room temperature to cool.

4. In a bowl, add eggs, milk, a pinch of salt, and a few grinds of black pepper and beat until well combined. Place milk mixture over squash mixture in each jar evenly.

5. With a damp towel, wipe off sides and tops of jars. Tap the jars on a counter firmly to remove air bubbles.

6. Cover each jar with the lid. (Do not over-tighten jars because air will need to escape). Place jars in sous vide bath and set the cooking time for about 1 hour.

7. Remove the jars from the sous vide bath and carefully remove the lids. Place jars onto a wire rack to cool for about 5 minutes. Top with potato chips and serve immediately.

8

FRUITS & DESSERTS

PUMPKIN BREAD

Preparation Time: 15 mins
Cooking Time: 3 hours
Cooking Temperature: 195 °F

INGREDIENTS:

1 cup all-purpose flour

1 teaspoon baking powder

¼ teaspoon baking soda

2 teaspoons ground cinnamon

½ teaspoon ground nutmeg

pinch of ground cloves

½ cup vegetable oil

⅓ cup granulated sugar

¼ cup dark brown sugar

¾ cup canned pumpkin puree

½ teaspoon salt

2 large eggs

DIRECTIONS:

1. Attach the sous vide immersion circulator using an adjustable clamp to a Cambro container or pot filled with water and preheat to 195 °F.

2. Generously grease 4 half-pint canning jars.

3. In a bowl, mix together flour, baking powder, baking soda and spices.

4. In another bowl, add oil, both sugars, pumpkin puree and salt and beat until well-combined.

5. Add eggs, one at a time, beating until well-combined.

6. Add flour mixture into pumpkin mixture, and mix until just combined.

7. Divide mixture evenly into prepared jars. (Each jar should be not full more than two-thirds full).

8. With a damp towel, wipe off sides and tops of jars. Tap the jars onto a counter firmly to remove air bubbles.

9. Close each jar. (Do not over-tighten jars because air will need to escape).

10. Place jars in sous vide bath and set the cooking time for 3 hours.

11. Remove the jars from sous vide bath and carefully remove the lids. Place jars onto a wire rack to cool completely.

12. Carefully run a knife around the inside edges of the jars to loosen the bread from the walls.

13. Cut into slices and serve.

CHOCOLATE RICOTTA MOUSSE

Preparation Time: 15 mins
Cooking Time: 1 hour 5 mins
Cooking Temperature: 172 °F

INGREDIENTS:

4 cups whole milk

6 tablespoons white wine vinegar

4 ounces semisweet chocolate chips

2 tablespoons Grand Marnier liqueur

¼ cup powdered sugar

1 tablespoon fresh orange zest, grated

DIRECTIONS:

1. Attach the sous vide immersion circulator using an adjustable clamp to a Cambro container or pot filled with water and preheat to 172 °F.

2. ***For the ricotta:*** in a large cooking pouch, place milk and vinegar. Seal pouch tightly after squeezing out the excess air. Place pouch in sous vide bath and set the cooking time for 1 hour.

3. Remove pouch from sous vide bath carefully open it. Carefully, skim curds from the top of pouch and place in a cheesecloth lined strainer, keeping aside to drain for at least 10 minutes.

4. Discard remaining liquid, and refrigerate curds for at least 1 hour.

5. For a double boiler: arrange a bowl over a small pan filled with 1 inch of water. Bring to a gentle simmer over medium heat.

6. In the bowl of the double boiler, place chocolate chips and cook until just melted, stirring occasionally. Remove from heat and keep aside to cool slightly.

7. Into a food processor, add chocolate, ricotta, Grand Marnier, sugar and orange zest and pulse until smooth and fluffy.

8. Transfer mousse into serving bowls and serve.

Saffron Pears

Preparation Time: 15 mins
Cooking Time: 1 hour
Cooking Temperature: 181 °F

Ingredients:

4 pears, peeled, cored and halved

½ cup caster sugar

⅓ cup white wine

1 vanilla bean, cut in half and then sliced lengthways down the center

½ teaspoon saffron threads, crumbled

Directions:

1. Attach the sous vide immersion circulator using an adjustable clamp to a Cambro container or pot filled with water and preheat to 181 °F.
2. Into a cooking pouch, add all ingredients. Seal pouch tightly after squeezing out the excess air. Place pouch in sous vide bath and set the cooking time for 1 hour.
3. Remove pouch from sous vide bath and carefully open it. Remove pears from pouch, reserving cooking liquid.
4. Divide pears into serving plates and top with a few spoons of reserved cooking liquid.

Zucchini Bread

Preparation Time: 15 mins
Cooking Time: 3 hours
Cooking Temperature: 195 °F

Ingredients:

½ cup packed dark brown sugar

1 large egg

2 tablespoons extra-virgin olive oil

½ teaspoon vanilla extract

¾ cup all-purpose flour

12 ounces zucchini, grated and squeezed

¼ cup whole wheat flour

½ teaspoon baking soda

½ teaspoon baking powder

1½ teaspoons ground cinnamon

¾ teaspoon salt

Directions:

1. Attach the sous vide immersion circulator using an adjustable clamp to a Cambro container or pot filled with water and preheat to 195 °F.
2. Generously grease 4 half-pint canning jars.
3. Into a bowl, add sugar, egg, oil and vanilla extract and beat until well-combined.
4. Fold in zucchini.
5. In another bowl, mix together flour, baking soda, baking powder, cinnamon and salt.

6. Add zucchini mixture into flour mixture, and mix until well-combined.

7. Divide mixture into prepared jars evenly. (Each jar should be not more than half-full.)

8. With a damp towel, wipe off sides and tops of jars. Tap the jars onto a counter firmly to remove air bubbles.

9. Cover each jar with the lid tightly. Place jars in sous vide bath and set the cooking time for 3 hours.

10. Remove the jars from sous vide bath and carefully remove the lids. Place jars onto a wire rack to cool completely.

11. Carefully, run a knife around the inside edges of the jars to loosen the bread from the walls.

12. Cut into slices and serve.

PECAN PIE JARS

Preparation Time: 20 mins
Cooking Time: 2 hours 15 mins
Cooking Temperature: 195 °F

INGREDIENTS:

1 cup light brown sugar

2 cups whole pecans

1 cup maple syrup

½ cup heavy cream

1 tablespoon molasses

¼ cup unsalted butter

½ teaspoon salt

6 large egg yolks

freshly whipped cream, for topping

DIRECTIONS:

1. Attach the sous vide immersion circulator using an adjustable clamp to a Cambro container or pot filled with water and preheat to 195 °F.
2. Generously grease 8 half-pint canning jars.
3. Preheat oven to 350 ºF.
4. Spread pecans onto a rimmed baking sheet in a single layer. Bake for 7-10 minutes.
5. Remove from oven and keep onto a wire rack to cool. After cooling, chop pecans roughly.
6. Meanwhile in a medium pan, add brown sugar, maple syrup, cream and molasses over medium heat and cook for 5 minutes or until sugar dissolves, stirring occasionally.
7. Remove from heat and keep aside to cool for 5 minutes.
8. To the sugar mixture, add butter and salt, and beat until butter is melted.
9. Add egg yolks and beat until smooth.
10. Stir in chopped pecans.
11. Divide mixture evenly into prepared jars. (Each jar should be not more than half-full.)
12. With a damp towel, wipe off sides and tops of jars and then close each jar with the lid just tight. (Do not over-tighten jars, as air will still need to escape).
13. Place jars in sous vide bath and set the cooking time for 2 hours.
14. Remove the jars from sous vide bath and carefully remove the lids. Place jars onto a wire rack to cool completely.
15. Top with whipped cream and serve.

KEY LIME PIE

Preparation Time: 20 mins
Cooking Time: 30 mins
Cooking Temperature: 180 °F

INGREDIENTS:

For Filling:

1 x 14-ounce can sweetened condensed milk

½ cup fresh key lime juice

4 egg yolks

For Crust:

⅓ cup plus 1 teaspoon butter, melted and divided

1½ cups graham cracker crumbs

2 tablespoons granulated sugar

For Topping:

½ cup heavy whipping cream

2 key limes, cut into slices

DIRECTIONS:

1. Attach the sous vide immersion circulator using an adjustable clamp to a Cambro container or pot filled with water and preheat to 180 °F.
2. *For the filling:* in a bowl, add all ingredients and beat until well-combined.
3. Into a cooking pouch, add filling mixture. Seal pouch tightly after squeezing out the excess air. Place pouch in sous vide bath and set the cooking time for 30 minutes.

4. ***Meanwhile, for the crust:*** evenly grease an 8-inch, round springform pan with 1 teaspoon of butter.

5. Into a bowl, add remaining butter, graham crackers and sugar, and mix until well-combined.

6. Place the mixture evenly into the prepared pan.

7. With the back of a spoon, press crust mixture evenly to a smooth surface. Refrigerate until hard and set.

8. Remove the pouch from sous vide bath and carefully massage it to mix the filling mixture.

9. Carefully open the pouch and place filling mixture evenly over crust.

10. Keep aside to cool for 30 minutes.

11. After cooling, transfer the pie into refrigerator for at least 2 hours (or until set).

12. Into a bowl, add whipped cream and beat until soft peaks form.

13. Transfer whipped cream into a piping bag. With a medium nozzle, decorate pie according to your style.

14. Garnish with lime slices. Cut and serve.

CHERRY CHEESECAKE

Preparation Time: 20 mins
Cooking Time: 1 hour 35 mins
Cooking Temperature: 176 °F

INGREDIENTS:

For Topping:

2 cups fresh cherries, pitted

¼ cup granulated sugar

cornstarch, as required

whipped cream, as required

For Cheesecake:

Graham cracker crumbs, as required

16 ounces Philadelphia cream cheese

½ cup granulated sugar

¼ cup heavy cream

1 tablespoon vanilla extract

2 eggs, lightly beaten

DIRECTIONS:

1. ***For the topping:*** add cherries to a pan over a medium heat and cook until they begin to release their liquid. Stir in sugar and bring to a boil, stirring occasionally.

2. Reduce heat and simmer until cherries become tender.

3. Slowly add cornstarch, stirring continuously.

4. Cook until mixture becomes thick, stirring continuously.

5. Remove from heat and keep aside to cool.

6. Attach the sous vide immersion circulator using an adjustable clamp to a Cambro container or pot filled with water and preheat to 176 °F.

7. *For the cheesecake:* arrange a thin layer of Graham cracker crumbs into the bottom of your desired number of canning jars.

8. Into the bowl of an electric mixer, place cream cheese and beat until slightly softened.

9. Add sugar, heavy cream and vanilla extract, and beat until well-combined.

10. Add half of the beaten eggs, and beat until well-combined.

11. Add the remaining beaten eggs, and beat until well-combined and smooth.

12. Place the cream cheese mixture evenly into the jars.

13. Screw the canning jar lids closed tightly. Carefully arrange jars into sous vide bath and set the cooking time for 1½ hours.

14. Carefully, remove jars from sous vide bath and place onto a wire rack to cool slightly.

15. After cooling, refrigerate to chill completely.

16. Remove the lid from each jar and place cherry topping evenly over each cheesecake.

17. Top with whipped cream and serve.

Vanilla Bean Pots de Crème

Preparation Time: 15 mins
Cooking Time: 50 mins
Cooking Temperature: 180 °F

Ingredients:

½ cup granulated sugar

8 large egg yolks

1 teaspoon vanilla bean paste

pinch of kosher salt

1 cup heavy cream

½ cup whole milk

Directions:

1. Attach the sous vide immersion circulator using an adjustable clamp to a Cambro container or pot filled with water and preheat to 180 °F.

2. Into a food processor, add sugar, egg yolks, vanilla bean paste and salt, and pulse until smooth.

3. Transfer egg mixture into a large bowl.

4. Into a small pan, add cream and milk over medium-high heat and bring to a boil.

5. Remove from heat and keep aside to cool slightly.

6. Slowly, add warm milk mixture into egg mixture, beating until well-combined.

7. Keep aside to cool for 20 minutes.

8. Divide mixture into 6 sealable glass jars evenly. Screw the canning jar lids closed tightly.

9. Carefully arrange jars into sous vide bath and set the cooking time for 45 minutes.

10. Carefully, remove jars from sous vide bath and place onto a wire rack to cool for 10 minutes.

11. Transfer the jars into an ice bath to cool and set further.

12. Refrigerate for at least 4 hours or up to 1 week before serving.

PUMPKIN PIE

Preparation Time: 20 mins
Cooking Time: 1½ hours
Cooking Temperature: 163 °F

INGREDIENTS:

2 cups canned pumpkin (not pumpkin pie filling)

4 large eggs

1 cup dark brown sugar

⅔ cup whole milk

⅔ cups heavy cream (for cooking), plus more, whipped (for serving)

2 teaspoons ground cinnamon

2 teaspoons ground ginger

1 teaspoon ground nutmeg

¼ teaspoon ground cloves

½ teaspoon salt

9 honey Graham crackers, broken into medium pieces

2 tablespoons granulated sugar

5 tablespoons unsalted butter, melted and kept warm

DIRECTIONS:

1. Attach the sous vide immersion circulator using an adjustable clamp to a Cambro container or pot filled with water and preheat to 163 °F.

2. Preheat oven to 325 °F.

3. Into a food processor add pumpkin, eggs and brown sugar, and pulse until smooth.

4. Transfer pumpkin mixture into a large bowl and add milk, cream, spices and salt into pumpkin mixture. Mix until well-combined.

5. Into a cooking pouch add pumpkin mixture. Seal pouch tightly after squeezing out the excess air. Place pouch in sous vide bath and set the cooking time for 1½ hours.

6. Meanwhile for the crust: into a clean food processor add Graham crackers and sugar, and pulse until a fine crumb-like mixture is formed.

7. While motor is running, slowly add melted butter and pulse until a wet sand-like mixture is formed.

8. Transfer crust mixture into a 9-inch pie dish and, with your hands, spread the mixture evenly across the bottom and sides of pie dish.

9. With the back of a spoon, press crust mixture to smooth surface.

10. Bake for 15-18 minutes. Remove from oven and place onto a wire rack to cool completely.

11. Remove pouch from sous vide bath. Place the pouch onto a plate and keep aside to cool for 15 minutes.

12. After cooling, use scissors to cut one of the bottom corners and pipe pumpkin mixture into the cooled crust. With a spatula, smooth the surface.

13. Transfer the pie into refrigerator for at least 8 hours (or until set).

14. Bring the pie to cool room temperature before serving.

15. Cut into desired wedges and serve and serve with a topping of whipped cream.

CARAMEL PINEAPPLE WITH SORBET

Preparation Time: 20 mins
Cooking Time: 1 hour
Cooking Temperature: 149 °F

INGREDIENTS:

For Caramel Pineapple:

1 pineapple

1½ cups sugar

2 tablespoons glucose

10 pink peppercorns

1 star anise

For Sorbet:

15½ ounces banana, peeled and sliced

1⅓ cups sugar

2 cups passion fruit juice

14⅓ fluid ounces water

1 tablespoon orange juice

2 tablespoons plus 1 teaspoon glucose

For Garnishing:

edible flowers

pink peppercorns

pistachio nuts, crushed

DIRECTIONS:

1. Attach the sous vide immersion circulator using an adjustable clamp to a Cambro container or pot filled with water and preheat to 149 °F.

2. With a large sharp knife, cut pineapple in half along the core and cut each half into 6 long rectangles.

3. Remove the hard core from the pineapple rectangles and place into a deep tray.

4. *For the caramel:* into a pan add sugar, glucose and a touch of water, and cook until mixture becomes brown (but not burnt), stirring continuously.

5. Pour caramel mixture over pineapples pieces and keep aside to cool.

6. Into a cooking pouch add cooled pineapple pieces with caramel, peppercorns and star anise. Seal pouch tightly after squeezing out the excess air. Place pouch in sous vide bath and set the cooking time for 1 hour.

7. *For the sorbet:* in a blender, mix all ingredients and pulse until smooth.

8. Strain the mixture through a fine sieve.

9. Transfer mixture into an ice cream machine and process according to manufacturer's directions.

10. Remove the pouch from sous vide bath and carefully open it. Remove pineapple from the pouch.

11. Transfer the caramel from the cooking pouch into a small pan and cook until becomes thick. Keep aside to to cool until just warm. Coat pineapple again with this thick caramel.

12. Transfer pineapple pieces onto serving plates and garnish with edible flowers and some pink peppercorns. Place a spoonful of crushed pistachio on the side.

13. Add a scoop of sorbet to each plate and serve.

PUMPKIN CHEESECAKE

Preparation Time: 20 mins
Cooking Time: 5 hours 10 mins
Cooking Temperature: 180 °F

INGREDIENTS:

2 ounces butter, melted

4¼ ounces gingersnap cookies, crushed

24 ounces cream cheese, room temperature

1 cup canned pumpkin

1 cup sour cream

1⅓ cup sugar

1 teaspoon ground cinnamon

½ teaspoon ground cloves

½ teaspoon ground ginger

1 teaspoon vanilla extract

4 eggs

DIRECTIONS:

1. Attach the sous vide immersion circulator using an adjustable clamp to a Cambro container or pot filled with water and preheat to 180 °F.
2. Preheat oven to 350 ºF.
3. *For the crust:* in a bowl, mix together butter and cookies.
4. Transfer mixture into the bottom of 9-inch springform pan and, with the back of spoon, press to smooth the surface.
5. Press a piece of foil around bottom of springform pan and bake for 10 minutes.

6. ***Meanwhile for the filling:*** into the bowl of a stand mixer add the cream cheese and pumpkin, and mix until smooth.

7. Add sour cream, sugar, spices and vanilla extract, and mix until well-combined.

8. Add eggs one at a time, and mix until smooth.

9. Place filling mixture into prepared crust evenly. Seal top of pan tightly with a piece of foil.

10. In an extra-large cooking pouch, place the pan. Seal pouch tightly after squeezing out the excess air. Place pouch in sous vide bath and set the cooking time for 5 hours.

11. Remove pouch from sous vide bath. Remove pan from pouch and keep onto wire rack to cool for 30 minutes.

12. After cooling, refrigerate overnight.

13. Carefully, run a knife around the sides of pan to loosen the cheesecake from the walls.

14. Cut into wedges and serve.

CRÈME BRÛLÉE

Preparation Time: 20 mins
Cooking Time: 30 mins
Cooking Temperature: 180 °F

INGREDIENTS:

3 egg yolks

½ cup cream

½ cup milk

¼ cup sugar

¼ cup vanilla bean (seed scraped out separately)

DIRECTIONS:

1. Attach the sous vide immersion circulator using an adjustable clamp to a Cambro container or pot filled with water and preheat to 180 °F.

2. Into a bowl add egg yolks, cream and milk, and beat until well-combined.

3. Add sugar and beat until well-combined.

4. Stir in vanilla bean seeds.

5. Into a cooking pouch, add cream mixture. Seal pouch tightly after squeezing out the excess air. Place pouch in sous vide bath and set the cooking time for 20-30 minutes.

6. Remove pouches from sous vide bath and immediately plunge into a large bowl of ice water.

7. Through a fine sieve, strain the mixture into a bowl.

8. Refrigerate until chilled before serving.

CREAMY CHOCOLATE INFUSED WITH BLOOD ORANGE

Preparation Time: 15 mins
Cooking Time: 40 mins
Cooking Temperature: 180 °F

INGREDIENTS:

For Pots de Crème

 1 cup heavy whipping cream

 juice of one blood orange

 ¼ cup milk

 2 tablespoons plus 2 teaspoons granulated sugar

 ⅛ teaspoon kosher salt

 3½ ounces bittersweet chocolate, chopped

 3 large egg yolks

 2 dashes Angostura bitters

For Whipped Cream:

 ½ cup chilled heavy whipping cream

 1 tablespoon maple syrup

 1 tablespoon bourbon

 ¼ teaspoon vanilla bean paste

DIRECTIONS:

1. Attach the sous vide immersion circulator using an adjustable clamp to a Cambro container or pot filled with water and preheat to 180 °F.

2. Into a small pan add whipping cream, orange juice, milk, granulated sugar and salt, and beat over medium heat until well-combined.

3. Bring to a gentle boil, stirring continuously.

4. Remove from heat and immediately add chocolate, beating continuously until smooth and completely melted.

5. Keep aside to cool for 2 minutes, stirring occasionally.

6. Add egg yolks, one at a time then, beating until well-combined.

7. Add Angostura bitters and beat to combine.

8. Through a fine mesh strainer, strain the mixture.

9. Divide mixture into 4 canning jars evenly and close the lids tightly.

10. Place jars in sous vide bath and set the cooking time for 35 minutes.

11. Remove the jars from sous vide bath and place onto a wire rack to cool completely.

12. After cooling, transfer the jars into refrigerator for at least 2 hours (or until set).

13. ***Meanwhile, for the whipped cream:*** pre-chill the bowl of a stand mixer for at least 10 minutes.

14. In the chilled bowl, add all ingredients and, with whisk attachment, mix on medium speed until soft peaks form.

15. Place whipped cream over pots de crème and serve.

Honey Bourbon Cranberries

Preparation Time: 10 mins
Cooking Time: 1 hour
Cooking Temperature: 183 °F

Ingredients:

1 cup honey

7½ ounces fresh cranberries

½ ounce bourbon

1 tablespoon orange zest

Directions:

1. Attach the sous vide immersion circulator using an adjustable clamp to a Cambro container or pot filled with water and preheat to 183 °F.

2. Into a cooking pouch, add all ingredients. Seal pouch tightly after squeezing out the excess air. Place pouch in sous vide bath and set the cooking time for 1 hour.

3. Remove pouch from sous vide bath and, with a towel, smash the cranberries in the pouch.

4. Serve warm.

PEACH WITH LAVENDER

Preparation Time: 10 mins
Cooking Time: 20 mins
Cooking Temperature: 185 °F

INGREDIENTS:

2 peaches, halved and pitted

¼ cup honey

¼ cup water

1 tablespoon dried lavender buds

DIRECTIONS:

1. Attach the sous vide immersion circulator using an adjustable clamp to a Cambro container or pot filled with water and preheat to 185 °F.

2. Into a cooking pouch, add all ingredients. Seal pouch tightly after squeezing out the excess air. Place pouch in sous vide bath and set the cooking time for 20 minutes.

3. Remove pouch from sous vide bath and immediately plunge into a large bowl of ice water for 15-20 minutes.

4. Open the pouch and transfer peaches into a bowl. Through a fine-mesh sieve, strain the poaching liquid into a bowl. Discard the lavender buds.

5. Serve chilled peach halves chilled, along with pouching liquid.

POACHED PEARS

Preparation Time: 10 mins
Cooking Time: 1 hour 10 mins
Cooking Temperature: 176 °F

INGREDIENTS:

brandy *

white wine *

water *

sugar *

2 strips orange peel

cinnamon stick *

star anise *

vanilla extract, as required

4 pears, peeled and cored

whipped cream, as required

DIRECTIONS:

1. Attach the sous vide immersion circulator using an adjustable clamp to a Cambro container or pot filled with water and preheat to 176 °F.

2. In a pan, mix brandy, wine, water, sugar, orange peel strips, cinnamon stick and star anise over a low heat and cook until heated sugar is dissolved.

3. Stir in vanilla extract and remove from heat. Keep aside to cool.

4. Into a cooking pouch, add pears and cooled syrup. Seal pouch tightly after squeezing out the excess air. Place pouch in sous vide bath and set the cooking time for 1 hour.

5. Remove pouches from sous vide bath and immediately plunge into a large bowl of ice water to cool.

6. Place pears onto a plate, transferring cooking liquid into a pan.

7. Place pan over stove and cook until a syrupy consistency is reached.

8. Pour syrup over pears and serve with a dollop of whipped cream.

WINE & MAPLE POACHED PEARS

Preparation Time: 10 mins
Cooking Time: 1 hour 5 mins
Cooking Temperature: 176 °F

INGREDIENTS:

2 cups white wine

2 cups water

1 cup maple syrup

1¼ cups sugar

4 pears

DIRECTIONS:

1. Attach the sous vide immersion circulator using an adjustable clamp to a Cambro container or pot filled with water and preheat to 176 °F.

2. Into a pan, add all ingredients except pears and simmer until sauce reduces a little.

3. Remove from heat and keep aside to cool.

4. Into a cooking pouch, add pears and syrup. Seal pouch tightly after squeezing out the excess air. Place pouch in sous vide bath and set the cooking time for 1 hour.

5. Remove pouch from sous vide bath and carefully open it.

6. Transfer pears onto a plate, drizzle with sauce, and serve.

CINNAMON APPLES

Preparation Time: 10 mins
Cooking Time: 40 mins
Cooking Temperature: 185 °F

INGREDIENTS:

4 medium apples, peeled, cored and sliced

1 tablespoon brown sugar

2 tablespoons unsalted butter

¼ teaspoon ground cinnamon

DIRECTIONS:

1. Attach the sous vide immersion circulator using an adjustable clamp to a Cambro container or pot filled with water and preheat to 185 °F.

2. Into a bowl, add all ingredients and toss to coat well.

3. Into a cooking pouch, add apple slices in a single layer. Seal pouch tightly after squeezing out the excess air. Place pouch in sous vide bath and set the cooking time for 30-40 minutes.

4. Remove pouch from sous vide bath and carefully open it. Transfer apple mixture onto a plate and serve immediately.

MAPLE WHISKEY APPLES

Preparation Time: 10 mins
Cooking Time: 4 hours
Cooking Temperature: 190 °F

INGREDIENTS:

3 cooking apples, peeled, cored and sliced

1 tablespoon sugar

1 tablespoon maple whisky

pinch of salt

DIRECTIONS:

1. Attach the sous vide immersion circulator using an adjustable clamp to a Cambro container or pot filled with water and preheat to 190 °F.

2. Into a bowl, add all ingredients and toss to coat well.

3. Into a cooking pouch, add apple slices in a single layer. Seal pouch tightly after squeezing out the excess air. Place pouch in sous vide bath and set the cooking time for 4 hours.

4. Remove pouch from sous vide bath and carefully open it. Transfer apple mixture into a plate and serve immediately. Alternatively, serve apples after chilling.

STUFFED APPLES

Preparation Time: 10 mins
Cooking Time: 2 hours
Cooking Temperature: 183 °F

INGREDIENTS:

4 tart apples, peeled

juice of 1 lemon

3 tablespoons unsalted butter

2 tablespoons light brown sugar

2 tablespoons raisins

2 whole fresh dates, pitted

1 tablespoon ground cinnamon

¼ teaspoon nutmeg, grated

¼ teaspoon fine sea salt

⅛ teaspoon vanilla extract

freshly whipped cream or ice cream, for serving

DIRECTIONS:

1. Attach the sous vide immersion circulator using an adjustable clamp to a Cambro container or pot filled with water and preheat to 183 °F.

2. With a sharp knife, core the apples, leaving the base of the apple intact.

3. Drizzle apples evenly with lemon juice.

4. Into a bowl, add all ingredients except cream and mash into a chunky paste using a fork.

5. Stuff the center of each apple evenly with chunky paste and press gently to compact the filling.

6. Between 2 cooking pouches, divide apples. Seal pouches tightly after squeezing out the excess air. Place pouches in sous vide bath and set the cooking time for 2 hours.

7. Remove pouches from sous vide bath and carefully open them. Transfer apples to serving plate.

8. Serve warm with whipped cream or ice cream.

FLOURLESS CHOCOLATE CAKE

Preparation Time: 15 mins
Cooking Time: 1 hour 15 mins
Cooking Temperature: 115 & 170 °F

INGREDIENTS:

½ pound semisweet chocolate squares, chopped

⅛ cup coffee liqueur or orange liqueur

4 ounces butter

4 large eggs

2 tablespoons unsweetened cocoa powder

DIRECTIONS:

1. Attach the sous vide immersion circulator using an adjustable clamp to a Cambro container or pot filled with water and preheat to 115 °F.

2. Into a cooking pouch, add chocolate, coffee and butter. Seal pouch tightly after squeezing out the excess air. Place pouch in sous vide bath and set the cooking time for 15 minutes.

3. Remove pouch from sous vide bath every 5 minutes and, with your fingers, massage the mixture to mix.

4. Remove pouch from sous vide bath and carefully open it.

5. Set sous vide bath to 170 °F. Generously grease 6 x 4-ounce canning jars with nonstick spray.

6. Into a bowl add eggs and, with a standing mixer, beat at high speed until volume doubles.

7. Slowly add chocolate mixture, beating on low speed until well-combined.

8. Transfer mixture evenly into prepared jars and smooth the surface by tapping each jar on the palm of your hand.

9. Close the canning jar lids tightly. Carefully arrange jars into sous vide bath and set the cooking time for 60 minutes.

10. Carefully, remove jars from sous vide bath and place onto a wire rack to cool. After cooling, refrigerate covered for at least 6 hours.

11. About 30 minutes before serving, carefully run a thin knife around the edge of each cake to remove from jars.

12. Serve with your desired garnishing.

GINGER CRÈME BRÛLÉE

Preparation Time: 15 mins
Cooking Time: 55 mins
Cooking Temperature: 185 °F

INGREDIENTS:

⅔ cup whole milk

2 cups heavy whipping cream

4 teaspoons peeled and fresh chopped ginger

4 large egg yolks

½ cup superfine sugar

pinch of salt

DIRECTIONS:

1. Attach the sous vide immersion circulator using an adjustable clamp to a Cambro container or pot filled with water and preheat to 185 °F.
2. Into a medium pan add milk, cream and ginger, and warm through on a low heat.
3. Remove from heat and allow liquid to steep for 30 minutes.
4. Through a fine mesh sieve, strain the mixture and discard the solids.
5. Return the liquid to another pan and cook until just heated.
6. Into a bowl, add egg yolks and beat well.
7. Slowly add sugar and salt, beating continuously.
8. Slowly add ginger mixture, beating continuously until well-combined.
9. Place ⅔ cup of mixture into each ramekin. With a piece of plastic wrap, cover each ramekin and secure with a rubber band.

10. Carefully arrange ramekins over the rack in sous vide bath (water level should come ⅔ up the sides of the ramekins). Set the cooking time for 50 minutes.

11. Carefully, remove ramekins from sous vide bath onto wire rack to cool slightly.

12. Remove plastic wrap and keep aside to cool completely.

13. After cooling, refrigerate until chilled.

14. Before serving, spread a thin layer of sugar on top of each chilled custard. With a torch, caramelize top of each custard.

15. Serve immediately.

FLAN CUSTARD

Preparation Time: 15 mins
Cooking Time: 2 hours
Cooking Temperature: 180 °F

INGREDIENTS:

¾ cup granulated sugar

1 x 14-ounce can condensed milk

1 x 12-fluid-ounce can evaporated milk

12 large egg yolks

1 teaspoon pure vanilla extract

DIRECTIONS:

1. Attach the sous vide immersion circulator using an adjustable clamp to a Cambro container or pot filled with water and preheat to 180 °F.

2. Into a pan, add sugar and heat until liquefied completely. Pour liquefied sugar evenly into 4 x ½-pint jars and keep aside to cool.

3. Into a bowl, add condensed milk, evaporated milk, egg yolks and vanilla extract, and gently stir to combine.

4. Through a cheesecloth, strain mixture.

5. Pour strained mixture over liquefied sugar in each jar, leaving just enough room for the lid to close tightly.

6. Carefully arrange ramekins over the rack in sous vide bath. Set the cooking time for 2 hours.

7. Carefully, remove ramekins from sous vide bath. Place ramekins onto wire rack to cool completely.

8. After cooling, refrigerate to chill before serving.

CHOCOLATE ZABAGLIONE

Preparation Time: 15 mins
Cooking Time: 30 mins
Cooking Temperature: 165 °F

INGREDIENTS:

1 cup sugar

½ cup dry Marsala

8 large egg yolks

pinch of salt

⅓ cup unsweetened cocoa powder

¼ cup whipping cream

1 pound fresh strawberries, hulled and quartered

DIRECTIONS:

1. Attach the sous vide immersion circulator using an adjustable clamp to a Cambro container or pot filled with water and preheat to 165 °F.

2. Into a bowl add sugar, Marsala, egg yolks and salt, and beat until well-combined.

3. Add cocoa powder and beat until well-combined.

4. Add cream and beat well.

5. Into a large cooking pouch, place egg mixture. Seal pouch tightly after squeezing out the excess air. Place pouch in sous vide bath and set the cooking time for 20-30 minutes.

6. Remove pouch from sous vide bath occasionally and, with your fingers, massage the mixture to mix.

7. Meanwhile, divide strawberries into dessert bowls evenly.

8. Remove pouch from sous vide bath and carefully open it.

9. Place warm zabaglione over the strawberries, cover, and refrigerate to chill before serving.

MEXICAN CHOCOLATE POTS

Preparation Time: 15 mins
Cooking Time: 30 mins
Cooking Temperature: 180 °F

INGREDIENTS:

1 x 3½-ounce bar Mexican chocolate, chopped

1 tablespoon sugar

⅓ cup whole milk

1 cup heavy whipping cream pus more for topping

3 egg yolks

2 teaspoons cocoa powder

¼ teaspoon vanilla extract

⅛ teaspoon sea salt

chocolate shavings, for serving

DIRECTIONS:

1. Attach the sous vide immersion circulator using an adjustable clamp to a Cambro container or pot filled with water and preheat to 180 °F.

2. In a heatproof bowl, mix together chocolate and sugar. Keep aside.

3. Into a pan, add milk and cream and cook until heated completely.

4. Remove from heat and pour mixture over chocolate and sugar. Keep aside for 5 minutes.

5. Meanwhile, in another small bowl, add egg yolks, vanilla extract, cocoa powder and salt, and beat until well-combined.

6. After 5 minutes, stir the chocolate mixture until well-combined and smooth.

7. Add egg mixture and beat until well-combined.

8. Fill the ramekins evenly with chocolate mixture.

9. Arrange ramekins on a rack in the sous vide bath. (Water level should be halfway up the sides of ramekins). Using plastic wrap, cover the ramekins.

10. Set the cooking time for 30 minutes.

11. Remove from sous vide bath and keep aside for 20 minutes to cool.

12. Refrigerate for at least 2 hours before serving.

13. Top with chocolate shavings and a dollop of whipped cream, and serve.

CHOCOLATE PUDDING

Preparation Time: 20 mins
Cooking Time: 30 mins
Cooking Temperature: 180 °F

INGREDIENTS:

3 eggs

2 egg yolks

1 cup milk

½ cup sugar

¼ cup cocoa powder

½ cup bittersweet chocolate chips

1 cup heavy cream

DIRECTIONS:

1. Attach the sous vide immersion circulator using an adjustable clamp to a Cambro container or pot filled with water and preheat to 180 °F.

2. Into a medium bowl add eggs and egg yolks, and beat well.

3. Add milk and cream and beat until well-combined.

4. Add sugar and beat until well-combined.

5. Into another small bowl, add cocoa powder and a few tablespoons of egg mixture and beat until smooth.

6. Add cocoa mixture into remaining egg mixture and mix well.

7. Into a large cooking pouch, place egg mixture with chocolate chips. Seal pouch tightly after squeezing out the excess air. Place pouch in sous vide bath and set the cooking time for 20-30 minutes.

8. After 2 minutes, remove pouch from sous vide bath and, with your fingers, knead slightly to mix chocolate into the pudding.

9. Return the pouch into sous vide bath for the remainder of the 20-30 minutes.

10. Remove pouches from sous vide bath and immediately plunge into a large bowl of ice water for 1-2 minutes.

11. With your fingers, knead pouch slightly and return to ice water to cool completely.

12. After cooling, transfer mixture into a food processor and pulse until smooth.

13. Transfer pudding into a serving bowl. Using plastic wrap, cover the bowl and refrigerate before serving.

14. Serve with a topping of cream.

STICKY TOFFEE PUDDING

Preparation Time: 20 mins
Cooking Time: 3 hours
Cooking Temperature: 195 °F

INGREDIENTS:

½ cup boiling water

¼ cup figs, chopped

¾ cup dates, pitted and chopped

1½ cups all-purpose flour

½ teaspoon baking soda

1 teaspoon baking powder

¼ teaspoon ground cinnamon

pinch of salt

14 tablespoons unsalted butter, softened and divided, plus extra for greasing parchment

1¾ cups packed light brown sugar, divided

2 large eggs

1 tablespoon unsulphured molasses

1½ teaspoons vanilla extract, divided

¼ cup plus 2 tablespoons heavy cream

DIRECTIONS:

1. Attach the sous vide immersion circulator using an adjustable clamp to a Cambro container or pot filled with water and preheat to 195 °F.
2. Grease 6 ramekins with nonstick oil spray.

3. Cut parchment paper into circles to fit just inside the lip of the ramekins. Grease parchment circles with extra butter.

4. Arrange a rack in the bottom of the sous vide bath.

5. Into a heatproof bowl, add boiling water and soak figs and dates until rehydrated.

6. In another bowl, mix together flour, baking soda, baking powder, cinnamon, and salt.

7. In a stand mixer fitted with a paddle attachment, add 8 tablespoons of butter and 1 cup of brown sugar, and mix at medium speed until light and fluffy.

8. Add eggs one at a time and mix until well-combined.

9. Add molasses and 1 teaspoon of vanilla extract and mix until well-combined.

10. Add flour mixture and mix on low speed. Slowly increase speed to medium, beating continuously until just combined.

11. Into a food processor, add soaked fruit with soaking water and pulse until well-combined.

12. Transfer fruit mixture into flour mixture and, with a spatula, stir to combine.

13. Pour mixture evenly into prepared ramekins until half-full.

14. Place 1 parchment circle over top of mixture in each ramekin, butter-side down.

15. With a small piece of foil, cover each ramekin and use a rubber band to secure the foil lid over the top.

16. Carefully arrange ramekins over the rack in sous vide bath (water level should come ¾ of the way up each ramekin). Set the cooking time for 3 hours.

17. ***Meanwhile, for the toffee sauce:*** into a heavy, deep pan, add remaining ¾ cup of sugar and 6 tablespoons of butter over a medium heat and cook until sugar melts, stirring occasionally.

18. Add cream and stir until well-combined.

19. Remove from heat and stir in remaining ½ teaspoon of vanilla extract. Keep warm for serving.

20. Remove ramekins from sous vide bath. Carefully, uncover each ramekin.

21. Carefully, flip pudding onto serving plates.

22. Drizzle with toffee sauce and serve warm.

MAPLE RAISIN RICE PUDDING

Preparation Time: 10 mins
Cooking Time: 2 hours
Cooking Temperature: 180 °F

INGREDIENTS:

3 cups skim milk

2 cups Arborio risotto rice

½ cup maple syrup

½ cup golden raisins

1 tablespoon butter

2 teaspoons ground cinnamon

½ teaspoon ground ginger

DIRECTIONS:

1. Attach the sous vide immersion circulator using an adjustable clamp to a Cambro container or pot filled with water and preheat to 180 °F.

2. Into a cooking pouch, add all ingredients. Seal pouch tightly after squeezing out the excess air. Place pouch in sous vide bath and set the cooking time for 2 hours.

3. Remove pouch from sous vide bath and carefully open it. Transfer rice mixture into a serving bowl.

4. With a fork, fluff the rice and serve.

ORANGE CURD

Preparation Time: 10 mins
Cooking Time: 45 minutes
Cooking Temperature: 180 °F

INGREDIENTS:

1 cup ultrafine sugar

6 egg yolks

8 tablespoons unsalted butter, melted

¼ cup fresh orange juice

pinch of kosher salt

DIRECTIONS:

1. Attach the sous vide immersion circulator using an adjustable clamp to a Cambro container or pot filled with water and preheat to 180 °F.

2. Into a blender, add all ingredients and pulse until smooth and frothy.

3. Into a cooking pouch, add butter mixture. Seal pouch tightly after squeezing out the excess air. Place pouch in sous vide bath and set the cooking time for 45 minutes.

4. Remove pouch from sous vide bath occasionally and, with your fingers, massage the mixture to mix.

5. Remove pouch from sous vide bath and immediately plunge into a large bowl of ice water for 2 hours.

6. After cooling, transfer curd into a bowl and refrigerate for at least 2 hours before serving.

LEMON CURD

Preparation Time: 10 mins
Cooking Time: 1 hour
Cooking Temperature: 165 °F

INGREDIENTS:

½ cup sugar

3 large eggs

4 tablespoons butter, melted

¼ cup fresh lemon juice

2 tablespoons lemon zest

1½ teaspoons gelatin

DIRECTIONS:

1. Attach the sous vide immersion circulator using an adjustable clamp to a Cambro container or pot filled with water and preheat to 165 °F.

2. Into a cooking pouch, add all ingredients. Seal pouch tightly after squeezing out the excess air. Place pouch in sous vide bath and set the cooking time for 45-60 minutes.

3. Remove pouch from sous vide bath and carefully open it. Transfer mixture into a blender and pulse until well-combined and smooth.

4. Transfer mixture into a bowl and keep aside to cool.

5. Transfer into a container and refrigerate before using.

DULCE DE LECHE

Preparation Time: 5 mins
Cooking Time: 13 hours
Cooking Temperature: 185 °F

INGREDIENTS:

3 x 14-ounce cans sweetened condensed milk, labels removed

DIRECTIONS:

1. Attach the sous vide immersion circulator using an adjustable clamp to a Cambro container or pot filled with water and preheat to 185 °F.

2. Arrange cans in water bath while the machine is still preheating.

3. When temperature of sous vide bath reaches to 185 °F, set the cooking time for 13 hours.

4. Remove cans from sous vide bath and place onto a wire rack to cool for 20 minutes.

5. After cooling, refrigerate for up to 3 months.

9

SAUCES & OILS

BÉARNAISE SAUCE

Preparation Time: 15 mins
Cooking Time: 60 mins
Cooking Temperature: 174°F

INGREDIENTS:

¼ cup white wine

¼ cup white wine vinegar

1 tablespoon scallion, chopped

2 tablespoons fresh tarragon, chopped and divided

salt and freshly ground black pepper, to taste

4 large egg yolks

6 tablespoons unsalted butter, melted and cooled at room temperature

DIRECTIONS:

---

1. Attach the sous vide immersion circulator to a Cambro container or pot with water using an adjustable clamp and preheat water to 174°F.

2. In a large pan, add wine, vinegar, scallion, 1 tablespoon of tarragon, salt, and black pepper over high heat and bring to a boil. Reduce heat to medium-low and simmer for about 5 minutes.

3. Through a fine-mesh strainer, strain wine mixture into a bowl and set aside to cool for about 5 minutes.

4. In the bowl of wine mixture, add egg yolks and beat until well combined. Slowly add melted butter, whisking continuously until smooth.

5. In a large cooking pouch, place egg mixture. Seal pouch tightly after squeezing out the excess air. Place pouch in sous vide bath and set the cooking time for about 45 minutes.

6. Remove pouch from the sous vide bath and carefully open it. Transfer mixture into a bowl. With an immersion blender, blend sauce until smooth.

7. Stir in remaining tarragon and serve.

CARAMEL SAUCE

Preparation Time: 15 mins
Cooking Time: 2 hours
Cooking Temperature: 179°F

INGREDIENTS:

1/3 cup sugar

4 large egg yolks

½ teaspoon vanilla extract

¼ teaspoon fine sea salt

DIRECTIONS:

1. Attach the sous vide immersion circulator to a Cambro container or pot with water using an adjustable clamp and preheat water to 179°F.

2. In a bowl, add all ingredients and beat until well combined.

3. Place sugar mixture in a cooking pouch. Seal pouch tightly after squeezing out the excess air. Place pouch in sous vide bath and set the cooking time for about 2 hours.

4. Remove pouch from the sous vide bath and carefully open it. Transfer into a bowl and keep aside to cool slightly. Transfer sauce into a jar and refrigerate until cold before serving.

Cauliflower Alfredo

Preparation Time: 15 mins
Cooking Time: 2 hours
Cooking Temperature: 181°F

Ingredients:

2 cups cauliflower florets, chopped

2 garlic cloves, crushed

½ cup chicken or vegetable broth

2 tablespoons milk

2 tablespoons butter

salt and freshly ground black pepper, to taste

Directions:

1. Attach the sous vide immersion circulator to a Cambro container or pot with water using an adjustable clamp and preheat water to 181°F.
2. Place all ingredients in a cooking pouch. Seal pouch tightly after squeezing out the excess air. Place pouch in the sous vide bath and set the cooking time for about 2 hours.
3. Remove pouch from the sous vide bath and carefully open it.
4. Pour pouch mixture into a blender and pulse until smooth.

HERB INFUSED OLIVE OIL

Preparation Time: 10 mins
Cooking Time: 3 hours
Cooking Temperature: 131°F

INGREDIENTS:

2 cups mild olive oil

5 fresh herb sprigs (of your choice)

DIRECTIONS:

1. Attach the sous vide immersion circulator to a Cambro container or pot with water using an adjustable clamp and preheat water to 131°F.

2. Place all ingredients in a cooking pouch. Seal pouch tightly after squeezing out the excess air. Place pouch in sous vide bath and set the cooking time for about 3 hours.

3. Remove pouch from the sous vide bath and carefully open it.

4. Discard herb sprigs from oil. Store oil in a glass bottle or jar.

LEMON OLIVE OIL

Preparation Time: 10 mins
Cooking Time: 1 hour
Cooking Temperature: 131°F

INGREDIENTS:

2½ cups extra-virgin olive oil

peel of 1 Meyer lemon

1 large bunch lemon thyme

DIRECTIONS:

1. Attach the sous vide immersion circulator to a Cambro container or pot with water using an adjustable clamp and preheat water to 131°F.

2. Place all ingredients in a cooking pouch. Seal pouch tightly after squeezing out the excess air. Place pouch in sous vide bath and set the cooking time for about 1 hour.

3. Remove pouch from the sous vide bath and carefully open it. Strain oil through a fine-mesh strainer into a bowl.

4. Store oil in a glass bottle or jar. Oil can be refrigerated for up to 2 months.

COFFEE BUTTER

Preparation Time: 15 mins
Cooking Time: 3 hours
Cooking Temperature: 194°F

INGREDIENTS:

500g salted butter (17.6 ounces)

250g coffee beans (8.8 ounces)

DIRECTIONS:

1. Attach the sous vide immersion circulator to a Cambro container or pot with water using an adjustable clamp and preheat water to 194°F.

2. In a cooking pouch, place butter and coffee beans. Seal pouch tightly after squeezing out the excess air. Place pouch in sous vide bath and set the cooking time for about 3 hours.

3. Remove pouch from the sous vide bath and carefully open it. With a sieve, strain the butter into a bowl. Discard coffee beans.

4. Place butter into sealed bag and refrigerate until serving.

Raspberry Infused Vinaigrette

Preparation Time: 25 mins
Cooking Time: 2 hours
Cooking Temperature: 140°F

Ingredients:

For Raspberry Vinegar:

1 cup fresh raspberries

1-1/2 cups white wine or champagne vinegar

For Raspberry Vinaigrette:

3 tablespoons infused raspberry vinegar

1 tablespoon honey

1 tablespoon orange juice

1 shallot, finely chopped

5 tablespoons olive oil

salt and freshly ground black pepper, to taste

Directions:

1. Attach the sous vide immersion circulator to a Cambro container or pot with water using an adjustable clamp and preheat water to 140°F.

2. Place raspberries and vinegar in a cooking pouch. Seal pouch tightly after squeezing out the excess air. Place pouch in sous vide bath and set the cooking time for 1-2 hours.

3. Remove pouch from the sous vide bath and immediately plunge into a bowl of ice water for about 15-20 minutes. Strain vinegar and transfer into an airtight container.

4. For raspberry vinaigrette: in a bowl, add infused vinegar, honey, and orange juice and beat until well combined. Stir in the shallots and let sit for about 10 minutes.

5. Slowly add olive oil, beating continuously until well combined. Stir in salt and black pepper and serve.

GARLIC CONFIT

Preparation Time: 15 mins
Cooking Time: 7 hours
Cooking Temperature: 180°F

INGREDIENTS:

2 jars peeled garlic

2 tablespoons apple cider vinegar or sherry vinegar

1 tablespoon dried thyme

olive oil, as required

DIRECTIONS:

1. Attach the sous vide immersion circulator to a Cambro container or pot with water using an adjustable clamp and preheat water to 180°F.

2. In 2 mason jars, divide garlic, vinegar, and thyme. Fill jars with olive oil to the brim and cover with the lid tightly. Place jars in sous vide bath and set the cooking time for about 7 hours.

3. Remove the jars from the sous vide bath and place onto a wire rack to cool completely.

4. Store in the refrigerator for no more than a week.

INFUSED RASPBERRY SYRUP

Preparation Time: 5 mins
Cooking Time: 2 hours
Cooking Temperature: 140°F

INGREDIENTS:

1-2/3 cups white wine or champagne vinegar

1 cup raspberries

DIRECTIONS:

1. Attach the sous vide immersion circulator to a Cambro container or pot with water using an adjustable clamp and preheat water to 140°F.

2. Place vinegar and raspberries in a cooking pouch. Seal pouch tightly after squeezing out the excess air. Place pouch in sous vide bath and set the cooking time for about 1-2 hours.

3. Remove pouch from the sous vide bath and immediately immerse in a large bowl of ice water for about 15-20 minutes. Strain the vinegar. Store in a sealed container.

Blackberry Vinegar

Preparation Time: 5 mins
Cooking Time: 3 hours
Cooking Temperature: 153°F

Ingredients:

4 cups white balsamic vinegar

3 cups blackberries

Directions:

1. Attach the sous vide immersion circulator to a Cambro container or pot with water using an adjustable clamp and preheat water to 153°F.

2. Place vinegar and blackberries in a cooking pouch. Seal pouch tightly after squeezing out the excess air. Place pouch in sous vide bath and set the cooking time for about 2-3 hours.

3. Remove pouch from the sous vide bath and immediately immerse in a large bowl of ice water for about 15-20 minutes. Strain the vinegar. Place in a sealed container and store in refrigerator for up to 6 weeks.

BLACKBERRY BASIL VINEGAR

Preparation Time: 15 mins
Cooking Time: 3 hours
Cooking Temperature: 153°F

INGREDIENTS:

4 cups white balsamic vinegar

3 cups blackberries

½ cup basil leaves

DIRECTIONS:

1. Attach the sous vide immersion circulator to a Cambro container or pot with water using an adjustable clamp and preheat water to 153°F.

2. Place all ingredients in a cooking pouch. Seal pouch tightly after squeezing out the excess air. Place pouch in sous vide bath and set the cooking time for about 2-3 hours.

3. Remove pouch from sous vide bath occasionally and with your fingers, massage the mixture to mix.

4. Remove pouch from the sous vide bath and carefully open it.

5. Strain vinegar through a fine mesh strainer into a container. Discard the solids.

6. Keep in refrigerator for up to six weeks.

Ricotta Cheese

Preparation Time: 10 mins
Cooking Time: 40 mins
Cooking Temperature: 195°F

Ingredients:

8 cups whole milk

1 cup heavy cream

1 teaspoon sea salt

1 teaspoon citric acid

Directions:

1. Attach the sous vide immersion circulator to a Cambro container or pot with water using an adjustable clamp and preheat water to 195°F.

2. Add all ingredients to a bowl that fits into a cooking pouch. Arrange bowl inside cooking pouch and seal tightly after squeezing out the excess air. Place pouch in sous vide bath and set the cooking time for about 35-40 minutes.

3. Remove pouch from the sous vide bath and carefully open it. Remove bowl from cooking pouch.

4. With a slotted spoon, gently scoop out curd from top and transfer into straining vessel.

5. Strain ricotta until desired consistency of cheese is achieved.

Crème Fraiche

Preparation Time: 10 mins
Cooking Time: 12 hours
Cooking Temperature: 149°F

INGREDIENTS:

- 1 cup heavy whipping cream
- 2 tablespoons low-fat buttermilk

DIRECTIONS:

1. Attach the sous vide immersion circulator to a Cambro container or pot with water using an adjustable clamp and preheat water to 149°F.

2. Place all ingredients in a mason jar. Cover with cap tightly. Place jar in sous vide bath and set the cooking time for about 8 and no more than 12 hours.

3. Carefully remove jar from sous vide bath and open it.

4. Transfer mixture into an airtight container. Seal tightly and refrigerate for up to 3 weeks.

PERSIMMON BUTTER

Preparation Time: 10 mins
Cooking Time: 1½ hours
Cooking Temperature: 185°F

INGREDIENTS:

2 pounds ripe fuyu persimmons, peeled, hulled and cut into ¼-inch thick wedges

¼ cup apple juice

1 teaspoon lemon juice

1 cinnamon stick

1 teaspoon vanilla

¼ teaspoon kosher salt

DIRECTIONS:

1. Attach the sous vide immersion circulator to a Cambro container or pot with water using an adjustable clamp and preheat water to 185°F.

2. Place all ingredients in a cooking pouch. Seal pouch tightly after squeezing out the excess air. Place pouch in sous vide bath and set the cooking time for about 1½ hours.

3. Remove pouch from the sous vide bath and set aside to cool slightly.

4. In a food processor, add mixture and pulse until smooth.

STRAWBERRY & GRAPEFRUIT COMPOTE

Preparation Time: 10 mins
Cooking Time: 30 mins
Cooking Temperature: 180°F

INGREDIENTS:

juice of ½ grapefruit

1 tablespoon honey

½ teaspoon vanilla extract

1 pound fresh strawberries, hulled

DIRECTIONS:

1. Attach the sous vide immersion circulator to a Cambro container or pot with water using an adjustable clamp and preheat water to 180°F.

2. In a bowl, add grapefruit juice, honey, and vanilla extract and beat until well combined.

3. Place strawberries and honey mixture in a cooking pouch. Seal pouch tightly after squeezing out the excess air. Place pouch in sous vide bath and set the cooking time for about 30 minutes.

4. Remove pouch from the sous vide bath and carefully open it. Keep aside to cool slightly.

5. In a blender, pulse strawberry mixture until desired consistency is achieved.

6. Serve immediately.

PEACH CHUTNEY

Preparation Time: 15 mins
Cooking Time: 5 hours
Cooking Temperature: 182°F

INGREDIENTS:

For Pickling Spice:

1 tablespoon whole mustard seeds

2 teaspoons ground cinnamon

1½ teaspoons whole allspice berries

1 teaspoon whole coriander seeds

½ teaspoon red pepper flakes

6 whole cloves

1 bay leaf, crumbled finely

For Chutney:

1/8 cup apple cider vinegar

1 tablespoon olive oil

¼ cup packed brown sugar

1 tablespoon pickling spice

1 teaspoon chili powder

¾ teaspoon mustard seeds

¼ teaspoon curry powder

½ pound peaches, peeled, pitted, and chopped

½ yellow onion, chopped

1 garlic clove, minced

1/8 cup preserved ginger, chopped

½ cup raisins, chopped roughly

DIRECTIONS:

1. Attach the sous vide immersion circulator to a Cambro container or pot with water using an adjustable clamp and preheat water to 182°F.

2. For pickling spice: in a spice grinder, add all spices and grind until powdered finely.

3. Keep in an airtight container.

4. In a small bowl, add vinegar, oil, brown sugar, pickling spice, chili powder, mustard seeds, and curry powder and mix until a paste is formed.

5. In a cooking pouch, place remaining ingredients and spice paste. Seal pouch tightly after squeezing out the excess air. Place pouch in sous vide bath and set the cooking time for about 5 hours.

6. Remove pouch from the sous vide bath and set aside to cool slightly. Mash pouch mixture roughly.

7. Transfer into an airtight container and keep in refrigerator.

TOMATO SAUCE

Preparation Time: 15 mins
Cooking Time: 57 mins
Cooking Temperature: 181°F

INGREDIENTS:

2 tablespoons olive oil

½ cup onion, chopped

½ cup shallot, chopped

2 garlic cloves, sliced

3 fresh oregano sprigs, stemmed

2 pounds ripe tomatoes

3 fresh thyme sprigs, whole

1/3 cup parsley leaves, chopped

6 large fresh basil leaves, chopped

salt and freshly ground black pepper, to taste

DIRECTIONS:

1. Attach the sous vide immersion circulator to a Cambro container or pot with water using an adjustable clamp and preheat water to 181°F.

2. In a pan, heat oil over medium heat and sauté onion, shallot, garlic, and stemmed oregano for about 5-7 minutes.

3. Remove from heat and keep aside to cool slightly.

4. In a cooking pouch, place onion mixture, tomatoes, herbs, salt, and black pepper. Seal pouch tightly after squeezing out the excess air. Place pouch in sous vide bath and set the cooking time for about 50 minutes.

5. Remove pouch from the sous vide bath and keep aside to cool slightly.

6. Transfer mixture into a bowl. Remove the tomato peels.

7. In a food processor, pulse tomatoes and remaining mixture until desired consistency is achieved.

8. Serve immediately.

Hot Sauce

Preparation Time: 15 mins
Cooking Time: 20 mins
Cooking Temperature: 210°F

Ingredients:

1½ pound fresh red jalapeño peppers, stemmed, seeded, and chopped roughly

9 garlic cloves, smashed

1 teaspoon sea salt

3 tablespoons simple syrup

⅓ cup rice vinegar

Directions:

1. Attach the sous vide immersion circulator to a Cambro container or pot with water using an adjustable clamp and preheat water to 210°F.

2. In a food processor, pulse peppers, garlic, and salt until puréed.

3. In a cooking pouch, place puréed mixture. Seal pouch tightly after squeezing out the excess air. Place pouch in sous vide bath and set the cooking time for about 20 minutes.

4. Remove pouch from the sous vide bath and carefully open. Transfer mixture into a bowl. Add simple syrup and vinegar and stir to combine.

5. Transfer into an airtight container and keep in refrigerator for up to 2 weeks.

HOLLANDAISE

Preparation Time: 15 mins
Cooking Time: 60 mins
Cooking Temperature: 149°F

INGREDIENTS:

3 large egg yolks, beaten well

½ cup butter

1 tablespoon fresh lemon juice

½ teaspoon salt

pinch of dry mustard

DIRECTIONS:

1. Attach the sous vide immersion circulator to a Cambro container or pot with water using an adjustable clamp and preheat water to 149°F.

2. Place all ingredients in a wide mouth glass jar. Cover with cap tightly. Place jar in sous vide bath and set the cooking time for about 45-60 minutes, shaking the jar once after 20-25 minutes.

3. Carefully remove jar from sous vide bath and open it.

4. With a stick blender, blend mixture until smooth.

ORANGE ROSEMARY VINEGAR

Preparation Time: 15 mins
Cooking Time: 3 hours
Cooking Temperature: 153°F

INGREDIENTS:

4 cups white balsamic vinegar

zest of 10 blood oranges

10 fresh rosemary springs

DIRECTIONS:

1. Attach the sous vide immersion circulator to a Cambro container or pot with water using an adjustable clamp and preheat water to 153°F.

2. Place all ingredients in a cooking pouch. Seal pouch tightly after squeezing out the excess air. Place pouch in sous vide bath and set the cooking time for about 2-3 hours.

3. Remove pouch from sous vide bath occasionally and with your fingers, massage the mixture to mix.

4. Remove pouch from the sous vide bath and carefully open it.

5. Strain vinegar through a fine mesh strainer into a container. Discard the solids.

6. Keep in refrigerator for up to six weeks.

LEMON GINGER VINEGAR

Preparation Time: 10 mins
Cooking Time: 3 hours
Cooking Temperature: 153°F

INGREDIENTS:

2 cups white wine vinegar

peel of 1 lemon

1 - 1-inch piece of fresh ginger root, peeled, and cut into ¼-inch-thick rounds

1 thick lemon slice

1 tablespoon granulated sugar

DIRECTIONS:

1. Attach the sous vide immersion circulator to a Cambro container or pot with water using an adjustable clamp and preheat water to 153°F.

2. Place all ingredients in a cooking pouch. Seal pouch tightly after squeezing out the excess air. Place pouch in sous vide bath and set the cooking time for about 3 hours.

3. Remove pouch from the sous vide bath and carefully open it. Strain the mixture through a cheesecloth-lined fine-mesh strainer into a jar.

4. Keep in refrigerator for up to six weeks.

10

DRINKS AND COCKTAILS

EGGNOG

Preparation Time: 15 mins
Cooking Time: 1 hour
Cooking Temperature: 140°F

INGREDIENTS:

8 large eggs

4 large egg yolks

4 cups whole milk

2 cups heavy cream

1½ cups confectioner' sugar

1 tablespoon pure vanilla extract

½ teaspoon nutmeg, freshly grated

pinch of salt

6 whole cloves

3 cinnamon sticks

DIRECTIONS:

1. Attach the sous vide immersion circulator to a Cambro container or pot with water using an adjustable clamp and preheat water to 140°F.

2. For eggnog base: in a stand mixer, beat eggs and egg yolks until thick and pale yellow.

3. Add milk, cream, sugar, vanilla, powdered sugar, nutmeg, and salt and beat well.

4. In a large cooking pouch, place base mixture, cloves, and cinnamon. Seal pouch tightly after squeezing out the excess air. Place pouch in sous vide bath and set the cooking time for about 1 hour.

5. Remove pouch from the sous vide bath and immediately immerse in a large bowl of ice water for at least 20 minutes.

6. Strain mixture into a sealable pitcher. Discard cloves and cinnamon. Refrigerate for several hours to overnight to chill before serving.

IRISH ICED COFFEE

Preparation Time: 15 mins
Cooking Time: 6 hours
Cooking Temperature: 165°F

INGREDIENTS:

For Coffee:

3 cups bourbon

½ cup whole coffee beans

2 tablespoons brown sugar

For Serving:

ice, as required

2 ounces infused whiskey

1 ounce heavy cream

DIRECTIONS:

1. Attach the sous vide immersion circulator to a Cambro container or pot with water using an adjustable clamp and preheat water to 165°F.

2. Place all ingredients in a cooking pouch. Seal pouch tightly after squeezing out the excess air. Place pouch in sous vide bath and set the cooking time for about 6 hours.

3. Remove pouch from the sous vide bath and shake well. Immediately immerse in a large bowl of ice water for at least 30 minutes.

4. Strain mixture through a fine strainer into a container.

5. For serving: in serving glasses, divide ice and whiskey. Add bourbon mixture in each glass. Top with cream and serve.

TONIC WATER

Preparation Time: 15 mins
Cooking Time: 2 hours
Cooking Temperature: 158°F

INGREDIENTS:

4 cups fresh water

4 teaspoons powdered cinchona bark

1 cup lemongrass, chopped roughly

zest and juice of 1 orange

zest and juice of 1 lime

zest and juice of 1 lemon

zest and juice of 1 grapefruit

1 teaspoon allspice berries

¼ cup powdered citric acid

1 teaspoon salt

¾ cup of agave syrup

DIRECTIONS:

1. Attach the sous vide immersion circulator to a Cambro container or pot with water using an adjustable clamp and preheat water to 158°F.

2. Place all ingredients in a cooking pouch. Seal pouch tightly after squeezing out the excess air. Place pouch in sous vide bath and set the cooking time for about 2 hours.

3. Remove pouch from the sous vide bath and carefully open it. Strain the mixture through a fine strainer into a container and discard solids.

QUICK LIMONCELLO

Preparation Time: 10 mins
Cooking Time: 3 hours
Cooking Temperature: 130°F

INGREDIENTS:

zest of 3 lemons

1-3/4 cups vodka

2-1/4 tablespoons sugar

DIRECTIONS:

1. Attach the sous vide immersion circulator to a Cambro container or pot with water using an adjustable clamp and preheat water to 130°F.

2. Add all ingredients to a sterilized mason jar. Cover with cap tightly. Place jar in sous vide bath and set the cooking time for about 1-3 hours.

3. Carefully remove jar from sous vide bath and open it. Strain vodka into a pitcher. Discard lemon zest.

4. Serve over ice with the garnishing of sparkling water and lemon twist.

OLD FASHIONED

Preparation Time: 10 mins
Cooking Time: 3 hours
Cooking Temperature: 130°F

INGREDIENTS:

zest of 1 orange

1-3/4 cups bourbon

2-1/4 tablespoons sugar

morello or maraschino cherries, as required

DIRECTIONS:

1. Attach the sous vide immersion circulator to a Cambro container or pot with water using an adjustable clamp and preheat water to 130°F.

2. In a sterilized mason jar, add all ingredients. Cover with cap tightly. Place jar in sous vide bath and set the cooking time for about 1-3 hours.

3. Carefully remove jar from sous vide bath and open it. Strain bourbon into a pitcher. Discard orange zest.

4. Serve over ice with an orange twist and cherries.

BOURBON BACON COCKTAIL

Preparation Time: 10 mins
Cooking Time: 3 hours
Cooking Temperature: 130°F

INGREDIENTS:

½ cup bourbon

2-1/4 tablespoons brown sugar or maple syrup

1 cooked bacon strip plus more for garnishing

zest of 1 orange

DIRECTIONS:

1. Attach the sous vide immersion circulator to a Cambro container or pot with water using an adjustable clamp and preheat water to 130°F.

2. Add all ingredients to a sterilized mason jar. Cover with cap tightly. Place jar in sous vide bath and set the cooking time for about 1-3 hours.

3. Carefully remove jar from sous vide bath and open it. Strain bourbon into a pitcher. Discard bacon strip and orange zest.

4. Serve over ice with a garnish of fresh cooked bacon.

ORANGE CREAMSICLE COCKTAIL

Preparation Time: 10 mins
Cooking Time: 3 hours
Cooking Temperature: 130°F

INGREDIENTS:

zest of 3 oranges

½ cup bourbon

2-1/4 tablespoons sugar

1 vanilla bean, split and scraped

DIRECTIONS:

1. Attach the sous vide immersion circulator to a Cambro container or pot with water using an adjustable clamp and preheat water to 130°F.

2. Add all ingredients to a sterilized mason jar. Cover with cap tightly. Place jar in sous vide bath and set the cooking time for about 1-3 hours.

3. Carefully remove jar from sous vide bath and open it. Strain vodka into a pitcher. Discard orange zest and vanilla bean.

4. Serve over ice with an orange twist.

CHILI VODKA

Preparation Time: 10 mins
Cooking Time: 2 hours
Cooking Temperature: 153°F

INGREDIENTS:

2 small red chilis

1 (12.68 fluid ounce, 375 mL) bottle of vodka

DIRECTIONS:

1. Attach the sous vide immersion circulator to a Cambro container or pot with water using an adjustable clamp and preheat water to 153°F.

2. Place all ingredients in a cooking pouch. Seal pouch tightly after squeezing out the excess air. Place pouch in sous vide bath and set the cooking time for about 2 hours.

3. Remove pouch from the sous vide bath and immediately immerse in a large bowl of ice water for about 15-20 minutes.

4. Remove chilis from vodka and transfer back into the vodka bottle.

CUCUMBER LEMONGRASS COCKTAIL

Preparation Time: 10 mins
Cooking Time: 3 hours
Cooking Temperature: 122°F

INGREDIENTS:

1 fresh lemongrass stalk, bruised and chopped

½ cucumber, thinly sliced

5 fresh mint sprigs, bruised

rind of 1 lime

¾ cup cane sugar

2 cups gin

3 cups water

juice of 2 limes

DIRECTIONS:

1. Attach the sous vide immersion circulator to a Cambro container or pot with water using an adjustable clamp and preheat water to 122°F.

2. Place all ingredients in a cooking pouch. Seal pouch tightly after squeezing out the excess air. Place pouch in sous vide bath and set the cooking time for about 3 hours.

3. Remove pouch from the sous vide bath and carefully open it. Strain mixture through a fine-mesh sieve.

4. Mix with tonic or fizzy water and serve.

Mulled Wine

Preparation Time: 10 mins
Cooking Time: 1 hour
Cooking Temperature: 137°F

Ingredients:

2 oranges, thinly sliced

2 cups apple cider

1 bottle full bodied red wine

1 cup orange juice

¼ cup honey

2 cinnamon sticks

1 teaspoon whole allspice

1 teaspoon whole cloves

Directions:

1. Attach the sous vide immersion circulator to a Cambro container or pot with water using an adjustable clamp and preheat water to 137°F.

2. Place all ingredients in a cooking pouch. Seal pouch tightly after squeezing out the excess air. Place pouch in sous vide bath and set the cooking time for about 1 hour.

3. Remove pouch from the sous vide bath and carefully open it. Strain wine through a fine-mesh sieve into a pretty punch bowl. Reserve orange slices and float them atop the wine. Serve hot.

GRAND MARNIER

Preparation Time: 10 mins
Cooking Time: 1½ hours
Cooking Temperature: 180°F

INGREDIENTS:

2 cups brandy

fresh zest of 8 large oranges

½ cup ultrafine sugar

DIRECTIONS:

1. Attach the sous vide immersion circulator to a Cambro container or pot with water using an adjustable clamp and preheat water to 180°F.

2. Place all ingredients in a cooking pouch. Seal pouch tightly after squeezing out the excess air. Place pouch in sous vide bath and set the cooking time for about 1½ hours.

3. Remove pouch from the sous vide bath and carefully open it. Strain brandy mixture and discard orange zest.

4. Transfer brandy into an airtight container and refrigerate for up to 1 month.

STRAWBERRY INFUSED TEQUILA

Preparation Time: 15 mins
Cooking Time: 2 hours
Cooking Temperature: 165°F

INGREDIENTS:

For Tequila:

    3 cups fresh strawberries, hulled and halved

    1 bottle tequila

    1/3 cup white sugar

    1/3 cup lime juice

    ¼ cup Cointreau

    ¼ cup agave syrup

For Garnishing:

    ½ cup fresh strawberries

    fresh mint leaves

DIRECTIONS:

1. Attach the sous vide immersion circulator to a Cambro container or pot with water using an adjustable clamp and preheat water to 165°F.
2. Place all ingredients in a cooking pouch. Seal pouch tightly after squeezing out the excess air. Place pouch in sous vide bath and set the cooking time for about 2 hours.
3. Remove pouch from the sous vide bath and immediately immerse in a large bowl of ice water for about 15-30 minutes.
4. Strain mixture through a fine-mesh strainer into a pitcher.
5. Fill a lowball glass with ice and add tequila infusion. Garnish with strawberries and mint leaves.

MINT JULEP

Preparation Time: 15 mins
Cooking Time: 1½ hours
Cooking Temperature: 135°F

INGREDIENTS:

2 cups bourbon

2 cups water

2 cups fresh mint

1½ cups coconut sugar

DIRECTIONS:

1. Attach the sous vide immersion circulator to a Cambro container or pot with water using an adjustable clamp and preheat water to 135°F.

2. Place all ingredients in a cooking pouch. Seal pouch tightly after squeezing out the excess air. Place pouch in sous vide bath and set the cooking time for about 1½ hours.

3. Remove pouch from the sous vide bath and immediately immerse in a large bowl of ice water for about 15-30 minutes.

4. Strain mixture through a fine-mesh strainer into a pitcher.

Orange Cream Cocktail

Preparation Time: 10 mins
Cooking Time: 1½ hours
Cooking Temperature: 130°F

Ingredients:

1/4 cup sugar

1 3/4 cups Vodka

Zest of 3 large oranges

1 vanilla bean, seeds from inside the pod

Directions:

1. Attach the sous vide immersion circulator to a Cambro container or pot with water using an adjustable clamp and preheat water to 130°F.

2. Place all ingredients in a clean mason jar. Seal tightly. Place the jar in the sous vide bath and set the cooking time for about 1½ hours.

3. Remove from the sous vide bath and immediately immerse in a large bowl of ice water. Strain the mixture through a fine mesh sieve. This is to remove the orange zest and vanilla bean pieces Place in a sealed container and store in refrigerator up to 1 month.

Pumpkin Spice Bitters

Preparation Time: 10 mins
Cooking Time: 2 hours
Cooking Temperature: 122°F

Ingredients:

1/3 cup dark rum

3 thumbs of ginger, peeled

2 cinnamon sticks

½ teaspoon black peppercorns

½ teaspoon whole cloves

1 nutmeg, roughly chopped

Directions:

1. Attach the sous vide immersion circulator to a Cambro container or pot with water using an adjustable clamp and preheat water to 122°F.

2. Place all ingredients in a cooking pouch. Seal pouch tightly after squeezing out the excess air. Place pouch in sous vide bath and set the cooking time for about 2 hours.

3. Remove pouch from the sous vide bath and carefully open it. Strain the mixture and store in a small bitters bottle.

BERRY VODKA

Preparation Time: 10 mins
Cooking Time: 3 hours
Cooking Temperature: 130°F

INGREDIENTS:

2 cups mixed berries (cranberry, blueberry, raspberry and blackberry)

vodka, as required

DIRECTIONS:

1. Attach the sous vide immersion circulator to a Cambro container or pot with water using an adjustable clamp and preheat water to 130°F.

2. Place berries in a mason jar. Add enough vodka to leave about ½-inch space from top and cover with the lid tightly. Place jar in sous vide bath and set the cooking time for about 3 hours.

3. Remove mason jar from the sous vide bath and carefully open it. Strain the mixture and serve over ice.

CRANBERRY VODKA

Preparation Time: 10 mins
Cooking Time: 2 hours 15 mins
Cooking Temperature: 153°F

INGREDIENTS:

For Vodka:

4 cups vodka

¾ of a pound fresh cranberries

For Simple Syrup:

2½ cups water

2 cups sugar

DIRECTIONS:

1. Attach the sous vide immersion circulator to a Cambro container or pot with water using an adjustable clamp and preheat water to 153°F.

2. Place vodka and cranberries in a cooking pouch. Seal pouch tightly after squeezing out the excess air. Place pouch in sous vide bath and set the cooking time for about 2 hours.

3. Remove pouch from the sous vide bath and carefully open it. Through a strainer, strain the mixture and transfer into a stoppered bottle.

4. For simple syrup: in a pot, add water and sugar over medium-high heat and bring to a boil.

5. Simmer for about 15 minutes, stirring occasionally. Remove from heat and keep aside to cool.

6. After cooling, add sugar syrup into vodka and stir to combine.

Mojito

Preparation Time: 10 mins
Cooking Time: 1½ hours
Cooking Temperature: 158°F

Ingredients:

2/3 cup fresh mint leaves, plus extra for serving

3.17 fluid ounces silver rum

simple syrup, as required

fresh lime juice, as required

lemon-lime soda, as required

Directions:

1. Attach the sous vide immersion circulator to a Cambro container or pot with water using an adjustable clamp and preheat water to 158°F.

2. In a pan of boiling water, blanch mint leaves for about 10-15 seconds.

3. Strain mint leaves and transfer into a bowl of ice water.

4. Place mint leaves and rum in a cooking pouch. Seal pouch tightly after squeezing out the excess air. Place pouch in sous vide bath and set the cooking time for about 1½ hours.

5. Remove pouch from the sous vide bath and bath and immediately immerse in a large bowl of ice water. Strain the mixture.

6. For 1 serving: in a rocks glass, place 2½ ounces infused rum with simple syrup, lime juice and 2-3 fresh mint leaves and stir to combine.

7. Fill glass with carbonated soda and serve with a garnish of a watermelon chunk.

CHOCOLATE CHERRY MANHATTAN

Preparation Time: 10 mins
Cooking Time: 1 hour
Cooking Temperature: 122°F

INGREDIENTS:

For Chocolate Bourbon Infusion:

1 cup dried cherries

2 cups bourbon

¼ cup cacao nibs

For Chocolate Cherry Manhattan:

2 ounces cherry chocolate bourbon infusion

3 dashes chocolate bitters

1 ounce sweet vermouth

3 sous vide cherries

DIRECTIONS:

1. Attach the sous vide immersion circulator to a Cambro container or pot with water using an adjustable clamp and preheat water to 122°F.

2. For cherry infusion: place all ingredients in a cooking pouch. Seal pouch tightly after squeezing out the excess air. Place pouch in sous vide bath and set the cooking time for about 1 hour.

3. Remove pouch from the sous vide bath and bath and immediately immerse in a large bowl of ice water. Strain the mixture and reserve cherries for garnishing.

4. For 1 serving: fill a short glass with ice. Add bourbon, bitters, and vermouth and stir to combine.

5. Garnish with reserved cherries and serve.

APPLE & CARDAMOM GIN

Preparation Time: 10 mins
Cooking Time: 2 hours
Cooking Temperature: 136°F

INGREDIENTS:

1 pink lady apple, cored and sliced into rings

1 cup gin

1 green cardamom pod

DIRECTIONS:

1. Attach the sous vide immersion circulator to a Cambro container or pot with water using an adjustable clamp and preheat water to 136°F.

2. Place all ingredients in a cooking pouch. Seal pouch tightly after squeezing out the excess air. Place pouch in sous vide bath and set the cooking time for about 2 hours.

3. Remove pouch from the sous vide bath and carefully open it. Strain the mixture and transfer into a sterilized bottle.

4. Freeze to chill. Remove from freezer and keep at room temperature for about 20 minutes before serving.

GINGER BRANDY

Preparation Time: 10 mins
Cooking Time: 2 hours
Cooking Temperature: 135°F

INGREDIENTS:

1.68 fluid ounces brandy

1½ cups fresh ginger, grated

1¼ cups sugar

1 cup water

DIRECTIONS:

1. Attach the sous vide immersion circulator to a Cambro container or pot with water using an adjustable clamp and preheat water to 135°F.

2. Place brandy and ginger in a cooking pouch. Seal pouch tightly after squeezing out the excess air. Place pouch in sous vide bath and set the cooking time for about 2 hours.

3. Meanwhile in a pan, add sugar and water and boil until desired consistency of syrup is achieved.

4. Remove pouch from the sous vide bath and carefully open it. Strain the mixture and transfer into a stoppered bottle.

5. Add cooled syrup and mix.

ROSE SYRUP

Preparation Time: 10 mins
Cooking Time: 2 hours
Cooking Temperature: 122°F

INGREDIENTS:

---

3 cups sugar

1 cup water

½ cup dried roses

1 teaspoon fresh lemon rind

DIRECTIONS:

---

1. Attach the sous vide immersion circulator to a Cambro container or pot with water using an adjustable clamp and preheat water to 122°F.

2. In a cooking pouch or clean mason jar, place all ingredients and mix gently. Seal tightly and place in the sous vide bath. Set the cooking time for about 2 hours.

Made in the USA
Middletown, DE
04 February 2018